TURTLE SOUP PRESS

This book is dedicated to the author's late parents,
David A. and Margaret A. Schwalb.

TURTLE SOUP PRESS

LIBRARY OF CONGRESS CATALOGING-IN-PUBLICATION DATA:
Schwalb, Eric J.
The East Side, A Novel / by Eric J. Schwalb. – 1st ed.
p.   cm.
I. Title
ISBN: 978-0-9886141-0-9 (hard copy); 978-0-9886141-1-6 (e-book)

For their help with this book, the author is particularly grateful to
Christy Schwalb and Craig Schwalb; to Robert Hasenstab, David Donahue,
Raymond Kowalski, Alan Sanders, and Jennifer Gold;
and to Matthew Johnson.

the

EAST SIDE

A NOVEL

Prologue

March, 1994

JACK SPELLMAN EXITED THE ELEVATOR into the lobby of the courthouse. He passed through revolving doors and braced for the cold outside. The fountain bays along the plaza walkway were empty save for a few stray leaves and cigarette butts.

A bank of microphones with local radio and television flags affixed to them stood waiting on the legal defense team in State of Illinois v. Timothy Spellman. Seeing Jack and his partner Nelson Bleaker exit the courthouse, the reporters left the warmth of their vans parked along the street and headed into the plaza. As Jack approached the microphones, three unmarked dark blue sedans circled the dormant Memorial Fountain in the town square and pulled alongside the news vans at the edge of the traffic circle.

Jack had commanded the St. Clair County courthouse for over twenty years, winning dozens of civil lawsuits inside, and wowing the press outside. But now, in considering the jury's verdict in his son's trial, he searched for something to say.

"Mr. Spellman," a reporter finally asked, "what did you tell Tim after the verdict was read?"

"I think that's between a father and his son," Jack replied. He looked past the reporters to the men in suits emerging from the blue sedans. Federal agents, Jack figured, heading in to testify in a local drug case.

"Most of you who know me know that I am rarely at a loss for words," Jack finally began. The men in suits passed around the reporters and microphones.

"But the sobering fact, of which we all remain mindful, is that a young boy—" The agents pushed through the assembled reporters, and shouldered in past Nelson. Two agents each placed a hand on Jack's shoulders, while another stepped in front of the microphones.

With cameras rolling, and a federal prosecutor watching from the curb, the agent recited the charges against Jack Spellman:

"John David Spellman, upon indictment secured by the United States Attorney, Ruth Whittaker, you are hereby under arrest for conspiracy to bribe a federal official; bribery of a federal official; and nine other federal crimes. You have the right to remain silent," the agent began.

"Hold on! Hold on!" Jack yelled, as he attempted to shrug the hands off of him. "What the hell is this? Who is behind this?"

"—and anything you say, counselor, can and will be used against you—"

"I waive my Miranda rights. Shut the hell up! I know my goddamned rights!"

"Who orchestrated this?" Nelson called out to the agents.

In handcuffs, Jack was pushed quickly down the sidewalk towards a waiting car. The television cameramen gave chase.

"I'm going with you, Jack," Nelson called out, running alongside Jack until the federal prosecutor stopped him.

"Not a good idea," the prosecutor cautioned, stepping in front of the older, shorter man and nearly knocking him to the ground.

"Who the hell are you?" Nelson said, recovering his balance.

"Managing Assistant United States Attorney Xavier Holden. Mr. Bleaker, here are your papers. You are an unindicted co-conspirator of Mr. Spellman, as laid out in this indictment. I will not allow you to get in that car with him."

"You are a piece of work, Holden," Nelson said as he swatted away the prosecutor's hand. "In the middle of all of this, up here, Jack's son's life in the balance, and with the cameras going live, you drop this shit? Media whores. You and Ruth Whittaker both." He poked his finger into Xavier's chest.

Knocking away the finger, Xavier shouted: "Did you hear me say *unindicted* coconspirator, Mr. Bleaker? Did you hear that? You best hope to keep it that way and step away from me. I'll be in touch. Watch it." He stepped past Nelson and headed to the convoy of federal vehicles.

With flashing lights, the three cruisers darted into the traffic circle and for the benefit of the assembled cameras circled the dormant fountain before heading south down Illinois Street. The cameras caught through the rear window of the third car Jack's steeled expression. The cameramen then turned to capture the view of Kathy Spellman, who stood in the plaza with her hands over her mouth, either too cold or too scared to move, watching her husband retreat from view.

PART I

1

Fall, 1993

ON ALL FOURS, WINDED AND BEATEN, Jason Flowers offered up his wallet. "Here, take it. Take it, just take it. Take it," he pleaded.

"I don't need your money," came the response, followed by a kick into Jason's ribs.

The black leather wallet dropped with the boy to the dirt. Six more words came, each punctuated by another kick, the last to his face:

"I. Don't. Want. Your. Fucking. Wallet."

Blood seeped from his lip and nose, leaving small black drops in the dirt. He laid motionless in a defensive curl, his hands and arms covering his head from further damage. The first ring of observers, all wearing remnants of black eye smudge under their eyes, themselves complicit in allowing the fight to move forward, now deemed it over. Two of the football players lifted Jason from the dirt and carried him through the parting crowd onto the farmhouse porch. Three more players held back one of their own, who put up a mock struggle as if the boy he whooped needed more of what he had left to give.

Jason watched from the floor of the porch through the legs of classmates as his torn, maroon letterman's jacket was thrown up into a tree. "You stay the fuck away from her, from this place," came the final words from the victor Chad Johnson, who watched the jacket he had thrown hang by its leather sleeve from a branch.

Rain began to fall in earnest and the crowd poured into the graying Stupes farmhouse. Chad was in no mood to settle into the castoff furniture or to rejoin his drinking game at the cracked red Formica table in the kitchen. He asked his friend Tyreese Jackson if he was agreeable to heading back into Belleville and getting something to eat at the all-night burger and milkshake place. So long as Chad was paying, Tyreese said, he was willing to go anywhere. The two loaded into Chad's car and followed a gravel road towards the center of the rural village of Millstadt.

Exiting Millstadt was a delicate business. The village police knew full-well that the town was host to a variety of high school parties on weekends out on the distant farms, which they rarely visited. Instead, when the parties ended in the early morning, the police settled into the two main exit routes and waited, looking for anything that raised their suspicion. The bar was not set particularly high.

Making Chad's exit through town even more precarious on this night, however, were two factors. First, his buzz had returned. Driving straight and true, while keeping up conversation with Tyreese, and thinking about the fight, proved difficult.

The second concern was his passenger, Tyreese, the star running back for the football team. Despite Tyreese's local notoriety, having any young black kid in a car while driving through Millstadt was more likely than not to be noticed by the police.

A half-mile past the village's only blinking red light, and just before the speed limit shifted from 25 to 45 mph, Chad saw the lights. He looked down and saw that he was already at 43; 18 mph over by a few hundred feet. Chad slowed his car and pulled off the two-lane road.

"Shit," Tyreese said.

"It'll be okay," Chad reassured him.

"Dude, are you drunk?" Tyreese had seen the beers his friend shotgunned when they first got to the farm after the game.

"No, I'm fine. Don't worry, I know half these guys; I used to get pulled over every weekend. They know me, man."

"So then why are we being stopped?"

Chad thought that was a fair question, but before he could answer it, he saw the bright beam of a flashlight as an officer approached. The light shone down into the car, searching for contraband, slowly washing across the front floorboards under the boys' shoes, then along the backseat and its floorboard, then into Tyreese's face, where it lingered, then to Chad.

"Anything in the trunk?" the officer asked Chad.

Chad shaded his eyes from the light, and knew the game was on. If he said the officer had no right to search his trunk, the officer would get in his face, threaten to call in a dog to sniff out some old pot smell and create that right. Or Chad could consent, because, as he knew from experience, only idiots would dare head through this town with anything in their trunk late on a weekend night.

"No, sir," Chad said, opting for a formality that usually helped grease the skids with the local police.

"Then you won't mind if I take a peak?" the officer asked.

"No sir. Let me open it for you." Chad got out and unlocked the trunk. It contained a jack, flares, and other safety items his dad had supplied. Football gear, a school bag, a baseball bat, and some motor oil completed the officer's tour.

During the inspection of the trunk, a second officer came to the passenger side of the car, tapped on the glass, and asked Tyreese for some identification. Tyreese rolled down his window and handed up his driver's license. The officer read it aloud: "Ty-reese Jackson. Now, why do I know that name?"

"I play for West."

"You play what for West?"

"I play football; I'm the running back."

"That right? I thought I heard that name. So let me ask you a couple things Tyreese. How come this license of yours says you live in East St. Louis?"

"I used to live there; now I live in Belleville."

"That right? How long you lived there?"

"Like two years, or 18 months or something."

"'Like 18 months or something?' You happen to know it is the law in Illinois that a driver update his address with the state within 30 days of moving?"

"No…sir."

"No, sir? Well, let me ask you one other thing, Tyreese, was that how you pronounce that name of yours? Why do I feel staple holes?"

"Excuse me?"

"Your license, dummy." He held his flashlight to the license, flashing its beam through the laminate into Tyreese's face, "it has staple holes. See here? Well, only one reason for that—your license must have been taken before for something. What was it?"

"Um, I guess when I got a speeding ticket?" The ticket was for 34 mph in a 30, he recalled, a harassment earned in Belleville's west end.

"You guess when you 'got a speeding ticket'?" The recitation was starting to grate on Tyreese, as was the inquisition from a cop looking maybe four years his senior.

"Yeah, that's what I said."

"Get out of the car."

"What?"

"I said get out of the car. Your buddy is standing out here in the rain, and you don't need to be falling asleep in here. Get out."

Tyreese exited the car and hustled over to where Chad was standing. The two officers stood a dozen feet away, talking to one another. Then, the younger of the two headed back to the police car and got on his radio.

Chad knew what the officer was doing and whispered to his friend: "They are running the plates on the car, and our licenses, for warrants. You have any outstanding shit?"

"No way," Tyreese responded, "I paid that ticket."

Tyreese's memory proved wrong. He had also been ticketed during a campus visit in Columbia, Missouri. He had forgotten about that ticket, for driving too fast in a school zone. His failure to pay, or appear in court, on the ticket had resulted in a bench warrant being issued in Missouri, which was now being honored in Illinois.

The older police officer broke the news. "Son," he said sympathetically, once having played on the same football team and knowing full-well who Tyreese was, "turns out this isn't your night." He informed Tyreese of the warrant, explained that he had no option but to take him in to the police station and to hold him there pending a response from Missouri.

Tyreese was incredulous—and scared. He remembered the ticket, but he thought the athletic department had told him that campus police tickets weren't for real. But he couldn't remember if it was campus police, or the real police, or if there really was any difference. In either event, he was heading to the Millstadt jail, and he'd never been locked-up anywhere, nonetheless in this all-white small town.

The officers told Chad he was free to go. He and Tyreese spoke briefly. Neither boy had a portable phone. They whispered, debating whether Tyreese might be given the opportunity to make a phone call at the police station. They agreed quickly, as handcuffs were being placed on Tyreese, that Chad would drive to Tyreese's house to let his parents know that he was under arrest.

Chad waited in his car as the police left with his friend. He pulled onto the road and sped away, turning onto 59th Street towards Belleville. He shook his head and then placed it on the steering wheel as he drove. Had it not been for the confusion over the Missouri warrant, he knew that he could have been the one headed to jail. He lifted his head and focused his blurred vision on the slick country road ahead of him.

When the officers had pulled him over, Chad had felt a strong need to relieve himself, and the feeling returned with an urgency. He pulled over, leaving enough of his car in the roadway to keep his wheels off of the muddy roadside. He turned off the engine, cut the lights and got out, closing the door behind him.

Chad slipped down the muddy embankment and into the field. The night was near black save for the flame glowing above the garbage dump maybe a mile in front of him. As he unzipped, he wondered if the dump would explode if the flame ever went out. He watched over his shoulder as a car passed along the road. He looked to see if it was the police or anyone he knew coming back from Stupes, but he couldn't tell in the darkness.

Chad headed back up the hill. He reached the front of his car and felt a lurch in his gut where the remnants of alcohol churned with adrenaline.

He took a moment to assess his stomach and figured he would vomit. He kneeled down and gripped his side, looking at the grill of his vintage Camaro, which wore an "SS-355" that he had found at a salvage yard and welded into place.

His stomach leveled. He decided to stand. Chad then heard the loud, long blast of a car horn, which he figured was emanating either from someone he knew returning from the farm, or someone angry at his car having taken up some of the road. Either way, he instinctively looked up and moved towards the road to confront the sound and the approaching headlights.

The on-coming vehicle didn't slow. As Chad walked forward, the leather sole of his cowboy boot slipped on wet oil sealer at the edge of the road.

Chad teetered and his considerable size hastened his fall towards the roadway. His hand reached back for the car, but the smooth wet hood provided no grip. As he fell towards the road, the steel bumper of the passing vehicle clipped the side mirror of his car and then struck him squarely. The force of the impact sent the young football player careening off the side of the road and down into the ditch.

2

"I REMEMBER WALKING THESE STREETS AS A GIRL, over thirty years ago. My family, we would come down to the Avenue for lunch after church. That building's gone. My neighbor, he was an accountant. His brother was a doctor. They had a shared office that was just over there. Gone too. And my daddy, he worked in the stockyards, not so far away from right here. Gone."

Ruth Whittaker looked out over the crowd. The collective wealth assembled on the makeshift stage sat in stark contrast to the squalor viewable to her in all directions. At precisely noon, in front of the United States District Court for the Southern District of Illinois, and before the barons of the region's industry who had placed her there, she took the oath of office as the United States Attorney for the Southern District.

"There have been tough days in all cities. And there have been tough years in many. But here, in this place, there have been tough decades. Tough entire lives," Ruth said as she looked up and down Missouri Avenue, along which the hulking stone and brick federal courthouse behind her sat in what remained of East St. Louis. Indeed, the courthouse was one of the few remaining landmarks on a main street that once hosted a bustling commercial and entertainment district, but now mostly served as an abandoned strip used by outsiders on their way to the bridges to downtown St. Louis.

"No one person caused all that pain. And no one person can eliminate it. But I am here to do what I can, with the help of a great team of attorneys, and everyone in law enforcement, to try and right the ship and get this city back, get the East Side, all of it, back on its feet." The crowd stood, the risers vibrating with their applause. As they regained their seats, the new lead prosecutor asserted her agenda.

"Now, I am just a prosecutor. And my only tool is the law." She paused, glancing at the neat lines of white wooden chairs, filled with court workers, assistant prosecutors and politicians. She nodded towards the Chief Judge of the Southern District, William J. Flood, who was seated to her right and had just sworn her into office. Flags of the United States, State of Illinois, St. Clair County, and the City of East St. Louis started to whip about in their wooden stands, rain threatening again as it had all morning.

"But the law is a formidable tool," Ruth said, wagging her right finger. "And we will wield it as we must, where we must.

"So, I say to criminals: we are coming for you." She started a cadence: "Drug dealers: we are coming for you. Murderers, gang bangers: we are coming for you. And to those who would prey on our children, or on the elderly: we are coming for you."

Ruth again paused, listening to the applause. She turned towards the gentlemen seated to her left. These were her backers—the men who moved her name up through the office of Illinois's junior Republican U.S. Senator, and who lobbied the new Republican administration hard for her installment in this post. They included: Matthew Lambreth, heir to the brewery of the same name just across the river in St. Louis; Sydney Driscoll, chairman of the southern Illinois ammunition and firearms giant; Guy Sampson, the CEO of the Class I railroad headquartered in the area, and, closest to the podium, J. David Meirs, the president and

CEO of AgriFarm, the area's formidable agrichemical company.

"But my office won't focus only on gangs, drugs and violence. For indeed, crime doesn't have to involve guns or drugs to be worthy of our attention—or merit the use of our tools.

"This region is full of non-violent crime—corruption, bribery, pay-to-play politics—that has done as much to damage life here over the years as anything else. And for far too long, the men in my position have done nothing to put an end to this—to lock up these criminals, to put a stop to this long-running graft and greed.

"That stops now. We will prosecute crimes that arise in a fancy office building on Main Street just the same as we would if they arose in a crack house off State Street.

"If you are breaking the law, we are coming for you," she said, regaining her cadence. "Mayors who accept bribes, we are coming for you. And to judges who favor their friends over the law, we are coming for you. If you abuse the public's trust, if you tarnish the shine of your office, we are coming for you."

Again, the crowd applauded. As the sun began to creep behind the courthouse roof and the wind picked up in the shadows of the stage, Ruth concluded:

"Some would say the best days of this region are behind it. The jobs gone, the hope lost. I don't buy that. We need to make people feel safe in their homes, and make them believe in their systems of government again. If we do that, and if we keep doing that, people will stay, and jobs will stay. And soon, you mark my word, more people will come, and more jobs too.

"And so, with the law as my tool," Ruth thundered, "I intend to help make this East Side great again."

3

THROUGH THE WIDE CONFERENCE ROOM WINDOWS of the top floor of the Railroad Commerce Building, Jack Spellman could see the iron railroad bridges spanning the Mississippi River, allowing freight into the rail yards of East St. Louis and beyond. The federal courthouse was just beyond those yards, the green glass of its rear addition reflecting the setting sun.

For years, Jack had spent his days and nights laboring against the nation's few remaining big railroad companies, including the St. Louis & St. Paul Railway, in whose headquarters he now sat. Jack had represented railroad workers, mainly locomotive engineers, who had been exposed to asbestos, were injured in train accidents, or were mentally spent after running their locomotive over a family that failed to heed warnings at a grade crossing.

This case was altogether different and far more damaging to the railroad.

"Alright Jack, what's left is the press release. We can't agree to this language, that our actions were 'unauthorized.'"

"You buried tens of thousands of miles of telephone lines, rented them out, and never paid the landowners. That is about as unauthorized as it comes, Tom," Jack said, turning away from the window.

Tom Rahn was the general counsel for the railroad, and was the most anguished of the railroad lawyers sitting on the west side of the table. He continued: "For Christ sake, Jack. You are getting $100 million of our money in a settlement. You personally are getting another 25. Give us our damned language."

"Fine," Jack relented, his mind now elsewhere.

Jack considered the good fortune that had led him to this case. He was visiting a rail line several years earlier during an inspection of track conditions. While on a stretch of mainline he noticed a Baby Bell boring into the railroad's right-of-way and running cable down into the ground. He asked his photographer, who was present to take pictures of the line, to snap a few shots of the spools of cable and the machines feeding the cable into the ground. He had an associate search to see what property rights the railroad had to allow the phone company to be there. They had none.

Under the law, that lack of permission was a trespass and the damages were real and substantial—if they could be grouped into a class. Thus, where the SL&SP had run over 25,000 miles of lines, even valuations of only a few dollars per foot amounted to millions in potential damages, plus interest.

Jack tried hard to conceal his excitement at this settlement, which was his biggest to date by far. He watched as a corporate vice president signed the settlement documents. Jack had hoped the railroad CEO Guy Sampson might appear for the signing, but he had apparently delegated the task to a subordinate officer. The $125 million figure was a difficult pill for the railroad to swallow, Jack knew. It was not only the largest class action settlement in railroad history, but it was an embarrassment to Sampson who had instigated a "no settlement" litigation policy since taking the helm of the railroad five years earlier.

The railroad's lead counsel spoke up from his computer monitor: "Jack, okay, I think we are done here. The release will issue tomorrow morning. We've signed the settlement in triplicate. Here is your stack, here is the court's, which you can file on Monday, and we will retain this last stack. Is there anything else?" The pain in the voice of the railroad's attorney brought a rush of color to Jack's pale, 50-year old face and balding head.

"You are going to make me ask for my fee?" Jack asked, smiling.

"No, not at all. It is in the envelope, on your stack."

Jack grabbed the envelope, opted not to peek inside, and slid it into his suit coat pocket. He lifted the stack of papers into his litigation case and departed the executive floor of the railroad. He descended in an art deco elevator to the lobby of the building, smiled to the security guard at the front desk, and headed out into the early evening. He contemplated stopping for a celebratory drink, but he wanted nothing more than to cross the river and to deposit his check, making him one of the wealthiest trial lawyers in the area.

He gunned his Cadillac up the ramp and onto the Poplar Street Bridge, thinking about his new fortune. The things he wanted—elite colleges for the kids, a summer place in the Outer Banks, an athletic field for his old grade school—all were now obtainable. As he crossed into Illinois, Jack tapped the lapel of his suit where underneath a check with six zeros to the left of the decimal rested. He made a celebratory fist and smiled.

4

THE CALL TO THE SCENE of a potential vehicular homicide had come into the County Sheriff's office early on Saturday morning. The dispatcher paged Sgt. Cliff Schaefer, the head of the major case unit of the sheriff's office, at his home.

When his pager chimed and rattled, it was sitting on the kitchen table, next to the Sports section of the News-Democrat which was open to coverage of the West football team's defeat the prior night. Sgt. Schaefer called his dispatch while he headed down the hall from the kitchen to his bedroom closet. He grabbed his County Sheriff windbreaker and sidearm from his closet. Homicide calls were infrequent in St. Clair County, even more so in Belleville on a Saturday morning.

When he arrived at the scene 20 minutes later, it was a shambles. There was no body in the field and the field itself was a muddy mess.

An old, restored Camaro was parked on the street. Sgt. Schaefer started his investigation there. Noticeably missing was the driver's side mirror, but the car otherwise looked impeccable. As he waited on the forensic team and photographer to arrive, Sgt. Schaefer peered into the car. He could see it was unlocked and the keys were still in the ignition.

He walked around the car. The road was now closed to traffic, and he searched the roadway looking for any bits of glass, metal or plastic that could have broken off the offending car. He found only discarded fast food bags, cups, and beer cans.

All told, he thought this was one of the least helpful crime scenes he had seen in quite a while. He radioed back to dispatch to ask the EMTs who had first arrived at the scene to report back so that he could take their statements. He needed to learn from them the location of the body and anything else they could offer.

The forensics van arrived and the photographer began to shoot pictures of the area. Sgt. Schaefer scanned the horizon of nearby houses, small businesses, and the garbage dump. From none of these distant places, he figured, would a witness arise.

The search of the car proved equally fruitless, although the registration in the glove box gave a name to the victim: Chad Johnson. The car's engine turned over on the first crank and its fuel tank was half full. The tires were fine. There was no apparent reason, it seemed to the sheriff, for the driver to have stopped at this spot or to have gotten out of the vehicle. Sgt. Schaefer watched in frustration as the forensic techs walked the fields, finding no evidence. After an hour, they had managed to gather only one worthy item—the missing side mirror.

The EMTs arrived in their ambulance, which they again parked in the field. Sgt. Schaefer hustled down the hillside, his windbreaker whistling as he pumped his arms, balancing himself as he slipped in the mud. "Are you assholes serious?" he screamed at the EMTs as they disembarked from their ambulance. "You already drove your rig through this goddamned field once and now you cross through the tape and park on this field again?"

Sgt. Schaefer walked up to the two men, both in their late 20s, as they came around the front of their rig. "Which one of you dumbfucks spotted the boy?"

"I did, sir." The taller of the two men answered first. "Pete was driving. I'm Brian. I spotted the boy, it was still dark. We just pulled up to where the kid was located."

"And then what?"

"Then we thought we detected signs of life, began CPR, and transported him to Memorial."

"And you turned around where?"

"In the field," answered the driver. "We drove forward to the driveway there, which made the quickest exit."

"And right through a crime scene."

"We didn't know that, sir. We were just doing our jobs."

"Right, well. What did you find when you reached the boy?"

"His head was wide open, he was bleeding into the field. He wasn't breathing, but we thought he showed some signs of life and we tried to resuscitate him, without success."

"Other than trauma to the head, anything else."

"Major contusion to the chest. Compact fracture to the left wrist. And bloody right knuckles."

"Bloody knuckles. OK. And he was DOA at Memorial?"

"Yes."

"OK, now show me where that body was located, as close as you can recall."

The three men walked further into the field. The area was off the road maybe eight feet, and just before the plowed-under corn rows began. It was a deep, muddy turnaround for the tractor before the road.

"Right here, around this tire rut," the taller man spoke. "Here, you can see the darker soil, from the blood."

"How was he aligned?"

"Excuse me? Aligned?" This was the first such interview the boy had ever participated in, and he appeared to be taking it seriously.

"How did you find him, face up, face down, what? Which way did his head point, was he laid out straight or all over the place? Describe the body as you found it."

"OK. His head was pointing east. He was face down, arms tucked under him, legs splayed. He looked like someone who got punched in the face and went cold on the way down."

"Good. That is a helpful description. Did you check his pockets for anything, meds, drugs? Any of that?"

"Yeah, we checked. Nothing." The other EMT shook his head in agreement.

"Anything else you can remember to tell me, seeing as I have no body and no discernable crime scene?" The two EMTs shook their heads. "No," Sgt. Schaefer confirmed. "Great, thanks. Next time, keep your rig up on the road and stay out of the field."

Sgt. Schaefer walked up to his car and pulled a paper mockup of a body out of the trunk. He walked back down the side of the road towards the rut where Chad was found and placed the paper generally as described by the EMTs.

He spoke with the forensic team, which began to register measurements between the car and the mockup, between the street and the mockup, and the like. The distance from the car to the mockup was perhaps 10 linear feet, but because of the drop from the road down to the field, the point where Chad Johnson was found was a good distance from his car. All of that information would be used to determine the speed of the car at the time of impact.

Sgt. Schaefer got on his radio and asked dispatch to send a deputy to the registered address of the car, where presumably the boy's parents would be waiting on the arrival of their son from the prior night. He informed dispatch to pass along that it was a hit and run, that it was high speed and high impact, resulting in immediate death. Whether that was true was impossible to know, but it was the only thing that was fair to tell the parents, he said.

The forensic team completed their work and came to the sheriff for final instructions: "I want the vehicle plastic you found on the roadside classified for make and model; state police will do that, but tell them to do it now, they can take forever. Also check the rearview mirror for paint and get that analyzed. And run the distance and speed calculations based on your numbers."

Once the car was towed, Sgt. Schaefer ordered the street reopened in both directions. He climbed back into his police cruiser and looked down at his notes. He radioed his dispatch to invite County Coroner Fred Donovan to join him for breakfast. He pulled his car out of the ditch along the road and headed for Mr. Donut.

The coroner walked into the pastry shop a half hour after the sheriff and sat down next to him at the horseshoe-shaped counter: "Good to see you Cliff. But we have to stop meeting like this."

"No shit," Sgt. Schaefer agreed. "Your folks been to Memorial yet?"

"I just stopped there myself to take a look. We took possession about a half hour ago. The preliminary autopsy is set for this afternoon. I'll be there for it, you bet."

"I've not seen the boy. Pretty bad, I imagine, he got tossed quite a ways."

"Looked about like what you would think if you got hit by a car going full speed at your head," the coroner muttered to the sheriff while staring at the wall of pastry in front of him. He gave his order to the waitress.

"Yeah, that's what I gathered from the EMTs, who messed up the crime scene something fierce."

"Mmm…hate that," the coroner said, biting into his fritter.

"Yeah, so I am looking forward to getting the results of your autopsy and tox screen to see what else you can tell me. I've got to go see the parents, and see what they know. Literally at square one right now."

"I'll try and have a preliminary report for you tomorrow on cause, which we already know, contents of stomach, all of that. Tox will take longer, you know that."

"That sounds good, Fred. Thanks for expediting. In fact, if you find anything out today, you get on the horn and give me a call. We need to put this case down as soon as we can."

"You got it."

———

Chad Johnson's father was across town at his transmission shop where he'd heard the news of his son's death hours earlier from a sheriff's deputy. He couldn't figure out what else to do; his other son was with his mother this particular weekend, and he didn't think heading to an empty house seemed like a good idea. He remained at work when another sheriff's car pulled into his lot.

The bay doors were open and Sgt. Schaefer saw what he presumed was Carl Johnson working under a minivan. "Mr. Johnson?" Sgt. Schaefer inquired of the man, who looked to be about 40, with a shock of black hair that nearly matched his oil-stained hands. The man looked up with red eyes. "My deepest sympathies on the loss of your son. I'm Sgt. Cliff Schaefer, a sheriff, and I'm in charge of finding out what happened. Can I talk to you for a few minutes?"

"Sure." Carl wiped his hands on a rag tucked into his jeans and directed the detective towards the office on the second floor of the aluminum-sided building. The office overlooked the rear parking lot that held cars in various states of disassembly.

"Quite an operation you've got here," Sgt. Schaefer commented, sitting down into a red vinyl and steel armchair.

"Largest transmission shop on the East Side. We've been here almost 15 years, but the bank still owns most of it."

"I imagine. Chad used to work here?"

"Sure. He and his little brother are always in here, helping sweep up, you know. Chad started working here when he was 14, mostly disassembling engines, that sort of thing. He ended up working most of the time on the old Camaro I found him, but I didn't pay him for that."

"That is a beautiful car."

"Yeah, well." The elder Johnson's voice fell off as he thought about working side-by-side with his son for years fixing that car. He looked out the window, and kept his gaze there as the sheriff began his questions in earnest.

"Did you expect Chad home last night?"

"Not really. I have custody of the boys, but I give Chad pretty much leeway. Hell, he's 18. I require him in his bed on weeknights, and no missed school, but the weekends were pretty much his."

"Did you see him on Friday night?"

"I saw him play football on Friday night. He gave me a thumbs up when he found me up in the stands after a third down sack, but that was it."

"Do you have any idea where he went after the game Friday night?"

"You'd have to ask his teammates. They usually all went out together afterwards, but I don't always know where. Parties somewhere, I imagine."

"He appears to have been coming back from Millstadt."

"Right, well he might have been out at the Stupes place. Brad Stupes. He's on the team with Chad. His dad has a farm out that way. Chad had told me before about going out there after games."

"Where you all live, near downtown, 59th wouldn't have been the obvious way home last night."

"Well, like I said, I don't always know where he was on weekends, just the weeknights is what I could manage, by myself. He could have been heading somewhere else, I guess. I just can't figure why he stopped there on that road. And how he'd get in the way of a car. He'd know better than that." He looked back at the sheriff with eyes that the sergeant had seen many times and always meant that the interviewee didn't want to talk any more. He respected that.

Sgt. Schaefer rubbed his bald head and smoothed the corners of his gray mustache. "Mr. Johnson," he said as he stood, "thank you for your time. I am terribly sorry for your loss. If there is anything that you think of that you need to tell me, here is my phone number and you should call any time." Carl Johnson took the sheriff's card, spun in his chair and reverted to his half-mile stare out his office window and said nothing more.

Sgt. Schaefer left the transmission shop and headed back to his car. He checked in with dispatch to find the address for Chad's mother. She lived out near Millstadt.

The path to her home in the country took Sgt. Schaefer past the crime scene. As he approached, he saw a farmer back in the field where Chad was found. Sgt. Schaefer pulled off the road and the farmer brought his tractor around to the road and idled, still atop his machine.

"Sgt. Cliff Schaefer. Good day sir," he yelled over the sound of the engine.

"Same to you. Paul Stanis. Hell of a day, though."

"Yep. I assume you called it in?" A nod. "Thanks for calling it in. I know you told 911 what you saw, but would you mind telling me again. I'm in charge of this investigation."

The farmer cut the engine and stepped down off his tractor. He told the sheriff to follow him and they walked towards the spot where the body had been found. "Well, I was out here just after the sun had come up and saw that car. And well—you look like a man about my age—when you see a car like that, you go take a look.

"So I started my work by driving the tractor down there to the street to give the Camaro a nice, slow drive by. But when I made the turn, that's when I saw the boy. He wasn't moving. I took him for being passed out, until I got closer and saw him."

"Was he face up or face down when you pulled up?"

"Face down. I rolled him over and saw he was dead. Bruised real bad and real bloody. So I got right up and drove up over there to the house and called it in."

"The EMTs seemed to think he had some life in him when they got here."

"I doubt that. One look at him, there was no doubt about that. Those ambulance guys were here and out in about five minutes."

"They do CPR?"

"Not that I saw. But once they arrived I headed back to my back fields to get out of their way."

"What time did you make it to bed last night?"

"9:30, after the early news."

"Did you see the car out front then?"

"Nope. I didn't see it until daybreak when I was out front here."

"Did you find anything out there near the body? Any car parts, or clothes? Anything unusual?"

"Nope. But I didn't go looking for nothing either."

"Right, sure. OK, listen, thank you for your help. Here's my card. Call if you think of anything else."

The farmer took the card and slid it under the flap of his front shirt pocket. "Shame what happened to that boy. The way the cars drive down here on weekends, kids half drunk and out of control, it's amazing it doesn't happen more often. Good luck."

Luck, indeed, Sgt. Schaefer thought. With a hit and run in the middle of the night, and in the middle of almost nowhere, that was exactly what he needed.

5

THE BROAD TABLE OF THE U.S. ATTORNEY'S MAIN CONFERENCE ROOM was set for lunch. Along the room's walls hung the oil likenesses of nearly every man to have served in the office since the courthouse had risen along Missouri Avenue in 1908.

Ruth took her seat at the head of the table as her small list of invitees joined her. She had met over breakfast with the judges of the district, as well as with the Democratic U.S. Congressman representing the area, who subsequently watched her take her oath of office. This luncheon, however, was intended as a thank you only for her sponsors—the men who had conceived of her for this position when the White House changed hands and the State of Illinois simultaneously elected a Republican to the U.S. Senate for the first time in half a century.

For their part, the sponsors had come to congratulate Ruth and to speak to their hopes for her. While the news reporters outside filed their reports on the historic installation of the first female—and first black—United States Attorney in the history of the Southern District, these men regaled in the fact that they had placed a corporate lawyer—a well known, well-connected and powerful corporate lawyer—into the seat of the lead prosecutor. Their concern wasn't with the crime around the courthouse, it was with what happened in the courthouse, and in the state courthouses all around the area.

Sen. Robert Padlow, the first term Republican from Peoria, stood to welcome the group. He rose from his seat next to Ruth, and gazed at her, then to each of the men in the room:

"When I was elected last Fall as the first Republican senator from the great state of Illinois in a long while, I proclaimed that we would change the way we did work in Washington; and I promised that I would bring that change all the way back home to Illinois. Today, we've all taken a major step in that regard." The men around the table raised and clinked their glasses with one another while the Senator continued: "You know, I grew up in the country, watching old spaghetti westerns on television with my dad. And as they used to say: 'Boys, there's a new sheriff in town.' Ruth," he said looking at the new U.S. Attorney, "I am pleased as punch you are our new sheriff." He sat to applause.

Sen. Padlow had made his fortune manufacturing plastic components sold to commercial farm equipment companies. He knew absolutely nothing about what U.S. Attorneys did for a living or that he was enabled to provide a name to the President. So, he delegated the task to a panel of three "advisors"—including two well-connected Republican defense trial lawyers from within the state and to David Meirs, a lawyer-by-training whose agrichemical company operated large manufacturing, distribution and corporate facilities in southern Illinois.

It was little surprise to the senator, then, when the top name that was returned to him was someone close to Mr. Meirs. He stood to speak next, barely able to hide his excitement.

"When I left the general counsel's office of AgriFarm fifteen years ago to take the reins as the chief executive, I knew that I left my legal shop in great hands. I left it to Ruth.

"Over the past fifteen years, Ruth has handled the expansion of our company abroad, and defended us against scurrilous lawsuits here at home. She has done so with laser-beam focus and incredible sense of purpose. I could not have asked for a better general counsel, or a better friend.

"I know that Ruth will bring her experience, and her discipline, to her new role. Ruth has lived in this district virtually her entire life; she was born here; and she knows what is fundamentally wrong here. I know she wants nothing more than to do what is best for all of us. My loss, I expect, will be all of our gain."

He raised his glass, and the others followed suit: "My congratulations to Ruth on this appointment. I know we all look forward to seeing her successes for many years."

While lunch was served, more informal remarks shot back and forth across the table. "How does it feel, Ruth," the CEO of the firearm company, Sydney Driscoll, asked, "to be in the belly of the beast?"

"Well, Syd, looking around at this room, and my office, and this whole building, I do have to say, it doesn't look like a 'judicial hellhole.'" The men laughed. Indeed the Southern District, and all of the state courts in the southwestern part of the state, were routinely placed atop the national lists of "judicial hellholes"—places where corporations did not want to be sued.

"Ruth, that is very funny," Guy Sampson interjected, "but don't let these trappings fool you. You know, as well as any of us, the fortunes lost in this building. Indeed, our railroad just lost quite a fortune, not a month ago—from the chief judge no less."

"So I heard, Guy. That was a tough one."

"Always a queen of understatement!" Guy harrumphed, his company's nine figure settlement still roiling inside him.

The young brewery chief, Matthew Lambreth, added his thought, "Ruth, I don't have much to say—and I don't know you as well as these other gentlemen. But let me say this: we at the brewery are very excited by the prospect of having someone from our side of the world in this office. And I understand from all of these men that you are under no false illusions: we expect great things from you."

The men all looked down the long table to Ruth, who put down her fork.

"Matt, David, Guy, Syd. Senator. I thank all of you for your part in getting me here. I understand the weight and importance of this appointment. I do. As I said today, I know there must be two facets to this job—where previously there was only one.

"We will go after crime, wherever we find it. And we will send a clear message to judges, and to lawyers, that we are watching. That the paybacks, and the gentlemen's agreements, which lay the foundation for these $100 million judgments—sorry Guy—cannot stand. That they are good for no one, they reflect the interests of no one, save for a handful of very powerful gentlemen up the hill," she pointed east.

"I know where we are," Ruth continued, "and I know where we need to head. And I know that we need to get there quickly. No one wants this place—our backyard, our home—to be a laughingstock for the nation. We need to take down that sign that says we are closed for business here; and we need to make equally clear that we are not going to be the beacon for class actions and lawsuits that have nothing to do with us.

"You all know the phrase that justice is blind. Well, I think here in the Southern District that this is no longer true. Who you are, and who your judge is, mean far more in this area than anywhere else in America. I'm not beholden to this 'wash-my-back' mentality. It needs to stop, and I will be the one to stop it."

6

JACK SPELLMAN HAD SLEPT POORLY, owing in no small part to his excitement over the deposit of $25 million into his firm's bank account the prior night. He also was excited about his 10:00 a.m. interview with a field reporter from the Wall Street Journal about his victory.

Barely dawn, and with his family asleep, Jack headed down to the kitchen and made himself coffee and toast. He ate at the sink, watching through the window as a few hardy golfers made their way down the slick fairway a hundred yards away.

By 7:30, Jack had showered and dressed in his weekend casual work attire of a pressed pair of khakis and white button-down oxford. He opened the double-garage door as he left, finding his car blocked by his son Tim's Ford Explorer in the driveway. He grabbed the spare keys to the SUV, which were hanging by the doorway to the garage, and headed out. He figured he'd be back by noon, which was a typical wake-up for his son on a Saturday.

The SUV was muddy on the outside, and smelled of campfire on the inside. Jack switched off the moaning sounds of Morrissey and turned on AM sports radio.

He had time to kill and opted for a leisurely drive around town. Except for college and law school in North Carolina, Jack had lived in Belleville his entire life. The city was the county seat and the offices of Spellman, Bleaker & Rock were located three blocks from the county courthouse. The firm was housed in a three-story mansion, built by famed architect James Hayes who had been hired from St. Louis to design the antebellum Victorian lady. The home boasted nine-foot tall windows between dark red brick under an intricate mansard roof. Although it survived periods as a boarding house, a bed and breakfast, and as an accounting firm, the home always had been known simply as Hayes House.

Jack circled through the town square, arriving at Hayes House a minute later. He pulled onto the apron driveway of the coach house. Inside the garage, blocking Jack's parking spot, was Randall Cutler. Randall tended to the grounds of Hayes House and also served as errand boy, copy boy, and general go-fer. It was an odd job for a man pushing sixty, but he enjoyed its variety and liked the people at the firm. The respect was mutual and he had been there nearly seven years.

"Good morning, Randall. How the hell are ya?" Jack asked. Randall was tightening a water hose onto a power washer.

"Just fine, Jack, just fine. You?" Randall winked, knowing that Jack had settled the firm's biggest case the day before.

"No complaints. Say, how'd West do last night?"

"Oh, my, not so good. I left at half and they were down 28-6. You can't compete with those Catholic schools and their scholarship athletes you know."

"I imagine. What are you up to this morning?"

"Well, it's fixin' to be nice. So once this dew burns off, I thought I'd cut the grass. Until then, I'm just goin' through my list. I'm going to spray-wash the sidewalks and driveway. You need anything?"

"No, I don't think so. I've got a reporter coming in an hour to interview me about the railroad case. Then, I'll be leaving."

"OK, well if you need anything, holler. I brought some donuts and gooey butter cake in from Hasenstab Bakery—the ones you like."

"Oh my, yes. That place will kill us both eventually. Thanks, I'll take you up on that."

Jack headed inside, grabbed a donut from the rear kitchen and headed through the dining room, officially the Lincoln Conference Room, across to the living room. The living room seemed to make the best impression on guests, Jack thought, so he set about straightening what was already a tidy room. He considered where the best view would be for his interviewer and decided it would be from the two armchairs in the front window, with a view to the flowers in the front yard, and back through the expanse of the entire living room to the library in the rear of the house. Jack headed upstairs to make sure his office was presentable should the reporter desire to see that space as well. It, too, was spotless.

Jack paced his office, looking out the window to the street, seeing a car pull into the driveway. Jack headed downstairs to the front door.

"Karen Whitman-Lee," the reporter said, extending her hand as she stepped into the front hall, "absolutely a lovely building."

"Thank you. Jack Spellman. Good to see you, Karen." The reporter declined Jack's offer of a donut, but agreed to a cup of coffee. Jack poured two cups and brought them over to the sitting area near the front window. She was from the Chicago regional office for the Journal, and this was her first visit to the southern part of Illinois.

"Tell me about this place. It is maybe the nicest little law firm I've set foot in."

"Well, thank you. We enjoy it very much. This is Hayes House."

"How did you find it?" the reporter asked, looking up to the high ceilings and into the rooms viewable from the foyer.

"I used to work a few blocks away, in one of the glass office buildings by the courthouse. But during lunches, I would walk by these old buildings, including this one, and I always thought, or dreamed, I guess, that one of these old ladies would make an excellent legal office someday.

"So, I finally decided to buy the place when it slipped into foreclosure. It was a B&B. My wife and I sunk quite a bit of time and money into returning it to what you see here."

"Very well done. What was your former firm?"

"Johnson & Demitri. It was—it is still—a railroad plaintiff's firm. They sue the railroads in worker injury cases mostly. That is where I cut my teeth."

"On the railroads?"

"On the railroads," Jack confirmed.

"Why did you leave Johnson & Demitri?" the reporter asked.

It was an easy question to answer, Jack thought. He wanted more money, more respect, more of everything his partners had, but didn't see fit to share with him. He had labored for years making them millions and although they paid him well, they had never offered him the chance to share in the profits as an equity partner. And so, once Hayes House was finished, he bolted. But he avoided all of that: "Johnson & Demitri is an excellent firm. Great lawyers. I was fortunate to be a lawyer there for over 15 years. I believed there was an opportunity to strike out into new areas—against the railroads and otherwise—but that was a risk my partners did not want to take."

"And that was, what? With class actions?"

"Precisely. Class actions typically required large start-up costs. Once a class action is filed, the crucial process of gaining class certification can take years and cost millions of dollars. Neither Johnson nor Demitri cared for these risks, and had no reason to, given the success they have had taking on the multitude of straightforward cases against the railroads."

"And speaking of success, how are you feeling about your fortune today?" Karen asked.

Jack thought that was a gutsy question, even from a Journal reporter with probably 20 years of experience. "I think the focus should be on the money to the class plaintiffs," he said coolly. "They were the ones defrauded in all of this."

Karen could sense Jack was slightly offended by her question, and retreated to some background information. "How many attorneys are in your firm today?" she asked.

"Seven; three partners and four associates."

"Tell me about your partners."

"My partners are Nelson Bleaker and Craig Rock. Both are former judges. Nelson was on the bench here in St. Clair County for fifteen years—five as chief judge. Craig sat in Madison County, the county north of here, for ten. Great lawyers. Great litigators. Excellent legal minds. Nelson joined the firm in 1984. Craig joined us about two years ago."

The Journal reporter moved along with questions about the class action against the St. Louis & St. Paul Railway, about how Jack had conceived of the suit, and about his lawsuits pending against other railroads.

"My research indicates," the reporter began, "that your case against the SL&SP was the first of its kind to be certified as a class action, and that in several other districts around the country, certification was routinely rejected in these sorts of cases."

"Yes, that's generally right."

"Judge Flood, I also determined, had certified only three class actions in his almost three decades on the bench. He refused certification in twenty times as many cases."

"Is that right?" It was closer to thirty times, Jack knew. He was nonetheless impressed by the reporter's research.

"Yes, how do you account for your good fortune?"

"We had a good case. The types of property and the types of easements were generally common among all plaintiffs, and Judge Flood recognized that. And once liability and a damage per foot figure could be determined, the class could be managed. I can't speak to the other cases he refused to certify. I just know we had good facts and the law backed us up."

"How much did your firm invest in this case?" Karen asked.

"We indicated in our filings with the court that we spent millions of dollars on finding and vetting our plaintiffs, and on land valuation work, title research, and all of that. We also spent thousands of attorney hours on briefs and discovery. Plus expert fees."

"Can you be more specific?"

"No, I'm afraid those documents were filed under seal with the court."

"Is it safe to say that the fee to your firm more than met your costs?"

"Yes," Jack said, breaking into his first smile.

"Have all of your cases been against the railroads?"

"No, no. We have filed actions against any number of companies, from makers of firearms for faulty safety devices to ATV manufacturers who encouraged dangerous modifications to their bikes. The railroads were where we started, and what we are talking about today, but they are just a part of the picture."

"And you've filed these cases, almost exclusively, here in southern Illinois, correct?"

"By and large, yes. We don't like to travel." Jack thought his comment was funny, but Karen didn't laugh.

"I presume you are aware of the reputation of these courts in and around the state, and even in the country?"

"No, what is that?" Jack asked coyly.

"Well, for one, the term "judicial hellhole" has been used to describe them."

"And you take that to mean what, exactly?" Jack had no interest in trashing the very courts where he was well-liked, and his cases were well-received.

"Well, just look at the some of the numbers the Journal reported on last year. The vast majority of asbestos cases, especially class action cases—for the whole nation, mind you—are filed right here. And the cases stay, even if the plaintiffs are from, I don't know, New Jersey. How is that possible?"

"The courts around here have reputations for understanding these types of issues—'mass torts,' they are called—and that is one reason cases are brought here."

"It doesn't have anything to do with the settlement rates and jury verdicts for cases here?" Karen asked.

"Certainly, if you are going to bring a case, you consider where your client will get the best result. But a jury verdict is something that is completely out of our hands as part of the trial bar. When they get back in that room for their deliberations, and we have said that we want 'x' and the defendant has said that we deserve 'nothing at all', well, that is up to the jury at that point."

"The Journal also reported, however—and I want to get your take on this—on the propensity for judges to move from law firm to the bench and back again. In fact, there was one judge that made millions, joined the bench, and then ruled on cases that brought in millions to his former firm. How can that be appropriate?"

"Did you come here today to talk about my case, or about the state of the courts in southern Illinois?" Jack was starting to tire of this line of questions and was mindful that he had hired a top jurist from each of the local counties.

"Well, I guess I am trying to figure out the extent to which the two are related."

"You want to know if this case could have been won somewhere else?"

"Sure," the reporter said, "that's a good place to start."

"Well, I think it is a good place to end—with this line of questions. In this case, I have a plaintiff—lots of plaintiffs—who are harmed. My named plaintiff lives in Illinois. I have a defendant who harmed him, and the defendant is located in Missouri. I pick the Southern District because the law lets me do that. But then I get—as you said—the hardest line judge there is, Judge Flood.

"So, we litigate the hell out of the case for almost two years until we finally prevail on getting our class certified. That decision is appealed by the defendant. But then—and here is the key—a very conservative Chicago appellate court agrees it was a proper class. Now, the value of that case goes up, and the railroad settles. Had we lost on appeal, you wouldn't be here today."

"OK. But that doesn't answer my question. Could this case succeed outside of this so-called hellhole for corporate defendants?"

"I did answer your question," Jack shot back. "Yes, it could have. That court in Chicago hears cases from many districts, in Illinois and other states. The fact that it started here means little—we had a good case and the appellate court agreed with us."

"Is your firm profitable?"

"Today, yes. Next year, who knows. Some cases cost tens of millions of dollars, and if we lose, we are out of business. So we don't bring these cases lightly."

Sensing Jack's agitation, Karen shifted gears again, "can you tell me a little about your life outside the office?"

"Sure. Married 21 years to Kathy. Two kids, Tim, 18; Wendy, 14. Always lived in Belleville. My mom was a cook at the junior high; my dad worked in a foundry that made stoves here.

"I went to the local high school here—the public high school. Then on to Duke for college and law school. Um, what else can I tell you? My son goes to West—that's the public high school. He is the student body president there, in fact. He was accepted under early admission to UVA and will begin there in the Fall with plans to walk-on to the soccer team. Wendy, my daughter, will start West in the Fall; she's a tennis player. She looks just like her mother."

"I understand you are a generous contributor to various causes in the area," Karen noted, "tell me about those."

"Sure. Well, I've been involved in a variety of local charities. I am on the board of the city and county historical societies. I am the main contributor to the sports booster clubs at the kids' schools. Our firm targets a million dollars per year for various charities. And we always take part in events at the Belleville Central Kitchen."

By noon, the reporter was gone. Jack sat for a few minutes and ran through in his head what he had said and how it would be portrayed in the Journal. Convinced he had done his best to defend himself, his practice, and his local lawyer brethren, he headed out to his son's red truck, which Randall had dutifully washed and left drying in the sun.

7

BRIGHT SUN TRIED TO BETRAY THE SOMBER MOOD in Township Stadium. School was closed for Columbus Day, but hundreds of students had nonetheless returned to the West campus for the Chad Johnson memorial service.

The end-zone stands of the concrete bowl were filled with mourners facing the podium beside the goalposts. Chad Johnson had been celebrated on this field, the senior captain of the defensive unit. He'd played hurt, he'd played with heart.

Off to the corner of the end zone idled a black hearse, its rear curtains pulled back to show a glimpse of a silver casket, draped in a maroon and white shroud. Some students had thrown flowers onto the hood of the car, others had jumped the side ropes to touch the vehicle. Now, the hearse sat, with Chad Johnson inside, awaiting the eulogies before leading the procession to the cemetery.

Chad's pastor opened the ceremony with a prayer from the prophet Isaiah. Then a soloist sang, the sound of her voice crackling over the stadium's speakers. When she finished, the stadium was quiet, save for the audible sniffs and sobs of students in the stands.

West's principal rose to the podium to welcome everyone and to thank them for coming to honor the boy he called a "fine young man." After a few minutes of tribute, he also delivered a message:

"While we remember and honor Chad today, we also remain mindful that a crime happened. Someone, somewhere, hit and killed our friend. And that someone drove away and did nothing to help him." The principal removed his glasses, rubbing his eyes. "And if that person is in this stadium today, I say to you this: shame on you. And damn you. Turn yourself in and face your reckoning.

"And to the rest of you, I say this: if you know who did this, or have heard rumors of who did this, come to my office and talk to me, or talk to any one of the sheriffs by the exits today. Your silence is as inexcusable as the person who drove away from the scene of this crime. The school board has authorized a reward of $10,000 for anyone with information that leads to the arrest and conviction of the coward who did this unspeakable act."

The principal sat and the student body president walked to the podium. "Mr. Johnson, Ms. Johnson," Tim Spellman began, looking towards Chad's parents, who sat with their eight year-old son between them. "I speak today on behalf of the 2500 students, and thousands of alumni of Maroon Nation, and I offer you our deepest condolences for the loss of your son Chad. You will hear today from Chad's football coach, and from his fellow players, about what a great football player Chad was and would have become, and you should treasure that. His death marks a sad day for all of us.

"One of the things that so inspired all of us at West was Chad's ability to fire up his teammates, to encourage, to prod, to goad them to fight on this field. From the tunnel leading from the locker room, all of us, if we listened from the stands as the band stopped and we awaited the team's entry onto the field, could hear Chad screaming at the top of his lungs, 'We WILL do this! You've got to BELIEVE! BELIEVE in yourself, BELIEVE in your teammates, BELIEVE in the MAROONS.'

"Earlier this week, our student council voted unanimously to approve funds for the creation and immediate installation of a brass plaque over the tunnel leading out of the home team locker room." Tim opened a brown paper wrapped rectangle, and held up the plaque, which shimmered in the sunshine. "It says:

BELIEVE
Chad Johnson Class of 1994

and it will be installed in a ceremony before Friday's night's East-West game.

"And from that day forward, as our football players exit their locker room and prepare to head into battle, this plaque will meet each of their hands, and remind those players, not only to BELIEVE, but to understand that life can be all too short, and to play like this was their last game on Earth."

Once the ceremony ended, the hearse slowly moved across the end zone and headed for the ambulance exit from the stadium. The hearse drove through the concrete grounds of the sprawling campus, past students who made way for it, then let their hands slide along the rear glass of the car. With a police escort, the hearse cut into traffic on Main Street and began its westward crawl. The processional was over 200 cars deep and took nearly an hour to reach the cemetery on 59th Street, not two miles from where Chad had been killed.

The funeral was the first for many of the students, who were struck by the size and heft of the casket as it was moved from the hearse by suited members of the football team. Most of the players lifting the casket wore sunglasses. Not so, Tyreese Jackson.

As he received the front of the casket as it rolled out of the hearse, tears began to stream down his cheeks. He walked through the crowd, with both hands on the ornate handle, unable to wipe away his tears. The sight of the casket, and of Chad's best friend sobbing, sent currents of cries through the crowd that had assembled around the small tent covering the open hole where Chad would be laid to rest.

8

Ruth took a hammer and nails to the plaster walls and picture rails of her office. She had boxes of photos and art sent over from her old office at AgriFarm, and was intent on personalizing the sprawling Office of the United State Attorney. She hung first her diplomas from the University of Illinois and the law school at Washington University in St. Louis. She hung a framed picture of her first year associate friends from her first legal employer, the top-flight St. Louis firm of Jones Reed, where she had spent seven profitable years.

Ruth looked at the picture of her friends, many of them now partners at the firm. She knew that she could have become a partner, but knew that the job never would have given her what she had wanted—autonomy and power. So, seven years into her career at Jones Reed, Ruth had considered what would give her that autonomy and power, but also protect her way of life, which had improved markedly from her days in East St. Louis. She decided a move in-house to a corporate law department might be her next step.

When she had made her decision that she wanted to leave, Ruth reached out to some of the in-house lawyers she knew to inquire as to job opportunities. David Meirs was one of the few to answer her call, and was the first to take Ruth up on her offer to meet for lunch. As general counsel for AgriFarm, David had hired Jones Reed to defend the company at the trial of a contentious employment dispute. Ruth had won the bench trial in glorious fashion—in front of a judge who rarely ruled in favor of corporate defendants.

When Ruth had called David, he had recalled their triumph. He agreed to meet for lunch at The Depot, the repurposed Belleville train station, where the two had shared a celebratory beer after that trial.

Lunch at The Depot turned quickly into a job interview. David knew his legal department was growing, and he recalled the tenacity with which Ruth had argued his company's case. He told her of the wide array of cases, corporate work, and regulatory puzzles that his company encountered each day. He told her that he could pay as well as her law firm, but could offer her more responsibility, more say, more everything that she could possibly want.

David made Ruth a job offer on the spot during lunch, which she accepted after picking up the check. Two weeks later and with a map spread across the passenger seat of her car, Ruth found her way to the secluded, corporate campus of AgriFarm where she began her role as one of the company's Assistant General Counsel.

Ruth thought back to that first day of work for AgriFarm as she settled into her new role. She was less nervous now, she thought, for she certainly knew her capabilities. And although this was a new role—and a public one—she knew the direction she wanted to head and she was ready for the challenge.

Ruth placed a few more frames on her desk and walls. She looked at the note David had inserted into her boxes from AgriFarm. "Thank you," the note read, "for all you have done, and all you are going to do. Best, Dave." She placed the note in the center drawer of her desk, where she knew she would see it every day.

Ruth collected the empty boxes and moved them to her secretary's space. She returned to her clean and orderly office and found it to her liking. It could use some new carpet and a fresh coat of paint, but generally it looked its part—it was a formidable space that echoed well the power of the office.

At noon, Ruth looked up to find Walter McDonnell at her door, holding a bag of sandwiches. She had invited the Managing Assistant United States Attorney, the second-in-command holdover from the prior administration, for a lunch meeting. Ruth was unsure she wanted him to stay on in that role, and his reluctance in accepting an invitation on a Saturday indicated to Ruth that he probably felt the same way.

After a few niceties, Walter gave Ruth a detailed summary of the direction the office had taken over the last four years. He also summarized the priorities for the office, as he saw them, concluding with a presumptuous, "and that's how I see us moving forward."

Ruth had listened attentively. The summary of open cases and investigations was helpful. The direction of the office, however, and Walter's belief that it would be no more than a continuation of the existing path led her to stop him short.

"That is not how I see it," Ruth declared.

"Really? OK. Then pray tell, how do you see this office moving forward?" queried Walter, who had served under three previous U.S. Attorneys—all Democrats.

Being the top assistant prosecutor meant a slightly higher salary for Walter, but more importantly, a real say in how the office was run. Most U.S. Attorneys arrived in the office without much criminal trial experience, knew nothing about the day-to-day operations of the office, and relied upon their managing attorney for everything from introductions to the other attorneys and staff, to detailed explanations of on-going investigations and prosecutions.

What was becoming very evident to Walter as he listened to his new boss, however, was that Ruth had no intention to rely upon him in any fashion.

"Walter, I understand where you are coming from. I understand what were your priorities, or what were the priorities of the men sitting in this office before I arrived," Ruth said, staring down Walter from behind an old walnut desk. Walter continued to harbor plans that the large desk would someday be his. Thus, he sat in his chair, his legs nestling his sandwich, trying to thread the needle between pressing hard enough for his power, while not risking the loss of his job.

Ruth continued: "I respect the fact that, for I don't know how long, the focus of this office has been on crime and on criminal investigations in and around East St. Louis. What I am asking you is this: what has it gotten us? When I grew up here, the town was split about fifty-fifty, black-white, and now it is pretty much 100 percent black. I've read the statistics over those decades—as the jobs left this city, as the whites left this city and moved up the hill to Belleville, the unemployment soared, and the crime followed.

"But let's be frank, Walter. Even if we had double the lawyers in this office, and double the law enforcement, we would be lucky to see even a slight reduction in violent crimes, in drugs, in gang activity."

"I disagree," Walter offered, "if we had more resources, we would have even more of an effect."

"How many lawyers were in this office when you started 15 years ago?"

"I don't know, maybe 20 or 25."

"15, split 13 to criminal, two to civil. Now we have 75, split 65 to 10."

"And what, you want to move more resources to civil?"

"I did not say that. How many cases do you think those 75 lawyers are handling at the moment? I'll tell you; close to 1500. Fifteen hundred cases, at all stages from arraignment to awaiting trial. And we plead-out the majority of those cases, resulting in what appears to be very impressive conviction rates."

"I will take that as a compliment, I think," Walter added.

"By all means, congratulations; you all have been very good at what you do. But where has it gotten us? Despite this huge increase in the size of this office, what difference do you see out there," she said, pointing to Missouri Avenue.

"Ruth, respectfully, you have no idea of the difference we have made. We have run many St. Louis gangs out of East St. Louis. We have shut down several drug channels, and put in prison thousands of men who would be out there, pushing coke, crack, heroin—right now—if it wasn't for us."

"And are coke, crack, heroin no longer available—"

"What, you want to legalize drugs?"

"Did I say that? Did I say that? No. We are sitting here today, you and me, eating these sandwiches and talking about the future of this office—a future I presume you still want to be a part of."

"Yes," he said. Walter was no longer so sure.

"Well, then. What I am talking about to you, and soon to the rest of this department, is where I see resources being redirected. Not to civil; not entirely away from drugs, but to areas where I believe we can make a difference."

"And that is what?" Walter pondered aloud.

"Here, I'll show you an example." Ruth slid a stack of papers across the desk. "Read that."

Walter picked up the stack of papers and saw that they were financial forms, IRS returns and the like, but the documents provided no name. He flipped through the documents, which showed modest income statements for a decade or more. He also found bank accounts, checks, again with the names blanked.

"What," he asked, "we are going to focus on tax evasion?" He couldn't imagine a more horrible turn of events for the office. People were out in the street gunning each other down, he thought, and here we have an Elliot Ness-type who wanted to throw people in jail for cheating on their taxes.

"And this," Ruth said, "read this." It was a HUD form, showing the closing on a million dollar house.

"OK." Walter still thought this looked like tax evasion and he was pretty sure the Southern District had prosecuted virtually none of those cases since he had been in the office.

"Walter, what you have there is a part—and believe me I have much more where that came from—of an investigation into an elected official in this district. What that shows, I am sure you can tell, is that this guy earned upwards of $50,000 per year, had no investments to his name of any kind, and yet, six months ago, closed on a million dollar home not fifteen miles from here.

"Here's another," she passed along another bundle. "This is the mayor in a town an hour from here. He and his board of alderman granted to his wife ten separate job contracts for the city—at once—netting her over $500,000 for what appears to be no work.

"And another: kick backs. Another: pay-to-play." Ruth hoisted a bankers box onto her desk, pulling out bundles of summaries of cases. "I've got a bunch of them."

"How come I've not heard of any of these apparently on-going, investigations?" Walter asked, slightly piqued at not knowing, but more relieved it was far juicier than tax fraud.

"Because your former boss did nothing to prosecute them, and the files sat in boxes. Judges, elected officials, you name it; I have it. To say the FBI was frustrated and appalled at the blind eye your boss turned to these cases would be a grave understatement. My briefing from the field director was scheduled for two hours last week. Once he understood I wanted to hear what he had to say, we scheduled meetings for two additional days this week, and he brought me all of these pending investigations yesterday to get me started."

Walter was dumbfounded. Not so much at the corruption; it was no secret to anyone who lived for any time in the East Side that it rivaled only Chicago's Cook County, at the other end of the state, for patronage, strong-arming, and other machine-style politics. He was not even surprised at the failure of his previous bosses to investigate; those men were products of that very machine.

What astonished Walter was that, by positioning her office so clearly against that machine, Ruth was now going to make Walter choose sides.

Walter had tied his cart to Democrats for decades, working on dozens of campaigns. How could he, he wondered, prosecute these cases that were going to be brought against those very same Democrats, he assumed, and expect to have a single friend remaining in the Democratic-bastion that was the East Side?

Indeed both Walter and Ruth knew the answer: he couldn't. Walter considered the extent to which Ruth knew he would not side against the establishment. Ruth had removed all names and other identifiers from the documents she showed him, Walter noted. Ruth brought the question to the fore:

"So, Walter, in answer to your question, while I still intend to go after drug crimes, and gang activity, and to continue to beat this office's head against the wall of drugs and violence, I do have larger plans. As you no doubt have discerned, I see a real opportunity to go after the greed, graft and corruption that have plagued this area since as long as I can remember.

"To do that, I need a team made up of attorneys who will not blink, who will not leak, who will not waiver, to take on this political crime enterprise that has existed in this district for so long.

"And if I can't find the lawyers in this office to do that," Ruth said, looking down her nose and over her reading glasses to Walter, "I will bring in those who will."

Ruth didn't ask Walter if he wanted to stay. The inference was enough. If he was not completely committed to bringing down considerable parts of the Democratic establishment with her, he would no longer be the second in command, and if he was lucky, would perhaps head the violent crimes division of the office.

As Walter returned Ruth's stare, he knew that she already had determined that he would leave. He wondered, then, why she even bothered to tell him this information. Perhaps she figured the news of her investigations would come out soon enough, or perhaps she simply couldn't resist boasting the new and wonderful direction she thought she was taking the office.

Or maybe, he considered, she was trying to help him. Perhaps, by laying all of this out, she was indeed offering him an opportunity at something great—the chance to head up an investigation that could give him a lasting legacy, or perhaps an appointment to the bench. But he doubted it; he sensed hers would be only name in lights when all was said and done.

Walter left Ruth's office without indicating either way his intentions, but he had already made up his mind. Not wanting to take on the enduring Democratic machine—which had survived similar attempts over the decades, Walter knew—and not wanting a demotion, Walter drafted his resignation.

Before delivering it, however, he took a day's vacation and scouted for office space. If Ruth was hell-bent on taking on the East Side political establishment, by all means do it, Walter thought. He would stand at the ready to represent those targeted judges, mayors, and anyone else caught in her net. There was no one better, Walter thought, to defend against the U.S. Attorney's office than the man who essentially ran it for years.

9

JACK SAT IN NELSON BLEAKER'S OFFICE waiting for his law partner to finish a phone call.

Jack had hired Nelson nearly a decade earlier to shore up his fledgling firm's class action credentials. In class actions, courts often demanded specific class counsel experience, which provided some level of assurance that the unnamed, but nonetheless equally bound, members of the class were well-represented. Thus, in the first few federal cases where his adequacy was challenged successfully, Jack was forced to tender his cases to experienced class action law firms.

Jack knew that he needed to expand his firm's class action expertise. He doubted, however, that well-known class counsel had any desire to join him, and he was certain that he had no interest in taking second seat to anyone if they did.

His solution was to target the bench, and he knew then—and now—that there were no local judges with the combination of class action experience, clout and brains possessed by Nelson, who was now off the phone.

"Sorry Jack, thought that would have ended by now."

"Not a problem, Nelson. You ready to go eat?"

"Yeah, yeah. Let's go. Do you want to grab anyone else?"

"No, let's just the two of us go."

As the two men descended the steps of Hayes House, Jack slapped his partner on the back. Jack remained in a grand mood, owing entirely to the class action settlement. He was ready to deliver Nelson's share of the settlement, and to tell Nelson about the next class action he had in mind.

Nelson and Jack had become good friends in their ten years working together. Prior to that, Nelson had been an admired judge and head of the county court. His stature had began to unravel due to three strains.

First, in a novel resolution of a lawsuit against a local city, where the local police had brutally beaten a traveler but had no funds or insurance to pay the jury's $10 million verdict, Nelson had awarded the plaintiff title to the town's city hall. Since that award, the city had been paying annual rent to the plaintiff. Although the award was upheld on appeal, it threatened Nelson's retention in the upcoming election because residents had planned to come out in droves to cast their votes against him.

Second, Nelson had been arrested for driving under the influence. Although during the arrest he refused the breathalyzer test, which confounded the case against him, the State's Attorney—up for reelection—had continued to move forward with a prosecution of the sitting chief judge.

Finally, Nelson had needed money. A nasty divorce settlement had taken most of his salary and had him on the hook for college tuition for his twin daughters who were headed to Stanford.

Jack had phoned Nelson in the midst of these problems in Summer of 1984, ostensibly to ask him to golf and to offer whatever assistance he could give to the judge with regard to the upcoming retention campaign. As the round of golf at the country club began, Jack was less than surprised to hear the judge lay out the reasons he did not plan to run for retention, including especially the deal he had made with the state's attorney to drop the DUI charge if he moved out of the courthouse. Judge Bleaker was, it turned out, ready to start talking to firms about entering private practice. Jack figured the judge needed look no further than his firm.

As they took their seats for lunch, Jack rubbed his hands together excitedly, then held them apart, grasping the world he could see between them. "Well, my friend," Jack said, "today is your day." Jack slid a white envelope across the table to his partner. Nelson peered inside to see a handwritten check made out to him for $5 million.

"My God," Nelson whispered to Jack, "I think lunch is on me." He looked again at the check. He was elated. "Thank you."

"Don't thank me. I thank you. I've taken seven, you and Craig will get 5—per our partnership agreement—and we will pour eight back into the firm."

"Well, Jack, this is amazing. Congratulations on this case, it was hard earned and you did an amazing job."

"Thank you; it took a lot of work by all of us."

"I guess you are going to want your keys back?" Nelson shook the keys in his pocket. He had been living, since joining the firm, in a condo owned by Jack. The condo sat on the same golf course as Jack's current home. Jack had offered him the condo as a way for him to have someplace to live after his divorce that was nice enough and big enough for his daughters to visit. Nelson had accepted the offer and resigned the following week from the bench. He had never paid rent, and Jack had never asked for any.

"No, no. You stay there as long as you want. But you know, paying a little rent might not kill you now!"

The two men laughed as they tucked into their sandwiches. They were an interesting pair. Jack Spellman was lanky and pale, especially at this time of year. Judge Bleaker had Jack by a good 75 pounds, and perhaps twenty years, but was short, stocky and olive skinned. Jack was fastidious in his appearance, while Nelson often arrived to work in mismatched loafers. As the two men ate, various members of the plaintiff's bar came up and slapped them on the back, offering "attaboys" for their settlement with the railroad.

After they finished the last of their chips, Jack leaned back and said to Nelson, "so, I've been thinking of what's next."

"I figured you would be. That's what I love about you, Jack. What, my friend, is next?" Nelson rarely conceived of class actions, but he excelled at shooting them full of holes, and then helping to close those holes.

"AgriFarm."

"First the St. Louis & St. Paul, now AgriFarm? Shit. You won't be winning any local chamber of commerce awards that's for damn sure."

"Yeah, but who cares. The shoe fits."

"And the shoe is, what? This new neutered seed I've read about in the Post-Dispatch?"

"No, no. Too soon on that. I don't know where the damages are—and everyone knows that seed is what it is."

"But…"

"But their main line of corn seed, Selector. It's used everywhere. Everywhere in this country and around the world."

"Sure. I've heard of it. I've seen the signs on farms along I-55. It's a popular seed, right?"

"Right. It produces a crazy yield. Yields like no one has seen before. And do you know why?"

"No idea."

"Because it is genetically modified seed. Cloned seed."

"What the hell is that?"

"I will show you this article from a German magazine a buddy of mine sent me. Apparently, someone over there has figured this all out. It isn't just seed. It is a specially engineered seed."

"And so what?"

"Well, the article makes several points. It is, first of all, incredibly susceptible to a major disaster—think Irish potato famine. The number of users of this stuff—if it gets hit by disease, it is game over for the industry for years. Across the world. No corn. No corn syrup. No ethanol. No cattle feed. Commercial farming brought to its knees."

"Wow. Okay. And what else?"

"No one knows what else. We are feeding this modified food to our kids. We press it down into oil. We make everything out of this stuff.

And we don't know what it means. Maybe it increases allergies in kids? Maybe it endangers the livestock that eats it? Or hell, us, we eat it.

"But my point is, this: they have never told anyone that this is genetically engineered. There is no U.S. regulation that requires that disclaimer. There are some in parts of Europe, but it doesn't get enforced, and the farmers there have clamored for this stuff. So the regulators ignore it."

"So, what is the class? The people who are eating the corn?"

"No, I think that is too hard, too attenuated. I think it is the farmers, because the science backs up the susceptibility of the seed to a catastrophic end."

"The German science?" Nelson asked, skeptically.

"The Germans, for one. They tested this very seed. But there is plenty of other science on genetically modified food and the dangers that come from it. The science is adaptable."

"So, U.S. farmers?"

"I think we start with that. Federal action. Southern District."

"AgriFarm doesn't mess around, Jack. They use Jones Reed and some East Coast firms for these kinds of things. And their general counsel, well, no, I guess she just left. But whatever, Dave Meirs was a lawyer back in the day. I recall that. And he is a nasty S-O-B. He will spend everything on this."

"I know, I know. They've yet to fill Ruth Whittaker's spot, from what I've heard. So if we get this case in there soon, it will literally blow up their legal department and take them a while to figure it all out. And Jones Reed, they aren't what they once were. We can handle them."

"Perhaps. Perhaps. But where is the harm, here, Jack? I mean, where are the damages. The farmers love this seed, and make money off this stuff, right? I assume they'd hate to see it taken off the market."

"Maybe, but I don't think that matters. They were lied to; they were sold a bill of goods. They didn't know the risks and didn't get to choose. A twenty percent better yield is a great thing, but not if it is followed by the decimation of their entire crop for years to come. So, I say, the damages are what they would have paid for this seed had they known the risk, coupled with any other breach and consumer action stuff we can throw in there."

"And I assume you've run the numbers?"

"Number one seed, dominates the market, sales in the billions. The number of users is domestically in the tens of thousands. Farmers of all sizes. Virtually all the seed is bought through farm wholesalers, who use the form agreement from AgriFarm for every sale."

"So the class is big, but similar. Same contracts, same seed. Just different purchase amounts."

"Right, exactly. It could be as big as the SL&SP, if not bigger."

Nelson started in on his peanut butter pie and thought about the class. As he ate, he was nodding his head in general agreement as Jack talked about the German article and how it would eventually make it into the general media. By then, Nelson knew, the suit would have been filed somewhere else by someone else.

"AgriFarm is going to regret being headquartered here on the East Side. There won't be much chance of getting out of the Southern District," Nelson said.

"Precisely," Jack said. "So, you are on board? We've got to get this thing filed."

"Jack. You just gave me five million reasons why I am on board. I can't believe I'm saying this, but hell yes, let's bring down AgriFarm."

10

"Ruth, it's Dave. David Meirs. It's around 5:15 on Friday afternoon. Give me a call when you get this message. I am holding in my hand a class action lawsuit filed against AgriFarm. Filed this afternoon, in your building there. The Southern District. I've read it. Unbelievable. It seeks $500 million on behalf of farmers who were not told Selector is a modified product. Class counsel is Jack Spellman in Belleville. We need to talk. I want to stop this guy. Give me a call at the office."

—

"Ruth. Sorry I missed your call. It's 7. I liked what you had to say, but wanted to talk some more. I thought I might catch you. Our stock is going to tank on this, and the press is going to be on this thing. I can't believe the gall of this Spellman. This is a good product, for Christ sake. Call me. We need fast action. I'm leaving the office, so try my car or the house later tonight. I definitely need to talk. Thanks. Call me."

PART II

1

THE PARKING LOTS OF TOWNSHIP STADIUM filled quickly as crowds arrived early in anticipation of the Friday night football game between cross-town rivals East and West. The stadium lights warmed as the sun continued a slow drop behind the end zone stands where just days earlier mourners had gathered for the Chad Johnson memorial service.

By 6:30 p.m., the bands were in place at opposite sides of the field, blasting their respective fight songs. Plumes of smoke rose from the charcoal grills in the alley beyond the stadium wall.

The north stands of West supporters in maroon and white stood in unison with the south stands of the blue and gray East fans for the national anthem. The superintendent for the two schools took to the microphone from the young man who had sung the anthem:

"One week ago tonight, our district, and this city, suffered an immeasurable loss. The death of Chad Johnson leaves a hole in our community fabric. We continue to grieve for this loss.

"Tonight, we honor Chad while we continue the search for answers surrounding his death. You will see officers of the sheriff's department in the stands and at the exits. Please, if you know anything, talk to them." The superintendent then turned and passed the microphone to a priest who offered a prayer.

As 'amen' murmured through the stadium, the visiting band started to play. A paper-lined hoop reading simply, "Beat West," stood in front of the path from the visiting locker room tunnel. The gray and blue Lancers ripped through the circle and continued onto the field towards their fans in the far stands. They stood along the visitor sideline and turned to watch the entry of the Maroons.

The West band overtook the last notes of the East march, and all eyes turned to the West hoop, which was papered in black, with a CJ underscored by 69—a replica of the patch on all the West jerseys. The first players, the captains, ran to the sign, but stopped before exploding through it, instead lifting it from the hands of the pep club boys. They carried the black circle to the center of the field, the entire team behind them, and held it up. The players on both teams raised their helmets.

After a coin flip, West kicked off, then brought their defense onto the field without its former leader. His loss showed; by halftime, East led 21-7.

If there was a place to find people who knew about the death of Chad Johnson just a week ago, Sgt. Schaefer figured, Township Stadium in an East-West game was it. He had brought with him eight deputies, outfitted in County Sheriff windbreakers and badges, to work their way through the crowd seeking answers.

So far, Sgt. Schaefer knew this much about the night of Chad's death: Chad had been at the Stupes farm. He had gotten into a fight with a kid, who later filed a report about the incident with the police. Chad had left the party after midnight, with his friend Tyreese Jackson, and the boys had been pulled over by local police. His friend was arrested and Chad had agreed to alert his friend's parents as to that fact. At some point, he decided to stop and get out of his car. He ultimately was hit by a car or truck, travelling somewhere close to 70 miles per hour.

The hit had broken his neck, crushed his face, and sent him into the ditch. Whatever his long-term prospects were for survival, he did not die instantly from his trauma. Rather, the autopsy had shown evidence—water in the lungs, dilated blood vessels in the eyes and brain—that indicated a death by drowning. Chad had apparently drowned in only a few inches of water pooled in a tractor-wheel rut. Chad's broken neck rendered him unable to move his head to gain an air passage. Thus, although death appeared to have come soon after Chad had been hit, had the driver stopped, Chad could have been flipped over—an airway secured—and survived.

The students in the stands were willing to talk about the accident and the dead boy. The problem Sgt. Schaefer and his deputies encountered, however, was that there were so many students who knew so little that the deputies found it nearly impossible to separate the useful information from the rumors.

When the deputies met at halftime to discuss their interviews, some themes had come up enough, however, that they provided decent

lines of additional inquiry. One was that Chad Johnson was not particularly popular outside of the football team. The beating he had put
upon Jason Flowers at the Stupes farm was a fairly typical occurrence.

Some said the fight out at the Stupes place was a boil over from a
bad relationship with one of the cheerleaders down on the field. Sgt.
Schaefer released his deputies and found someone to point out to him
that cheerleader, Courtney Stein, who had returned from the locker
room for the second half of the game.

"Miss Stein," the sheriff asked as he came up from behind her.

She returned her water bottle to her gym bag on the lower stands
and turned around. "Hi. Yes, I'm Courtney." She extended her hand,
not sure of the protocol of talking to the police.

"Can I have maybe five minutes?" he asked, shaking her hand.

"Let me check," she said looking up a few rows, making eye con-
tact with her coach. Her coach nodded and pointed over his back, indicating to Courtney that she find somewhere behind the stands to speak
with the officer.

"Courtney, I'm Sgt. Cliff Schaefer of the County Sheriff's Department. I'm investigating the death of Chad Johnson."

"Sure. OK."

"I understand Chad got into a fight with a boy named Jason Flowers last week at the Stupes Farm."

"Yeah, that's right. If you want to call it that. Chad pretty much
accosted Jason, pulled him out of the car we were in, and just beat him
up. It wasn't much of a fight."

"Right. So I've heard. Did you talk to Chad that night?"

"No, other than to tell him to leave us alone when we arrived. Chad
and I used to date—briefly. But I had nothing to say to him and--"

"And what?" the sheriff interrupted.

"And he left, like right after the fight."

"How do you know that?"

"I saw him leave."

"And what time was that?"

"I don't know. 12? We got there late and all of this didn't take all that long." Courtney looked away when she heard the crowd cheering, the game resumed.

"Just another minute, please. Did you leave with Jason that night?"

"No."

"When did you leave?"

"I left before him, like maybe around 1:30 in the morning. I was staying with a friend, and that's when she left."

"And was that always the plan—to come with Mr. Flowers and to leave with your friend?"

"Um, no? I mean, that was my back up plan, you know? Jason had gone back to his car and sat in there and we all just left him alone. We aren't dating, or anything, so I didn't know what to say, and I felt bad that maybe I had, like, caused this all to happen to him."

"So you left at 1:30 in the morning, and Jason was still at the Stupes place, in his car?"

"Yeah. We walked right by, he looked like he was asleep."

"And then where did you go?"

"Like I said, to my friend's."

"And that was where?"

"Further out in Millstadt, not that far from Stupes."

"So you did not return to Belleville that night?"

"Not until school on Monday. I don't live here in town—I also live out in Millstadt."

"Got it. OK. Anything else you have heard about Chad getting hit?"

"No, not really."

"What does that mean, 'not really'?"

"Well, I mean, you know, lots of people didn't like Chad. And lots of people are talking about people who would have liked to have done that. But what I mean, is, you know, not really has anyone said they know anything about it."

"OK. Well, thank you. If you think of anything, here is my card with my number on it. You call me anytime."

"Right. OK. I can go?"

"Yes."

Sgt. Schaefer followed Courtney into the stadium and sat to watch the game. He scanned the student section, wishing someone would sit down next to him and tell him something he didn't already know.

His already short list of potential suspects had shrunk to zero. And worse, nothing indicated the collision that night had been anything other than accidental.

If that were the case, he knew, and the person who had killed Chad was someone with no connection to him, then the crime would likely never be solved without someone walking into his office and confessing to it.

Sgt. Schaefer watched as the Maroons defense was pushed back eighty yards, allowing an easy score and a 42-10 East lead. His spirits now sunk in all regards, he headed for the exit.

2

RUTH DRIED THE CHAMPAGNE FLUTES over the kitchen sink as she looked through the window toward the St. Louis skyline. Several years earlier, she had decided to sell her Central West End condo in favor of more space and a connection to her roots on the East Side. She had heard that an executive from the St. Louis dog food conglomerate was selling his family's modernist home that sat on an Illinois bluff overlooking the flood plain of East St. Louis and the bigger city beyond it. The home had no neighbors to speak of, and its floor to ceiling windows offered views of nature, of the city skyline, a pool, and a carriage house. Few houses anywhere in the St. Louis area looked like this one, and that was what attracted Ruth to it. She had bought it the day it came on the market.

On this night, she would be entertaining a handful of prosecutors from her office. In addition to Xavier, her second in command, she had invited four young attorneys from the criminal and civil divisions. All had accepted the invitation, but none knew exactly what was in store for them.

The attorneys arrived promptly and migrated towards the west-facing windows, catching the last of the sunset. Ruth had not offered to her employees that they could bring guests, and they hadn't. They understood this was a work function.

Nonetheless, Ruth popped the cork on a bottle of sparkling wine and offered a toast to her office and to these attorneys, who began to wonder why they were there, and their coworkers were not. Everyone sipped their drinks and sat around the fire that was starting to take hold in the living room fireplace. Ruth called her prosecution team to dinner.

With the lights ablaze, the dining room windows reflected the six lawyers, smiling and laughing as they sat down and got to know one another. They made connections to places and people they had in common. Once the pink glow from the sunset faded, Ruth dimmed the lights, which transformed the window from a mirror into a show of the St. Louis skyline.

As the younger attorneys began to eat, Ruth talked of growing up just down the hill.

"I was born in '46. I grew up in East St. Louis with my two sisters, and our mother. We lived in a small apartment off of St. Clair Avenue—a two-flat.

"My parents weren't born around here, though. They both came to East St. Louis as kids in the early teens, I think it was. Anyway, my maternal grandpa, he died in the race riots right after that. So it never was easy.

"My momma, she met my father at a black speakeasy in St. Louis. They found out they both had family who had come from Arkansas, and they bonded over that."

Ruth talked about her mother, who had worked for years in St. Louis at a clothier downtown. Her father worked in the East St. Louis stockyards, mostly, but those jobs left not long after her parents were married. "And so he left too. He returned to Arkansas for seasonal work, but stayed for good," Ruth recalled with a shake of her head.

Ruth caught up with her soup as others chimed in about their growing up in the area. Xavier mentioned the similarities of his and Ruth's lives in East St. Louis, a generation apart.

That led to a spirited discussion about the downfall of East St. Louis, which had once been declared an All-American city in the 1950s, and had at that time a population of over 80,000. Now, they all agreed, there was nothing particularly great about the city, save for many of its residents who had stayed and tried to keep it great while the city lost more than half its population over the ensuing decades.

Xavier sensed the evening slipping away and so, while the other attorneys started to clear dishes, he segued into a discussion of the corrupt mayors East St. Louis had endured over the years. That opened the door for Ruth, who invited everyone back to the living room, as she stoked the fire.

"Well, thank you again for coming tonight. As I said, this was a work function, and we do have some work to do.

"You are all probably wondering why I've invited you here. Well, I have chosen you to be here tonight for a couple of reasons. First, I like what you had to say when I interviewed you about your cases. I liked what I read about you in the exit memorandum my predecessor left me. I like your energy.

"Before I agreed to accept an appointment to this position, I considered what it was that I could bring to this office that would be different—better—than the attorneys who sat here previously.

"I've been practicing law in this area for decades, and I've been reading the papers for even longer. And I know what you know, that this District, these counties, are awash in governmental malfeasance at virtually every level. And for years, despite the many tools at the disposal of this office, nothing has been done—no indictments, no trials, no convictions, nothing. And this, despite reams of evidence compiled by the FBI and local law enforcement.

"Well, that changes now, and I want each of you to help me bring about that change," Ruth said, as she took a sip of coffee.

"You've all now gotten to know Xavier a bit, and you may have read about him before. Summa cum laude from U of C. Undergrad at Princeton. U.S. Attorney's office in Chicago, then principal of Raines & Holden there.

"Xavier will head up what I am calling our Good Government

Group, or 3G. Xavier and I will make determinations based on what cases to go after, and he will determine what cases each of you will be a part of.

"And so, basically, I want all of you to join us. Becoming a part of 3G is not mandatory. If you prefer to remain in your existing caseload, no one will second guess you. But what I am telling you is that this is an opportunity to change the course of the way government has been run in this area for generations. You will leave work each day feeling that you are working to make things right in a way that affects every person in Southern Illinois."

The four young prosecutors looked at each other, subtly nodding their heads in unison. They were not tied to the political establishment and liked the idea of making a name for themselves. Without Ruth telling them, they already knew the success she and Xavier represented, and they hoped, could bestow upon them.

They submitted their unanimous agreement to become the inaugural 3G team. Xavier got up and retrieved four black three-ring binders, each with the individual attorney's name imprinted on the cover.

"We hoped you would say that," he said, "welcome."

Xavier distributed the binders to each attorney: "These are your binders. You are to keep them locked in your desks, or if you prefer, in my office. The goals and initiatives are set forth in Tab 1 and will be news soon enough, when Ruth has her first press conference as to this unit and its mission. Until then, your participation should be kept close to the vest, and any inquiries from your co-workers or anyone else should be directed to me. Tab 2 is a placeholder for your cases.

"Please look at Tab 3: Governing Rules. These are rules for 3G that expand upon, and in some cases supersede, those provided to you in your employee handbook. These run ten pages, and mainly focus on absolute protection of information regarding investigations and prosecutions arising out of 3G.

"I will give you the balance of this evening to review and sign the document. But let me point out one rule: 17.9: Termination for Unauthorized Release of Information. We know that you are all relatively young attorneys, and that in some instances, you will all make mistakes. The one mistake that will not be tolerated by any of you is the leak of information about cases handled by 3G to anyone outside this group. If information about an investigation is leaked to an outside party—a newspaper, a politician, your best friend, whomever—you will be terminated. And please note subsection (b); if the leaking party cannot be identified, all of you will be terminated.

"Now, please review the document, and let me know if you have any questions." Xavier was pleased that no one had balked as he spoke, and that instead they had silently begun to read the rules. "Oh, and one last thing, for your service to our government corruption unit, you've each been bumped up three steps within your pay level, effective now."

Ruth beamed as her assistants signed their rules. "And now that you have all sworn yourselves to our mission," she said, "I want you to know that you won't be sitting on your hands waiting for something to come. Beginning on Monday, and running for the balance of the week, we will announce a series of arrests emanating from this anti-corruption unit.

"We will move fast, and we will be noticed. For example, tomorrow night, at a fundraiser, we will arrest the mayor of Washington Park for accepting millions in bribes from out-of-state strip-club operators seeking to open in his hamlet. The following day, we have on tap a large bid-rigging case, and that will be followed by a straight-up government theft case.

"Further, Xavier and I will be working tomorrow on a highly-confidential investigation. I expect charges to be brought against a prominent official in a case that will reverberate throughout this district.

"So, again, welcome. Thank you for coming and for agreeing to be a part of this. This is going to get fun."

3

"DON'T GET ME WRONG, it sucks he died and all, but I mean, Jesus, what was with the whole stadium of people crying, and then all of that shit tonight. I mean, this guy was a dick, right?" Pete offered.

Tim Spellman sat in the backseat of his friend Pete's old car as it headed down 59th Street and into the country. Tim, Pete and Ben were en route to the Stupes farmstead slightly in advance of the end of the East-West football game.

"You are a dick. I mean, the dude died—right there," Ben volunteered. The three boys had the death of Chad Johnson on their minds as they passed the roadside memorial of laminated photos, a white cross and football helmet.

"Seriously," was all the comment Tim could muster. He stared out the window as the car passed the Stanis farm. His stomach churned. While he breathed slowly and tried to settle his nausea, he thought about what had transpired on the road only one week earlier.

That Friday night had marked six months in his relationship with his girlfriend Kate Shaw. Tim had convinced her to leave the football game after halftime, when her duties on the dance team had ended. Although she was expected to remain in the stands after her squad's halftime routine, she had agreed to head out to the Stupes farm before the crowds arrived. Brad Stupes had given Tim the okay to get there early, and the key to the farmhouse, and Tim had had plans.

His plans, as it turned out, were not Kate's plans. She didn't care for the creakiness of the farmhouse bed, or the musty smell of the upstairs bedroom. This wasn't the place, and it wasn't the time, Kate said, and she told him they could wait—they should wait—until prom at least, or maybe even later.

None of this was what Tim had wanted to hear. The house was fine, the bedroom was clean—he'd confirmed that with Brad. He'd brought a candle and some wine. They'd been dating for an eternity, he thought.

When it didn't happen, Tim spent the rest of the night ignoring Kate, heading from friend to friend, slamming beers and taking shots, all in hopes of forcing down his disappointment. As the booze took its effect, Tim started to spout off to his close friends about his inability to get laid. Chad Johnson, not in the circle, but close enough to hear the conversation, offered up his thoughts:

"Seriously, dude, Kate? I had her on the second date. We went to the Skyview. I crushed that in the back of the Camaro, dude. You guys, what's it been, like a year? What are you, gay?" Chad let out a laugh, backhanding his buddy Tyreese Jackson on his chest. "Gay!" They both said and laughed.

Tim knew Chad, but not well. Tim was in higher level classes, studying for AP credits and working on his class rank. Chad, meanwhile, was focused on keeping his grades above the level needed for football eligibility.

Despite rarely seeing one another, Tim had made a point of staying away from Chad over the course of the last several months because he could not wrap his head around how Kate had dated a guy like Chad—even briefly. Tim wasn't sure what that said about his girlfriend, or himself.

Tim told Chad to fuck off. He left the fireside in search of darkness and a spot in which to relieve himself. On his way to the open field beyond the barn, he found Kate sitting on the bumper of an old truck whispering and drinking with her friend Tara.

"Hey Tim," Tara offered. Silence. Tim headed further into the field.

"Man, I wish I could just whip it out and do that," Tara whispered to Kate as they watched the back of Tim and heard his beer depart him. Tara's whisper was plenty loud for Tim to hear.

"I wouldn't, Tara. Kate would run away from you if she saw it." Kate ignored the comment, but exchanged a look with Tara, who walked off leaving Kate and Tim in the field.

"Tim."

"What?"

"Tim, you know I'm right about this."

"You are such a hypocrite."

"What?"

"So, a nice old country house is somehow not good enough for you? I'm not good enough for you?"

"Tim, you know that isn't it."

"Then what? You are okay having sex at a drive-in theatre, with a dirtbag you barely know, but not with me, after six months? Jesus." Tim kicked at dirt, sending a clump into the side of the barn.

"Tim, stop it. Stop it. What are you talking about?" she asked, knowing full-well what he was talking about.

"Chad Johnson, you and him. The Skyview. Him 'crushing it' he just told me. Second date." Tim's voice cracked; he was as sad as he was angry.

Kate held back her tears and her words. She directed Tim back to the spot on the bumper where Tara had been sitting. She knew that he wanted to hear that Chad had been lying. The simple truth was, he hadn't lied; but the more complicated truth required more thought before she started down that path.

The two sat in silence, listening to thunder approach and watching the lightning in the distance. Kate considered her relationship with Tim. Had she been tired of him, she would have walked away and decided to end it. But she liked him and liked him more than anyone before.

Still, there was a limit to how much about that night with Chad, and particularly its aftermath, that she had planned to share with Tim or anyone, ever. And if she told him everything, well, then they had better be together forever, because she couldn't bear to think someone could know that Chad had gotten her drunk, her consent present but barely, and he'd gotten her pregnant.

No one knew that truth, not her mother, not Tara, not Chad, no one. She had intended to keep her pregnancy and its termination secret from everyone forever. But how could she reconcile to Tim, whom she wanted to keep forever but didn't want to have sex with, her relationship with Chad, whom she wanted nothing to do with even as she let him sloppily pursue her in his car.

Making matters a little worse was the fact that Tim was drunk. But she had seen him drunk before, and knew in fact that it was in that state that he often lowered his guard and was the most approachable. Kate decided to see if this could be one of those times. "Tim, will you walk with me?"

He nodded. The two grasped hands and headed slowly out into the field, which grew darker as they moved away from the bonfires and porch light of the farmstead. A slow rain started to fall, bringing up the smell of dirt. Tim could hear a commotion rising behind them at the farmhouse, it seemed, but he didn't look back. He listened while Kate began to share her secret.

Tim took in the information without comment. He closed his eyes, then stopped walking. He dropped his head. Kate continued to stare out into the field, stealing glances to decipher any hint at what her boyfriend was thinking.

Kate's revelation sent Tim's mind in two conflicting directions. The first was how he felt about Kate. He understood the traumatic experience she had endured, though he had never known anyone to have had an abortion. Not that it was really up to him, Tim realized, but he thought that he was okay with this having happened to his girlfriend. He also appreciated for the first time why Kate was hesitant at getting involved again with any guy, himself included.

The second direction his mind moved was towards a white hot anger, which made him shake with a rage Kate could feel as he gripped her hand tighter. His anger was directed only at Chad, whom he figured had used some combination of alcohol and force to steal Kate's innocence in the back of his ridiculous muscle car.

"That fucker," were the first words Tim spit out after minutes of silence.

Tim recognized these were the unfortunate first words out of his mouth. He started again, quietly, turning to Kate and pushing her hair out of her face: "God. I am so sorry this happened to you; that you had to go through that. That he did… that to you." Kate said nothing, but sunk her head into Tim's shoulder and cried.

The rain fell harder. Tim and Kate walked awkwardly in a grasp back to Tim's truck, which he had hidden off the back side of the rear road into Stupes farm. They ducked into the Explorer and Tim turned on the engine to get some heat started. Tim switched on a mix tape he had dubbed with the British alt-pop songs he knew Kate loved. The two sat in silence, listening to several songs. Their wet warmth fogged the windows.

As she sat with her eyes closed and her head on Tim's shoulder, Kate felt warm and safe. She felt relieved.

Tim, meanwhile, wiped his hand over the blurred windshield and continued to stew over the fact that there was nothing he could do about any of it. As much as he wanted to confront Chad, that would expose Kate's secret.

He decided he needed to get away from Chad and from the Stupes farm. Intoxicated, and full of pent up anger, frustration and tension, Tim pulled his truck out of the muddy field and headed for Kate's house.

By the time they had reached the blinking light in Millstadt, Kate had fallen asleep. Tim did his best to keep the Explorer between the lines, and went so far as to set his cruise control to make it out of town without worrying that he had broken the speed limit.

He made it past the village line and turned onto 59th street, heading toward central Belleville where Kate lived. He gunned the engine, passing 60 mph as he negotiated the turn. He was angry, certainly, at Kate having let herself be had, but that was a passing anger. What remained was a building rage at Chad.

As the fury continued to bang about in his head, and he began to envision the groping that Chad must have inflicted on Kate, Tim kept a two-handed grip on the wheel of his truck as it bounced along the slick two-lane road. The powerless feeling roiled his gut.

Then Tim saw what he thought might be Chad's car. He squinted and could indeed make out, at a distance and with his high-beams on, the unmistakable thick stripes on the rear of Chad's vintage Chevy, parked on the side of 59th Street. Tim looked down and saw that he was travelling nearly 75 mph. His mind sobered; his vision cleared. He gripped the wheel tighter.

Tim contemplated for a second what it was the football player was doing in that car, concluding that some other girl was meeting the same fate as Kate. He hastily considered his options, deciding to bring his truck and its steel bumper to bear on the protruding side mirror of the car. Knock it off, he figured, that would feel good. Deflower the blessed Camaro; how fitting.

Mere seconds into this not-fully-fleshed-out idea, Tim took solid command of his truck and barreled forward. As he came upon the car—which he knew from the CJ SS 69 plate was indeed Johnson's— he navigated the truck only slightly towards the road's crowned center.

Tim decided to blow his horn long and hard, hoping to interrupt Chad in coitus just long enough to see the mirror ripped off his car. Tim leaned on the horn, guiding his Explorer still closer to the car as he reached it.

Tim aimed his truck for the car's side mirror, but made out a shape of something emerging from the car's front. Tim had no time to steer away and didn't try. As his truck passed the car, he heard first a metallic tink—the mirror—then a sizable thud—the boy. As quickly as the truck had come upon the Camaro, it was clear and barreling into the darkness of the country road.

Tim looked in the rearview mirror and saw nothing but the retreating darkness. No other cars were on the road, and the road had no streetlights. He watched to see if a light would come on inside the now-distant Camaro, or if the headlights would be lit in pursuit. Nothing.

Tim passed into Belleville, now sick to his stomach. He stopped at the first gas station, pulled into the space by the payphone, got out of the truck, and proceeded to release the contents of his stomach onto the curb in front of the yellow bollards protecting the phone. Tim walked in the rain around his truck. He checked the front bumper. The black rubber covering the steel bumper appeared normal. There was no blood, no dent. The orange signal light was cracked, with a small beam of light shining through a missing speck of orange plastic. But that was it.

Kate had stirred from the feel of the impact and awoke as the bright lights of the gas station shone down upon her. When Tim got back into the driver's seat she asked, "Why are we stopped here?"

"I had to puke."

"Are you okay?"

"Yeah, yeah."

"Is everything ok? What were you checking?

"Hit a raccoon or some shit. No big deal, everything's OK."

"OK. You cool to drive?" she asked.

Tim nodded. Kate returned to sleep, her head resting against her window.

As Tim drove Kate home, his mind traded its preoccupation with the Chad and Kate saga in favor of the issue of what he had just done.

Tim pulled into Kate's driveway. They kissed their goodbyes, each preoccupied with other thoughts. Kate grabbed her bag from the backseat, gave a wave to Tim and bounded up her front sidewalk. The motion-detector lights came on across the porch and driveway and Tim caught a glimpse of himself in the rearview mirror. His blue eyes were a uniform red, his blonde hair a matted mess. He watched Kate open the front door, wave to him, close the door and kill the lights.

Tim pulled out of Kate's neighborhood and headed towards his home in the west end of town. He released a torrent of curses, growing louder as he drove. He pounded on his steering wheel. He resisted the urge to head back down 59th Street.

He headed home, drove up his driveway, and parked in front of the garage. He made his way upstairs and showered away the smell of bonfire, dirt and adrenaline. He crawled into bed and hoped for sleep. But for hours, his head spun each time he closed his eyes. Worse, when he closed his eyes his brain replayed for him in increasingly-clear detail that one second in time when he hit something or someone—and kept on driving like nothing much had happened.

By five in the morning, Tim's brain had recreated a crystal moment in time where he had killed Chad Johnson, though he didn't know if the hit had resulted in a death. That clarity brought with it an intermittent sleep, which was broken soon after by the footsteps of Tim's father moving about on the groaning wood floors of the upstairs hall.

4

Ruth had asked Xavier to meet for brunch far from the Southern District courthouse. They sipped coffee under the giant windows of the Palm House.

"So, Ruth, what do you have up that sleeve of yours?" Xavier asked.

"Flood."

"A flood?"

"Judge Flood."

"No! For what? You have got to be kidding me. I mean, for what?"

"Accepting a bribe in a case."

"Wow. Slow down," Xavier said, wanting to savor the details. "How did you even find out about this? This is incredible stuff. And this is stuff, I mean if we get this wrong, this will blow up in our faces and, well, you know, threaten everything else we are here to do."

"I know. And that is why this is going to be a very quiet path to indictment, and you and I are on this case, alone, and mainly outside of the courthouse."

"How long until he retires?"

"End of the calendar year, but then he has said he would take emeritus status, though what we know now might contradict that. Regardless, he knows every person in that building, has all the keys, and Lord knows what else."

"Jesus. The chief!" Xavier whispered, lowering his head. "You want to take down the chief."

"Not just the chief." Ruth stood and headed to the buffet, with Xavier in tow, still shaking his head.

"Just look at this brick work—isn't it amazing. You don't find this kind of work anywhere anymore," Xavier said, his comment earning him the nodding approval from the women in front of him in the buffet line.

The two prosecutors, apparently unknown to the entire room, looked at one another from each side of the long, narrow table of pastries and fruit, and shared a bemused look in recognition of the path they were now upon. They filled their plates and returned to their table overlooking the lily pond just outside.

"Ruth," Xavier said, "tell me more. Who paid the bribe?"

"Do you know the Spellman firm, in Belleville?"

"No, should I?"

"Well, it has been a growing firm over the last several years. Jack Spellman is the founder, and he added a couple of judges over the last several years. They practice in class actions and it looks like they are trying to add one more judge to their letterhead—the chief.

"Perhaps you recall the recent class action that settled against the SL&SP Railroad?" Ruth asked.

"Afraid not."

"Well, it was one of the bigger class settlements in this area—ever. The Spellman firm took the railroad for millions for misuse of their railroad easements—of all things," Ruth said, dismissive of the case. "And guess what judge certified that class?"

"I guess I don't have to."

"Now, the defendants sought appeal of the certification, but the judge's order was ironclad and admitted to no weaknesses in the class, the class counsel—nothing. The Seventh Circuit affirmed. And then, of course, the case settled. It was one of the only two or three classes he ever certified in all his years on the bench."

"So this was the first one in the money—and just in time for his retirement. Unbelievable. You know, now that you mention it, I think I do recall seeing the affirmation from the 7th Circuit in the digest when I was up in Chicago, some months back." Xavier picked at a scone, shaking his head and taking in all that Ruth was telling him. "What was the settlement?"

"$100 million to the class."

"Oof. And I hate to ask what was Spellman's take?"

"$25 million."

"Wow. And how much of that is going to the chief?"

"Well, that is where it starts to get complicated. When we get done here, I've got a tape for you to hear."

"Excellent. I can't wait to hear it. And I can't believe you had the gumption to get the guy on tape. Home? Car?"

"Chambers."

"Unbelievable!"

The two ate quickly, mostly in silence. Their minds were on moving forward against the Southern District's most powerful judge, and the most influential trial lawyer in the area.

"More coffee?" the waitress asked Ruth.

"No, no. Just the check, thank you."

Once Ruth had finished her meal, and the check arrived, Xavier dropped a $50 bill on the table, which more than covered the tab and tip. "Let's go hear that tape of yours."

Ruth stood, grabbed her purse and patted its side: "The greatest hits, right here." Xavier and Ruth walked out, past the lily pond and Xavier motioned her over to his car. He let her in the passenger door of his 7-series and she sunk into the black leather seat.

"Should we drive around?" Xavier asked, turning the key in the ignition.

"Sure." Ruth handed Xavier the cassette, which he placed in the player. He pulled the car out of its spot and headed out of Tower Grove Park.

Xavier decided upon a route, cutting through some of the city's grand old neighborhoods. They listened to snippets of Judge Flood, embroiling himself into a conspiracy.

"The older voice," Ruth said, "is Flood. The second voice is Nelson Bleaker, the former top judge in St. Clair County. He is a partner in the Spellman firm. This is, as I said, a greatest hits. There are hours and hours of tapes, from Flood's chambers phone."

"How long has the phone been tapped in his chambers?"

"Almost a year. It was put in there for investigation by the FBI of federal campaign finance violations, mainly soliciting contributions from his work phone. Well, there was some of that, but those calls led to this mess. Several of these are from months ago. Play it."

—

(Ring) Bleaker: "This is Nelson."

Flood: "Nelson, Bill Flood."

Bleaker: "Judge Flood, my friend! How the hell are you?"

Flood: "Can't complain. Good to talk to you. And it was nice to see you at the reunion. But listen, I won't keep you long. We are working on getting this D-PAC fund going."

Bleaker: "That's the PAC for St. Clair?"

Flood: "Right, supporting whatever Democrats in state and federal elections. It's a political action committee, so sky's the limit on funding it. I know you've done direct donations in the past to candidates, but this is more of an umbrella thing."

Bleaker: "Sure, I know about PACs. But you are right, I usually give when the candidate gives me a call, or looks me in the eye and asks for it. But what's the standard ask?"

Flood: "The standard? Uh, there is no standard. Just whatever you want, you know."

Bleaker: "Well, what is everyone else doing? I don't want to look like the jerk for giving too little, or too much, for that matter."

Flood: "I can tell you there is no 'too much'."

Bleaker: "Ha, right, I imagine. OK, well (pause). How does $100,000 work for you?"

Flood: "Nelson, wow. That is wonderful. You must be doing well."

Bleaker: "Sure as hell beats the bench, Bill. You should join us."

Flood: "If I had $100,000 to throw around, I wouldn't be working anywhere, I'll tell you that."

Bleaker: "That right?"

Flood: "Well, I mean, you know how it is."

Bleaker: "You've got your 20 in, right? You should just quit and come up here. We could use you."

Flood: "Well, I don't know if I have 2000 billable hours in me anymore. Hell, I've not even filled out a time sheet in decades."

Bleaker: "Me neither. That's not how we work it here. We are class counsel, we aren't corporate lawyers. Our fees are estimable! It truly was a revelation when I came over here. Think about it."

Flood: "I will. I mean, it sounds nice."

Bleaker: "And let me say this. It is nice. We make it easy to transition, to get yourself established. All of that."

Flood: "Right. Well, anyway, thanks for the pledge, that is incredible."

Bleaker: "Sure, and let's talk more about this other thing."

Flood: "Agreed."

—

Ruth motioned to Xavier to pause the cassette player. "So that, right there, that's a violation of the federal campaign finance laws. But he was doing that for years—and no one ever cared to do anything about it. He just shifted at his desk from case files to fundraising files, without so much as giving it a second thought. But what you heard, that was the beginnings of something more."

"It certainly appears to be," Xavier agreed.

"And don't forget, at the time this recording is going on, the Jack Spellman class action is pending certification before Judge Flood. So, my thinking is, Spellman has to be turning the wheels here," Ruth offered.

"Point taken. What's next?"

"The next call is from Bleaker to Flood, in his chambers, about two weeks later—still pre-certification of Spellman's class."

—

Female: "Chief Judge's Chambers. Diane."

Bleaker: "This is Nelson Bleaker. Is the judge in?"

Female: "Please hold. (pause). Transferring you now. Thank you."

Flood: "This is Flood."

Bleaker: "Judge, Nelson Bleaker."

Flood: "Nelson, how are you? Thanks for the D-PAC funds. I understand they were received by the PAC chairman."

Bleaker: "Certainly, and let me know if you need more. I can hit up my partners."

Flood: "A fine idea."

Bleaker: "Which gets me to the point of my call. Have you considered what we talked about last time we spoke?"

Flood: "Not in any real sense. I certainly feel I have ten years of practice in me, but I figured I would look over the river to one of the big firms. Some sort of figurehead role, trot me out, all of that. You know."

Bleaker: "They would be lucky to have you. But they don't need more show ponies, with all those congressmen and senators filling the corner offices. And wouldn't you want to be more active in a practice? Roll up your sleeves, knock down some guys."

Flood: "Perhaps, but not at the expense of taking on a risk as far as getting paid, or having to buck up funds to finance risky cases."

Bleaker: "Sounds like you have thought about it."

Flood: "Well--"

Bleaker: "But let me tell you, this place is the real deal. I left the pleasures of the bench for it—you know that. I walked down the street and into an office with keys to a new condo and a new Cadillac, and I've made more money in each successive year than I did in any ten years on the bench—combined."

(pause)

Bleaker: "I can promise you that you will be well provided for, well employed, and well regarded."

Flood: "Nelson, it was good to hear from you. You've given me some food for thought. I've got to be on the bench in five, and I need to use the restroom. So if—."

Bleaker: "Judge. Understood. I will talk with you soon. Have a good afternoon."

—

Xavier paused the cassette this time. "So, an offer of future employment. And an existing case with the law firm from whom the offer was sent. Impropriety all around. But, hell, we aren't the bar. This is the stuff of discipline, or disbarment, right? But beyond that…"

"We are only half way through, just wait. This next set of voices is Flood, and Manny Diaz, recorded a week later—still pre-certification."

"And he is?"

"Just listen, you'll know it in no time."

—

Female: "Chief Judge's Chambers. Diane."

Diaz: "Is the judge in? Tell him it's his cousin Manny."

Female: "Please hold. (pause). Transferring. Thanks."

Flood: "This is Flood."

Diaz: "Judge, Manny."

Flood: "I've been waiting for this call."

Diaz: "I bet. Rough game. Bills plus 4, and to lose by a touchdown in overtime. Rough one. So, that makes--"

Flood: "I know what I owe you. When do you need it?"

Diaz: "Well, last time, it was eighty grand, and we let that ride this week, but we can't let this one ri—"

Flood: "When?"

Diaz: "I need $160,000 by this Friday."

Flood: "That is impossible."

Diaz: "I don't think so, judge."

Flood: "I am telling you this is an impossibility. It will not and cannot happen by Friday. I can get you $15,000."

Diaz: "Nope. $160,000 or—"

Flood: "Or what?"

Diaz: "Judge, let's not get into that. You are going to pay us or we will have to make some other arrangement."

Flood: "Such as?"

Diaz: "We can work something out with your car or your house.

Something."

Flood: (inaudible)

Diaz: "Judge?"

Flood: "I will call you in two days."

Diaz: "Friday. C.O.B."

—

"Wow." From what little Xavier knew of the chief, garnered in only a few meetings in the courthouse, this was contrary to the judge he knew. He could not believe the chief was so heavily into gambling, and had six figure debts—in addition to the rest of what the tapes were starting to show. "Let me guess, he finds the boys at the Spellman firm to bail him out?"

Ruth watched the Victorian mansions pass, and the smaller lines of brick row houses resume as Xavier navigated through the streets of St. Louis.

"Well, that would certainly be neat and tidy, wouldn't it? But we don't have a tape of that—yet. What we do have, though, is evidence of a home equity loan the judge tapped on his home in Illinois, for $300,000."

"So he was able to get a loan in two days time? No way."

"Not quite. The loan was open a long time prior to this. Perhaps to fund his gambling endeavors over the years, who knows. But it appears, at this point, he already had maxed it out, and $300,000 is far more than his house is worth. So the $160 was going to have to come from somewhere else."

"So he was hurting."

"He was hurting. And needing some help, fast."

"OK, so now what?"

"So, now, the story moves along. We don't hear again from him on his phone to the bookie, and we don't have a call back to the chambers phone from the bookie. So that went away, somehow. But then, the following week, we have movement on the certification of the SL&SP

case—the railroad case. The motion had been sitting for almost three months, which isn't unusual from what I could tell of his docket.

"But what was unusual was the opinion itself. It was very well drafted, well researched and cited, and very long—far longer than any brief we've seen from his chambers in any case we could find. But very one-sided, which was not typically his drafting style." Ruth motioned to Xavier to restart the tape. "Then there's this: the female you will hear is one of his two law clerks, Andrea Tate, leaving a voicemail for the judge."

—

(beep) Tate: "Judge, this Andrea. I now you are out of court today, and I hope you are enjoying your day off. But Dianne left me a copy of the order in the SL&SP class action. (pause). Wow. That is a well-drafted opinion, but it isn't the direction we talked about or what I was working on. I guess you didn't care for my draft, which is okay of course, but I thought at least we would have talked about this some more. Anyway, when you are back in the office next week, I hope we can discuss this case. It will certainly be an interesting trial, if we get there I guess. Sorry this rambled. Have a good weekend, or if you get this Monday morning, I hope your weekend was a good one. Bye."

—

"We found a copy of Andrea's draft on the court system," Ruth said. "It was nowhere near complete, but it nonetheless had in the introduction the ultimate finding that certification was inappropriate for various reasons under Rule 23. She hadn't worked on it for weeks— she had been out a week for vacation, which was the time in which the judge issued his decision as to certification. But as you heard, it was an about-face from where they were heading with this case."

"Interesting." Xavier liked where this was going. He felt some passing sadness for the judge he hardly knew, but mainly, his thoughts went to finding holes in Ruth's case, at least based on what he had heard so far. "I see where you are going with this. And this tape will play well for the grand jury, I am sure you know, but for me, there is no conviction in this. Not yet, anyway."

"This is just the stuff on tape. What you haven't seen is the interrogation of the bookie, who stated he received a box of cash delivered by an unidentified courier."

"Of course he did! And the money came from where?"

"He didn't know, and didn't ask. And I don't know yet, either. That is our last piece."

"Well, Ruth. This is interesting. Very interesting. And I am glad you asked me to head it up. I'm blown away by this. The chief. Jesus, the chief! We need to get on linking this payment. I gather you've checked his finances and nothing on this?"

"No, nothing," Ruth confirmed.

"How are we going to get subpoenas in this case? I can't imagine you are working through the Southern District—there is too great of a chance of someone seeing or saying something."

"That is certainly true. I've been working it in two ways. One, I've been using John Doe's and partial account numbers for the financial stuff, and two, I've been using Judge Randolph."

"I don't know Judge Randolph. In the Southern District?"

"Emeritus judge from the Central District, who lives down here, and has an office in our building. He's a Nixon appointee, and a friend of a friend from my AgriFarm days. He doesn't know yet it's the chief, but I suspect he won't give a care when he does."

"Nice. I like that. So, I am thinking next we need to turn to the Spellman firm, and get to their computers, files, bank accounts, all of it. Maybe even the phones. How far will Judge Randolph let us go, do you think?"

"Based on what we've got at this point," Ruth said, "I have to figure some form of wiretap would be authorized at least for the firm, but I say we go for Bleaker's house, and Spellman's too. We need to focus as much on the firm, and those lawyers—especially Spellman—as we do the judge."

They sat in silence as Xavier drove west through midtown, completing his circle tour and returning into the park. He pulled his car alongside Ruth's silver Mercedes. She got out of the car, and Xavier stood outside his door, his hand on its roof: "One last thing, where are you keeping the document drafts, files, and all of that?"

"My house. Go get yourself a laptop computer, if you don't already have one, and use that. Nothing saved on the computer at the office."

"Alright. I'll start on the subpoenas tonight. Have a good one," Xavier said.

"Thanks Xavier. You too. See you tomorrow. And so it begins."

5

SIX WEEKS ON, SGT. SCHAEFER HAD NOTHING NEW regarding the Chad Johnson hit-and-run homicide investigation. Pressure remained on him to work the case, but no leads had materialized.

On this particular Monday morning, Sgt. Schaefer was expecting to head to East St. Louis on a different case to speak with acquaintances of a more recent homicide victim. He had stopped in at the department headquarters to pick up a deputy to join him. Two items on his desk, however, caught his attention.

The first was a letter from the Illinois State Police:

"Pursuant to your request, please find enclosed the analysis of the materials sent to our lab in the above-referenced matter. Illinois State Police Forensics Lab, Springfield, Illinois," it read. Sgt. Schaefer turned to the next page. He recalled the crime technicians had submitted about two dozen pieces of plastic to the lab, all found on the road or along the roadside near the Johnson crime scene. The report classified the pieces of evidence by location found, the type of material, and where known, the manufacturer of the material and vehicles using it.

Interspersed with numerous GM, Freightliner, Ford and other parts, all found on the roadside was a final entry: "VICTIM –

ORANGE PLASTIC – 3CM – MOTORCRAFT – TURN SIGNAL
LIGHT COVER – FORD TRUCK."

Sgt. Schaefer mumbled to himself. He had forgotten that the
autopsy unearthed a small piece of plastic from the victim, and now,
at least, he had a slightly narrower universe of vehicles that had hit the
boy—possibly a Ford truck. And there were only a few hundred thousand of those in the area, he thought.

The deputy that was to accompany him into East St. Louis sidled
up next to him, "what's up, Sarge? Ready to head down the hill?"

Sgt. Schaefer turned to the second item on his desk. "One sec.
Something else may have come up. Let me open this up, and see if we
can get rolling or not."

The second piece of mail was from a gasoline corporation, with
a return address in Texas. Sgt. Schaefer ripped into the padded envelope. Inside were two black VHS tapes, each with a white label: "Store
#6319", and then "Bay 2" on one and "Exit" on the other. The cover
letter was more helpful: "Dear Sgt. Schaffer," it read, misspelling his
name, but otherwise finding its mark: "Your request to the Manager
on Duty of United Petroleum, Store 6319, for surveillance footage of
closed-circuit cameras on the above-referenced date was forwarded to
this office for response. The requested October 8-9, 1993 footage from
the requested camera(s) is included from 11 pm to 6 am local time.
We also have preserved all tapes from all cameras from this station for
October 8 and 9. Please let the undersigned know if you require additional information. Note, United Petroleum reviews surveillance cameras in real time, and, excepting those mentioned herein, deletes taped
footage on a rolling, thirty (30) day basis." The letter was signed by a
security director for the national company.

Sgt. Schaefer handed the tapes to the deputy, "So much for our
trip, I need you to look at these videos. It's seven hours of footage from
a couple of cameras. Look for Ford trucks and anything else of interest.
Write down items of interest with the camera's time. And make a spare
copy. Happy Monday Jim."

Jim was Deputy James Birch, now in his second year with the sheriff's department. He was eager to get involved with anything having to do with homicides, though he took this for what it was—grunt work.

Birch took the tapes and headed towards the department's AV room. He deposited the first tape into the top of the silver VHS player and lowered the slot into the machine. The footage was low quality, black and white. The camera was stationary, with a view of the entrance to the station from 59th Street. It gave a clear shot of cars entering and leaving the gas station.

Birch recorded the time of any Ford trucks he saw exiting or entering the parking lot. After three and a half hours, with considerable fast-forwarding of the early morning hours when the station was closed, he finished the first camera's recorded footage.

The second camera's footage was taken from the vantage of the fueling bay and was focused on the pumps and the front corner of the lot where the payphone was located. Birch recorded the times Ford trucks came into this view, which corresponded with the exit footage. He also noted times when individuals used the phone, mainly because he didn't have much else to do with himself.

At the 1:27 time on the camera, a Ford Explorer, which was viewed and noted without additional comment on the earlier tape, stopped abruptly in front of the pay phone. The vehicle's driver, a white male, exited and then vomited on the curb in front of the phone. The man then proceeded to walk around the car, stopped in front of the vehicle, and kneeled down to inspect its bumper. The driver returned to his car, which idled for a moment, then drove out of the camera view. Birch confirmed from his notes that the car exited at 1:30.

Birch knew he had something. He watched the remainder of the video, advancing through the quiet hours of early morning. By this point, his shift was over and Sgt. Schaefer was gone.

Birch rewound the Bay 2 tape and watched the three minutes again of the driver getting out, vomiting, then checking the front of the truck. He then cued the same time in the Exit tape, finding the same truck exiting, turning left towards Belleville. From this view, Birch also thought he saw a passenger, possibly a female, slouched against the door. This was important, he decided, and called his boss.

Sgt. Schaefer was heading west down Main Street when the call came into his radio. Birch informed him as to what was on the videos, which Sgt. Schaefer agreed seemed potentially useful.

Upon his return, the two sheriffs repeatedly watched the three minutes of footage. They viewed the tape in real-time, then frame-by-frame. The truck appeared to have white plates, like those used in Illinois. The man driving the Explorer was fairly slight, but tall, and seemed young, with no beard and short blonde hair. Sgt. Schaefer agreed that the inspection of the vehicle was an odd fact, but also noted from the video that there was no apparent damage to the vehicle. "Any idea what those bumpers are made of on those Explorers?"

"Same as a Ranger, I think," offered Birch, "steel. But if you look, it seems like there is rubber on steel. Pretty solid."

"Well, the video ain't perfect," Sgt. Schaefer thought aloud, "but combined with the plastic taken out of the victim, it sure seems like that Ford Explorer—that driver—is our first real hit-and-run suspect."

The two sheriffs looked again at the exit video, watching the vehicle enter over and over. "Pause that," Sgt. Schaefer instructed. As the Explorer entered, the bright lights from the gas station were evident, shining down on the vehicle. The driver and passenger remained obscured. "I'll be damned. That, right there, those two stickers."

The first sticker was rectangular, on the passenger side, likely a city wheel tax sticker. But the second, smaller sticker, was circular, and above the city sticker.

"I know that sticker. That lower one, that's probably a City of Belleville permit. But the other one—the small round one—there was one of those in every other car at Township Stadium the night we went into the stands."

"Right, yeah. What color were those stickers?" Birch had been there, but he had no recollection of the stickers.

"They were two-toned, half maroon-half white." The sticker in the black and white video did not show any contrast, but it certainly was round.

"Any idea, Sgt. Schaefer, what shape East uses?"

"No idea. With our luck, probably the same one. Even still, this could really narrow it down."

"Nice catch. I guess we head over to West in the morning and get a look at their parking sticker rolls, or hell, just walk the parking lot after class starts."

"Yeah, or both."

6

"COUNSELOR, I'VE READ YOUR REQUEST for authority to wiretap. I am inclined to deny most of it. But I am willing to hear you on this matter." Judge Randolph leaned back in his old wood and leather desk chair, ready to listen.

Managing Assistant United States Attorney Xavier Holden had requested the in-chambers meeting with Judge Randolph, and had handed him his request for authority to allow the FBI to run audio surveillance on the law firm of Spellman, Bleaker & Rock, and in the homes and cars of the first two named partners. Xavier cautiously moved forward: "Thank you, your honor. As the brief indicates—"

"I've read the brief. What else do you have to say? You allege a conspiracy between an unnamed federal official, presumably a judge of some sort, whose name I frankly am getting tired of having remain anonymous, and one lawyer in the Spellman firm, which as far as I understand it, is quite reputable. So, I am inclined to grant you authority for just the one lawyer you have identified from the prior call— Bleaker, I believe it was—and no more."

"Your honor. The simple fact remains that these two men—Mr. Bleaker and Mr. Spellman, run this firm. So although Mr. Spellman is not heard on the tapes, we have every reason to believe he is complicit in the bribe of –yes your honor, you were correct—this unnamed judge. Further, these two men run their firm as much from their homes and their cars as they do their office. To the extent they have portable phones, please note we have requested wiretap authority for those as well."

"Again, I don't think you have shown me sufficient facts that would lead me to grant such a wide-ranging number of wiretaps. If, as you claim, the groundwork of conspiracy has been laid, and the acts—the bribe, I guess—has occurred in furtherance of that conspiracy, what are you hoping to prove now?"

Xavier sensed that he was about to lose his motion: "Your honor, what we believe is that the co-conspirators also agreed to the payment of a future bribe. We are hoping to find evidence of the mechanics of the overarching conspiracy and extant bribe; to determine the number of individuals involved with that conspiracy; and to determine whether there will be, or has been, a realization of that future bribe."

"And why do you need wiretaps to do that? Aren't you eyeing the bank accounts of these suspects of yours? I recall giving Ms. Whittaker that authority some time ago."

"Yes your honor, but with all due respect, these bribes may not be in cash, and they almost assuredly won't take the form of a check deposited into one account and merely drawn from another. We have every reason to believe the conspirators are more nuanced than that."

Judge Randolph leaned forward to give his decision. He removed his glasses and chewed on the earpiece. He nodded to himself, indicating he was sufficiently impressed by the performance. He flipped to the particulars of the wiretap request.

"I frankly do not believe it is possible for you to hope to capture every conversation on every phone of all potentially involved parties. But I will say this: I understand and agree that the single law partner may not be sufficient. So I will grant authority for the law offices and the cars of the two lawyers you have identified—but no home or otherwise personal phones. I will strike through the remainder of the request, including your request for wiretaps at the lawyers' homes." The judge pulled a thin, silver pen from the holder on the table and signed the warrant for wiretap surveillance.

"Thank you judge."

"And if those phones lead to the trove of information you believe they will, then by all means, come back."

"Thank you."

"But one more thing: the next time you come in here, on this John Doe case, I will require the name of this judge you are targeting."

7

THE TWO SHERIFFS PULLED INTO THE CIRCLE DRIVE in front of Belleville West High School, parking in a No Parking area directly in front of the doors to the administration building. Sgt. Schaefer headed up the steps, while Deputy Birch headed across campus to the parking lots surrounding the school.

A secretary in the assistant principal's office obliged his request to see the parking sticker roll. Expecting a detailed list of cross-referenced vehicle makes to permit numbers, Sgt. Schaefer was disappointed to find instead an index card catalog of permits, numbered from 1 to 400.

"Any chance you have a roll of these, searchable by make, or anything like that?"

"No. I'm sorry, why?"

"What possible good, then, is a system like this one?"

The secretary eyed the sheriff warily: "Well, if we see a car parked in violation, we check its sticker number and pull the card. Then we talk to the student. But mainly, this raises funds for the school."

Sgt. Schaefer softened his tone: "Gotcha. So this is it?"

"Sorry, hun, that's it."

"Thanks. Can you just keep this at the ready, I'll be back in a few minutes." Sgt. Schaefer left the administrative offices, and headed down a side staircase and out to the quadrangle of the school. He'd walked these stairs almost thirty years before, and not too much had changed, he noticed.

He could see Birch in the front parking lots on Main Street, so he headed to the rear lots. He passed through the faculty parking lot, and noted one Ford Explorer, a new white one. He took down the Missouri plate number. The faculty parking sticker was square, and had no year or number.

Sgt. Schaefer walked towards the back lots, nearest the railroad tracks that formed the southern boundary of the campus. These lots were full of El Caminos, Monte Carlos and other muscle cars. These were the cars of car guys, like Chad Johnson, he thought. There wasn't a new car or SUV among them.

He walked back towards the Main Street entrance to the campus, surveying other small lots for Ford Explorers, finding none.

"Birch!" Sgt. Schaefer yelled towards his fellow sheriff, who was now across Main Street in the overflow parking lot. Birch waved back that he would head over in a minute. Sgt. Schaefer looked up and down the front lot, which was a mix of faculty cars in the front row and student cars directly behind.

Sgt. Schaefer could see, peaking up over the sedans and pickup trucks, four SUVs. Two were Jeeps, and two were Explorers. One of the Explorers was red, the other green. He walked to the green one, in the rear of the lot. He walked around it, noting the City sticker, and the round student sticker. Sgt. Schaefer figured Birch already had taken it down, but he remembered the number: 37. He scanned the front bumper of the Explorer, noting a variety of scratches, but no dents, and no apparent broken plastic.

As Sgt. Schaefer headed towards the red Explorer, Birch joined him: "These two are it, from what I've seen. Did you find out anything inside?"

"No, they have a card catalog in order of permit number. Nothing you can check for vehicle type, color. Rudimentary. I did check the back lots and found a white one, but it was a faculty car with black Missouri plates."

"You are right about those round student parking stickers. So, we have 37 and 416, from my notes." Sgt. Schaefer approached the red Explorer, looking it over, and settling his eyes on the front bumper. "Nothing on either of these?"

"Not from what I can tell. That green one over there must not be much of a parker, it's all scraped up, but nothing consistent with a collision. This red one looks clean."

"All right, let's get back in there and pull these two cards."

The cards turned up the names of two students, Todd Wilson and Tim Spellman, both seniors. Sgt. Schaefer asked the secretary for a copy of the current yearbook, and she directed the sheriffs to the bookshelf at the corner of the room.

"Can I help you gentlemen?" came the booming voice of the assistant principal. He introduced himself as Ron Willis, and invited the sheriffs into his office.

Sgt. Schaefer grabbed the yearbook off the shelf, walked in and took a seat. Birch followed.

"What can I do for you men?" the principal asked.

Sgt. Schaefer sat down and answered: "We are investigating the Chad Johnson death, and running down some leads Mr. Willis."

"Is there anything I can do to help?" Willis asked.

"No, sir. Not at this time."

"Well, if I can be of assistance, you let me know. And of course, we would like to minimize the appearance of sheriffs running all over the place. I've already had questions from folks who saw the two of you scouring the campus."

"Well, sir, that is what we do when we are investigating a case."

"And I understand that. Believe me, I do. This isn't the first investigation, believe me, that I've been a part of at West. Sad to say. I just want to make sure I am kept abreast of what is going on here on this campus and with our students."

"Understood. And we will of course keep you apprised."

"Any developments?"

"A few leads. Just running them down. This case is still very much on our front burner."

"And so what brings you into our office here today?"

"This being a hit and run, we are running down cars, stickers, that sort of thing?"

"And you think you have reason to believe a West student was behind this?"

"Mr. Willis, as you say, you've been involved in these types of cases before. We run down leads. We don't comment on them, including to the administration, until the appropriate time. And this is not the appropriate time." Sgt. Schaefer shifted in his chair, visibly showing his lack of patience for any more conversation.

"Gotcha. Now, 'Birch.' That name rings a bell. You go to West?"

"Yes, sir," Birch said, looking up from his notes, while Sgt. Schaefer opened the yearbook to the Junior class, "you should remember me—I spent enough time in here over the years. Tardies, mostly. A coupla pink slips."

"Sure, sure. I remember, I remember. And now you are with the sheriff's office. Good for you. College?"

"Carbondale."

"Excellent. I bet that was a great time."

"Yes, sir."

"You play football here?"

"No, I wrestled. Class of 85."

"Good, good. Great to see you. Welcome back. I knew I knew that name."

"Thanks. And you know, Sarge is an alum too, what was it, Cliff, Class of '46?"

The two men had a good laugh at Sgt. Schaefer's expense, who had not heard anything they had said. He looked up from the yearbook, where he had ruled out Todd Wilson and his green Explorer. Todd was black; the person on the tape was not.

"What's that?" Sgt. Schaefer asked.

"When did you graduate here?" Willis inquired.

"64. Junior college here too, '66."

"So, you both know your way around here. And I will leave you to it. Good luck. And just be sure to let me know how I can help. And if you need to talk to anyone on campus, that has to go through me." Assistant Principal Willis stood and the sheriffs followed him out of his office.

Sgt. Schaefer asked the secretary who had first assisted him if he could use the copying machine behind her, and she agreed. He ran a copy of the two parking cards, and the two pages of the yearbook with the boys' photos. He returned the cards into the box and the yearbook to the shelf.

The sheriffs walked through the center hall of the administration building, past the bronzed basketballs, aging jerseys and other trophies to West's athletic teams, mainly from the era Sgt. Schaefer was a student.

Sgt. Schaefer stopped in front of one of the long displays, where he saw a picture of his baseball team. "See that, Birch?" he said, pushing his finger to the glass, "those were some great guys."

"I'll bet. They don't put any pictures of the wrestlers up here. I guess we were too ugly."

"Still are." The two men walked down the stairs and out to their car.

Sgt. Schaefer drove them into the parking lot and stopped in front of the red Explorer. He got out, snapped pictures of the truck from all angles, including the parking stickers and front bumper and lights. He peered inside, but the seats and dash were empty.

"You think that's it?" Birch inquired.

"Yeah, it might just be." Sgt. Schaefer pulled out a couple of stills from the gas station surveillance, and glanced from the photo to the truck. "That could be red, right?"

"Yeah, definitely. It looks lighter than the green one, anyway."

Sgt. Schaefer then pulled out the still of the driver, which was blurry, but certainly of a young, white man.

"And this? You think that looks like….him?" He pulled out the yearbook photo of Tim Spellman.

"Could be. What about the other kid?" Birch asked. Sgt. Schaefer showed Birch the photo of the young, black student. "Ah, definitely not him," Birch said, "so who's the white kid again?"

"Tim Spellman."

"Don't know him."

"Me neither, but there's a law firm in downtown with that name. You see the name on everything in town. They sponsor all the sports leagues, that sort of thing. Anyway, nice car for a high school kid, huh?"

"Yeah. Looks like they don't give all their money away. So what now?"

"Now we see if the State's Attorney agrees we have enough for a warrant to impound that vehicle for testing."

—

Sgt. Schaefer and assistant Illinois State's Attorney Monica Peterson had trouble finding a judge the afternoon before Thanksgiving in the St. Clair County courthouse. But they were tipped that Judge Alicia Briggs had yet to leave, and they found her in chambers, closing her briefcase and preparing to depart for the four-day weekend.

"Can this wait?" the judge asked Monica.

"Judge, I'm sorry, we will be brief. But no, we don't think it should wait. This is a request for a warrant to impound a vehicle suspected in the hit and run death of a high school student."

Judge Briggs exhaled, and sat back down into her chair. "Please have a seat. Tell me about the request."

Sgt. Schaefer, who had grabbed Monica out of the state prosecutor's office, filled the judge in on the purpose of the warrant. "Your honor, Sgt. Schaefer. I lead the major investigations with the sheriff's department." He'd testified in various felony cases over the years before Judge Briggs.

"Sure. I recall you Sergeant. Tell me about your investigation."

"We have considerable evidence, your honor, that we believe may lead to an arrest in the hit and run death of Chad Johnson, who was a 17-year old, high school senior," stated the prosecutor, emptying in one sentence the entire amount of information she knew of the investigation.

"The football player, I recall this," the judge added.

"Right," Sgt. Schaefer moved forward. "We have surveillance video from a business near the crime scene, taken in the time frame of the hit-and-run. These are the still photos of a Ford Explorer entering the property, a young man exiting and vomiting, inspecting his vehicle, then leaving the parking lot. We have video if you would like it played.

"We also have a close-up of the front windshield, which shows two parking stickers—one a city sticker and one a student sticker from West high school. We found a vehicle at West matching that description, containing those two stickers. Here are photos of that car, including pictures of the stickers." Sgt. Schaefer laid out each photo on the judge's desk.

"And who owns this vehicle?" the judge asked.

"It is registered to Tim Spellman, a senior at West."

"And he is how old?"

"17."

"And this 17 year-old, he owns this new SUV?"

"Yes, judge, it appears that way. There is no lien recorded on the VIN, and it is registered in his name."

"And where does Tim Spellman live?" the judge inquired.

"With his parents, Jack and Kathy Spellman, in the west end."

"Jack Spellman? The attorney?" she asked.

"Yes, your honor."

"So, you want me to sign a warrant impounding the vehicle of a minor, whose father is one of the most influential attorneys in this town?"

"Yes."

"And you don't see that as blowing up in all of our faces?"

"Well, judge, we—"

"And on Thanksgiving."

"Well, as we said, we have developed this information, and…" Sgt. Schaefer was at a loss. He failed to see how the judge couldn't approve such a simple request.

The young prosecutor tried to rehabilitate the request: "Your honor. The evidence here suggests that—"

"—you have found the vehicle of the boy who vomited on a parking lot?" Judge Briggs inferred.

"Well, we think that the evidence shows also—"

"It shows nothing else. You have visually inspected and photographed the vehicle. You believe you have matched it to one in a video, but that video shows no evidence of any crime. You want to learn more? Well, then, talk to the boy—with his father present. But this? This assuredly is not enough. Your request for a warrant is denied. Is there anything else?" The judge asked for the warrant, and searched in her desk drawer for her date stamp.

"Your honor. I should also note," Sgt. Schaefer looked to salvage his warrant, "that lodged in the body of the deceased was a piece of orange plastic, which the Illinois State Police crime lab traces to a turn signal plastic on a Ford truck. That is how we happened upon the search for Fords, and found this SUV and the activities of its driver, which we believe are notable."

"Denied. Denied. Denied. How many Ford trucks are there in this area?"

"Probably tens of thousands."

"Right. And let me see your photos… you don't show broken plastic on that Explorer anywhere. Denied." She marked the request denied, signed and stamped it, and stood to put on her coat. "If there is nothing else, have a wonderful Thanksgiving." She walked out, leaving the sheriff and prosecutor standing in front of their chairs, shaking their heads.

8

JACK AND TIM SPELLMAN SET ABOUT unloading the box truck of its contents into the arms of waiting volunteers. It was early on Thanksgiving morning and, as had been tradition for almost fifteen years, Jack, Kathy and now their two children worked at the Belleville Central Kitchen's first shift. Jack liked this form of giving back—direct, with the people and with his family—and he liked being done with it and back home in time to watch the Thanksgiving parade on television.

Jack sat on the board of the charity, and for years had cajoled his partners and others from his firm to take part. And this year, Tim, as head of his high school student council, had sponsored a canned food drive that had filled the truck with over five thousand pounds of food. Tim's girlfriend, Kate, was on hand to help unload as well.

Inside, ovens already were full with rolls and turkeys cooking. Kathy and Wendy Spellman, a spitting image of her mother in long, brown hair, stood before a large commercial mixer joining the ingredients for pumpkin pie fillings, ready to ladle them into the prepared pie shells that lined an entire table.

Outside, Jack turned to the assembly of boxes filled with canned goods, potatoes, and other staples, which would be distributed all morning.

"Jack." The voice came from above as Jack was bent over a box, taping and marking it ready for distribution. The voice belonged to William Flood, dressed for the cold in mustard colored coveralls and his camouflage hunting coat.

Jack looked up, hardly recognizing the judge outside of a courtroom and in his hunting clothes. But the shock of white hair was unmistakably the chief's. "Judge. How are you?" Jack extended his hand to the judge, shaking it perhaps for the first time. He was amazed at the size of the judge's fingers, and the roughness of his hands. These didn't seem like the hands of a man who had worked in a comfortable courtroom his entire life.

"Fine, fine. You got stuck out here, I see? Should have dressed for it, like I did."

"True enough. They figured I can't cook, and they are right. Kathy and Wendy are inside making pies, and Tim, Kate and I have been unloading the truck and filling boxes with the provisions needed for a full meal. Do you know my son, Tim? That's him over there in the rugby shirt. Tim! Wave! He organized that entire truck of food at West." Tim obliged with a wave and returned to unloading boxes to his girlfriend on the ground. The judge gave a half-smile and nod towards the younger Spellman.

"Can I assist you? I came to help. This is one of the DPAC charities we support, though I don't see anyone here."

"I think you all take over at 8 or so; I saw the schedule. But by all means. Grab a tape gun."

"A what?"

"The tape dispenser. I'm about finished filling these, and they need to be sealed up." The judge took the dispenser from atop a completed box and stared at its handle, teeth, and wheel of clear packing tape.

"Here's one." Jack lugged a box between the feet of the judge. "Tape it; I can lift it."

"I can lift a box, Jack." The judge improvised the tape gun, and managed to get the tape across the box with minimal effort.

"Jack, I should thank you..."

Jack shook his head. He knew there was a plan to offer the judge a job at his firm, but he did not intend to communicate with the judge about it until after he was retired from the bench. "You don't need to thank me. I haven't done anything."

"Well, whatever. I appreciate it."

"When are you retiring?" Jack inquired.

"December 31. The end of an era."

"Indeed. Listen, when that day passes, you come on up to Hayes House. We'll have a little party for you."

"I look forward to that."

Jack changed the subject back to the task at hand: "We need some more bags of potatoes. You mind filling these boxes per that list? And I'll go get some more?"

"Certainly."

"Thanks." Jack wandered off towards another truck, which contained the produce, and requisitioned as many bags as he could manage.

Jack rejoined the judge and the two men talked about the day's football games and Jack's kids. Soon enough, 8 o'clock had arrived and his family appeared before him, ready to head back home.

"Kathy, this is Judge Flood."

"It is nice to meet you, Judge."

"The pleasure is mine," he responded. "You have a wonderful family. And well done to you, Tim, on all the food you and West brought in. Very impressive."

Tim shrugged, "thanks."

"Well, we are off to get ready for Kathy's family. We've got about 20 for dinner, is that right, Kathy?" Jack asked.

"Not counting all the little ones, yes. Happy Thanksgiving," Kathy offered.

"And," Jack added, "if I don't see you, have a Merry Christmas, and New Year."

"The same to you, Jack. Happy Thanksgiving everyone. I'll keep up with these boxes until someone tells me otherwise."

The Spellmans walked to the back of the parking lot, loaded into Jack's Cadillac, and headed out of the parking lot, waving to others who were coming to volunteer at the kitchen.

Returning home, Jack was excited, as always, for the holiday. He was also nervous that he would field questions from his in-laws about the mountain of money his firm had taken in from the railroad class action settlement. He figured, if it was in the Wall Street Journal, and the local papers, they would have seen it.

If they had, they didn't mention it. Other than, "how's work, Jack?" inquiries, it never came up. Jack was relieved. The rest of the afternoon filled out a perfect day for him. Kathy and Wendy had made excellent food, the house looked splendid, and he got to play some pick-up football with his kids, nieces and nephews. Jack gave the blessing over the turkey, and told everyone it was for their company that he felt most thankful.

Meanwhile, only ten blocks north of the Spellman home, in a far less tony part of the west end, the remnants of the Schaefer Thanksgiving dinner sat on the kitchen table, while the family had moved a few feet away to the living room to watch the end of the football game.

Sgt. Cliff Schaefer and his wife, Brenda, were happy to have their two sons and the boys' wives home for the holiday. Still no grandchildren, but two were on their way. The boys occupied the couch while their pregnant wives laid out across the floor, moaning their sated bellies. Brenda moved about the kitchen, deboning the bird, placing leftovers in Tupperware for the kids to take with them.

For his part, Sgt. Schaefer hadn't said much. He was still bitter and stewing on the decision of Judge Briggs to deny his request to impound the red Explorer. He could feel how close he was to moving forward on an arrest, yet, he could not think of anything that would get him that warrant. He thought about driving over to Country Club and talking to the Spellman boy, but he was made painfully aware by Judge Briggs that he would need to be very careful moving forward with any case against the Spellman clan.

So, he sat. His boys offered to play cards with him, but he declined, citing the need to watch the game, and hoping they would all head home soon after it was over.

When it became clear they planned to stay even longer, and he saw his sons' baby albums being brought out, he had had enough. "I'm going to get some more beer."

"Hun, we have beer in the fridge, and the Main Street Market is closed," Brenda noted.

"I don't want that beer," which was true, it was an import that his sons had brought. "I want my beer." He headed out to his full-size white Ford pickup, now almost 15 years old, and parked in the street to make way for the sons and their pregnant wives, per his wife's orders.

Sgt. Schaefer headed past the closed market, across Main Street, and headed for Country Club Place. He knew the house number he was searching for, but had no idea where the house was in the neighborhood. He drove slowly by the large brick homes, and wondered if the Thanksgivings were all that different in these homes with their bigger televisions and formal dining rooms. He imagined they probably were.

He came upon house number 43 from the angle of its driveway, and he could see, in amongst other cars, the red Explorer. The home was a sprawling one, laid out across a double lot, with the tell-tale tall rear fence required of in-ground pools. The home was brick, two stories, with a third floor of dormer windows, built in a symmetrical, federal style. Built to impress, he thought, and it did.

As Sgt. Schaefer passed the home, he noted a game of touch football on the front lawn, and eyed what he figured was the Spellman extended family. They seemed a happy bunch. Middle-aged men, with their middle-age spread and thinning hair, appeared to be opposite younger versions of themselves—both boys and girls. The men attempted to play defense with beers in hand, while the children's team circled around and then past them. He pulled past the house and parked on the wrong side of the street, peering back through the rear window of his pickup, focusing on the blonde boy in the rugby shirt, who was the only boy in the game who seemed of high school age.

An errant pass sent the ball bouncing from the upper, flat portion of the lawn, down the hill, and in the direction of the street near the idling pickup. Tim Spellman scampered down the hillside to retrieve the football, and looked in the direction of the old truck. Sgt. Schaefer looked forward and down, as if searching for something, while stealing a glance in his side mirror. He was sure this was the boy on the tape. Whether all that meant was he had found the identity of a boy who vomited, like Judge Briggs had held, or had in fact found the culprit who had committed the lethal hit-and-run, he didn't know. But he decided it was time to bring this kid in for questioning as soon as was practicable.

Tim had not lingered in viewing the truck and Sgt. Schaefer did not immediately drive away. He idled and watched as Tim grabbed the football, spiraled it in his hands, patted it and heaved it up the hill towards a younger boy with his hands up and waiting.

The game ended when the family was called inside. Sgt. Schaefer sat for another minute watching the door close, then pulled away, headed to a convenience store for some light beer made just a dozen miles away.

9

"THREE MILLION, RUTH. THAT'S WHAT YOU'VE LOST."

"How do you know that? Or I guess, I know how, you are the Chief Executive Officer of the Company. But why are you telling me this?" Ruth sat across the café table from her former AgriFarm boss

David Meirs.

"Because I was curious. Since Jack Spellman filed his lawsuit against AgriFarm, our stock has dropped fifteen percent. And if this keeps up, it could fall by thirty-five more. So, I looked at your holdings. And that's the number—today. You've got a three million dollar paper loss so far."

"I hadn't looked at it like that."

"Well, you should. This has to stop. These class actions, these frivolous cases. They are a cancer on our company. No, strike that, not just on our company, but on our region, and on our way of life.

"They are driving the companies out of business, or out of town. And AgriFarm stands to be next. I can tell you that we are not planning to build our new distribution center here. Hell, I won't build anything here, not right now," David said in disgust, clanking his glass of bourbon onto the table.

"But this suit from Spellman is about the seed," Ruth said, "there's nothing to that claim, from what I recall."

"It doesn't matter. He draws a good judge—a chum of his or one of his partners—and this thing gets certified and we are paying $100 million, just like the railroad. This is straight-up corporate blackmail, Ruth. And you know that."

Ruth sipped from her wine glass, watching cars ease past on Euclid Avenue.

"Dave, I'll tell you a story. When I was first out and practicing, I had a case in St. Clair County. It was a motions call, and all the lawyers were standing in line, two-by-two waiting to be heard. The lawyer on the other side, representing some plaintiff claiming discrimination—I think it was—he says nothing to me as we wait fifteen minutes for the line to move us to the front.

"But we get there, and what does this guy do? He looks square at the judge and says, 'Judge, we still on for golf tomorrow morning?' And the judge says they are, and then he hears the motion. And guess who wins?"

"Not you."

"Not me, indeed. And guess who that judge was?"

"No idea."

"Nelson Bleaker."

"I'll be damned."

"Dave, I know all about the games over there. I know the lawyers hire the judges into private practice, and then they revolve back in again to make each other millionaires. I know how it goes down. I know how it is for companies; I lived it not that long ago. I get it. These trial lawyers, or plaintiff's lawyers, or whatever you want to call them, are a cottage industry on the East Side. It's been that way for generations. They have been the counterpunch to the big nasty corporate firms here in the city."

"That's true," David said, "but they've come into their own. They are the nasty ones now. They are the ones with the power, with the connections in the appellate courts, with the legislature," David said.

"I know. I know. And I'm sorry it has finally reared its head now with regard to the company, to AgriFarm. And I'm sorry I'm not there to lead the pushback on this class action you've got yourself embroiled in," Ruth offered.

"That makes two of us."

"But I can tell you, straight up, that my office is working on this. That I am working on this and that what my office is doing will have an effect on the things you are raising."

"I am glad to hear that. But what do you have?" David pressed.

"Dave, I don't think I can get into this, not now. But you will learn about it soon enough, I think, just keep watching your evening news. And I can tell you—I am not sweating the three million."

"That's all I needed to hear."

10

A DOZEN STUDENTS REMAINED ON THE WEST CAMPUS, preparing the school for the next evening's Christmas dance. Outside, Tim Spellman and two of his friends were fighting to untangle strands of lights in a brisk wind. None of the boys noticed the two sheriffs who had walked up behind them.

"Tim Spellman," Sgt. Schaefer surmised.

Tim turned around, unintentionally meeting the sheriff's eye. He turned back to his lights, "that's me."

"Mind if we talk to you?"

"Sure." Tim turned back around, and let the strand fall with a click to the ground. He stared at the sheriffs, wondering what would happen next. He could feel his throat constricting, and knew if he spoke at that moment, it would come out as a squeak, or something close to a sob, and he waited to say more until he had to.

"Why don't you come inside here, with us," Deputy Birch pointed towards the cafeteria entrance.

The two sheriffs and Tim walked into the building and out of the cold. Christmas songs streamed from a small radio near the door. Students were busy on ladders, decorating the floor-to-ceiling windows of the foyer.

"Tim, I'm Sgt. Schaefer, of the St. Clair County Sheriff's Department. We would like to ask you a couple of questions about Chad Johnson. Would you like to do that here, or perhaps come down to the sheriff's department for a few minutes?"

Tim scanned the room as all eyes turned to watch him talk to the sheriffs. He could feel his face turning red, both from coming in from the cold, and over this scene playing out in front of his peers. He opted to leave with three words he managed to force out of his clenched throat: "we can go."

The sheriffs turned around and exited. "We can take you, and bring you back, or you can follow us in your car."

"I'll follow." Tim gave a bemused look to his friends as he passed by that meant, "I have no idea what this is about, but what a pain in my ass," and walked out to his red Explorer. The sheriffs pulled by, and he followed them onto Main Street.

As he drove, Tim was occupied with thoughts as to what the sheriffs wanted to know—and what they did know. He was sick to his stomach and stemmed his nausea with measured breaths and turning on his CD player. He contemplated heading to his father's law office, but his dad was out of town for work. So he plowed forward, following the sheriff's vehicle.

The sheriff's building and county jail looked familiar. Tim recalled coming to the sheriff's department, in some form of summer school program where he and other students visited the juvenile lock-up, the jail, and ended their tour with lunch with the sheriffs. That was five years ago, he figured, and the place looked about the same.

Tim followed the officers to the rear lot, and parked his truck. The three men were buzzed into the rear entrance of the building. Deputy Birch showed Tim into a meeting room, asked him to have a seat, and if he wanted anything to drink. Tim declined.

And then Tim sat, for nearly an hour. This was some sort of tactic, he figured. But the delay gave him time to take in the room, the likely purpose of the interview, and his plan—to see what they knew, and to give them no new information.

After that hour, Sgt. Schaefer entered the room and sat in the chair opposite Tim. He had with him a manila file and a yellow legal pad. He placed his coffee on the wood-look, Formica table. He offered Tim a soda; Tim declined.

"Tim, I hear good things about you."

"Thanks."

"Senior stand out on the soccer team, class president, 'A' student. Going to Virginia for school next year. All of that."

He was student body president, Tim thought, but otherwise the sheriff had it right. "Thanks."

Sgt. Schaefer had spent weeks working up to this interview. As much as he had wanted to head to the West campus the Monday after Thanksgiving and talk to Tim Spellman, he didn't. As it turned out, Sgt. Schaefer's file reflected that the boy had an important birthday in a fortnight, making him 18—and eliminating the need for Sgt. Schaefer to talk with him in the presence of his parents. Sgt. Schaefer also had considered the best time to speak to Tim, and decided after school hours was the better choice than having to deal with the assistant principal again. And so here they were.

"I also understand you had some very nice things to say about Chad Johnson at his memorial service. In fact, the News-Democrat quoted you at length, I recall. You seemed to be fond of Chad Johnson."

Tim said nothing.

"But the story I get from most folks, which I find interesting in light of all of that, is that Chad really wasn't all that well-liked. Do you agree with that?"

"I don't know. Some people liked him, some people didn't."

"And what about you? What did you think of Chad Johnson?"

"I didn't know him all that much. West is a huge place."

"Yeah, but you are class president, right? I mean, you must know everybody."

"Not really."

"Well, okay, whatever you say. When was the last time you saw Chad Johnson?"

"I don't know."

"You were at Stupes Farm on the night he died, right?"

"Yeah, I think so."

"You think so? Well, I have talked to several people and your name appears on the list of everyone I spoke with as someone who was there."

"Okay."

"When did you leave the Stupes place?"

"No idea."

"Did you leave alone?"

"I don't remember."

"Before midnight, after midnight?"

"Don't know."

"You don't remember if you left alone?"

"No."

"Well maybe this will help you remember." Sgt. Schaefer reached into his manila folder. He hadn't thought he would have to go to the photos so soon, but he could tell his interview was not going anywhere. He placed before Tim three still shots from the gas station surveillance camera. They included a photo of the Explorer entering; a shot of Tim bent over, vomiting; and another of an apparent passenger in the truck.

Tim stared at the pictures. They were grainy. They were pictures of him, but he didn't know if this sheriff knew as much. So he sat.

"That you?"

"I have no idea."

"I mean, to me, that sure looks like you. Nice Explorer, a West parking sticker, looks like a pretty girl passed out in the passenger seat. And you puking your guts out."

Tim sat quietly, staring at the table. He decided he had nothing left to offer. "Can I go?"

"Well, no, not just yet. I have some more questions for you."

Tim looked at the clock. It was 6 p.m. He knew he could ask for a lawyer, but thought that might make him look guilty, and he figured that he was smart enough to deal with the police on his own.

Sgt. Spellman backtracked and asked Tim questions about school and about the victim's reputation. He was killing time, and trying to get his suspect talking.

Outside in the rear parking lot, Deputy Birch watched as a sheriff's evidence technician flooded the front of the Explorer with light, taking close-up images of the bumper and lights of the Explorer. The technician also placed a plastic-covered, tack board behind the bumper and up behind the grill of the truck. He blew high powered air at the grill, which sent all matter of bugs, dirt and other objects off the grill and onto the board. Finally, the technician tested various spots on the paint job for consistency, to see if the vehicle showed signs of having been repainted. He kneeled at each end of the car and looked along the side panels for scratches. The tech also dusted for fingerprints, to see if anyone else had run their fingers over these same spots, looking themselves for anything indicating the truck had hit something it shouldn't have.

Sgt. Schaefer came out to check on the progress. "How are we doing here, Birch?"

"Who needs a warrant? We got shots of everything, and Rick over here devised a way to get anything that was stuck in the bumper and grill out for us to inspect. And it was all in 'plain view,'" said Birch, who was clearly pleased with his part in the homicide investigation. "How goes it inside with Master Spellman?"

"Little bastard isn't giving us anything. Won't even agree that is him in the photos from the videotape. I'm going to let him sit for a while. Who wants dinner?" It was 7 p.m.

Dinner was not offered to Tim Spellman, and when the sheriffs rejoined him, it was nearly 9 p.m. Tim had laid his head down on the table.

"Can I go?" he asked Sgt. Schaefer when he returned. "I've been in here for hours and don't have anything else to tell you."

"Not just yet. A couple more questions."

"Can I go pee?"

"That you can do. Sgt. Birch will escort you." The men's room was across the hall, and Sgt. Birch stood outside of the door waiting on Tim. He escorted him back.

"Thanks for the escort," Tim said as he took his seat, which now faced shots of the Johnson corpse.

Sgt. Schaefer watched as Tim looked at the photos. "Shame isn't it?" he asked.

Tim said nothing. He nodded.

"Whoever hit this kid with their truck ought to come forward. Don't you agree?"

Tim sat motionless. He'd seen a few pictures of dead railroad workers in his dad's case files, but those looked like something from television. This was someone he knew and it turned his stomach. He was sick even before he considered that he had caused this outcome. Still, he sat, quiet.

"You have nothing to say?"

Tim was tired. He was hungry. He was scared.

"I am ready to go. Can I leave?" he asked.

"Tim, what do you think it felt like for Chad to get hit by a truck, speeding by at 70 miles per hour? Do you think it hurt to get hit like that? I bet it hurt like hell.

"Did you know he didn't die from getting hit? Did you? Nope? I didn't think so. Turns out, coroner's report says he died because his broken neck made it impossible for him to breathe when he was hit and fell into a shallow puddle of water. Chad drowned, Tim. He drowned."

Sgt. Schaefer stood. He rolled over the TV/VCR equipment and hit play. The video showed the Explorer entering the gas station parking lot and stopping. Then, the driver exited the truck and vomited.

"And had you turned around after you threw up all over the ground, Tim, had you just turned your pretty new SUV around, you could have gone back, found Chad, and gotten him some help.

"See, Tim. There was no crime in hitting him. It had to have been an accident, right? That's what I think. An accident. But your crime was in moving along, and never turning back. That was the crime. That IS the crime. And YOU, Tim, I think YOU did that crime."

Tim closed his eyes, shaking his head. He opened his eyes and watched the sheriff staring him down. "I want to make a phone call," Tim said.

"This isn't jail, son. There's no free phone call here."

"I want to make a phone call. To my dad. He is an attorney."

"Oh, we know your daddy, Tim. We know him. Why do you need a lawyer? What do you have to tell us, Tim?"

"I just need to make a call. Or leave. Can I leave?"

"Go make your call."

Birch showed Tim the door, and led him over to his desk. He punched 9, and told Tim to dial his number. Birch walked across to the other side of the bay of cubicles and desks, but kept watch of Tim.

The phone rang to voicemail and Tim dialed again. By the third ring, "Jack Spellman."

"Dad, this is Tim." His voice cracked.

"Tim, is everything all right?"

"I'm at the sheriff's department, Dad. They are questioning me about the Chad Johnson death."

"What kind of questions, Tim? What do you mean?"

"Um, questions, like they said I killed him."

"Tim. What have you said? Never mind. Just stop talking. Tell them you are done talking and stop talking. I mean not a goddamned word. Have they placed you under arrest?"

"I don't think so. I mean, they haven't put handcuffs on me or put me in a prison cell."

"Then leave, Tim. Just leave."

"They won't let me leave. I've been here for, like, six hours or something."

"Jesus. Tim. I will be there in a couple of hours. Have you eaten?"

"No. Dad, I'm scared. I didn't do this."

"I know you didn't. Is there an officer you can put on the phone?"

"I can try and see." Tim put the phone to his chest and called to Deputy Birch: "Can you talk to my dad?"

"No, I don't think so," Birch said.

"He won't talk dad," Tim reported back to his father.

"What the hell? Tim, you tell him to get on the goddamned phone and that I am your lawyer."

"My dad says to get on the phone—he's my lawyer." Deputy Birch, not knowing whether to talk to the lawyer or to go and get Sgt. Schaefer, decided on a middle approach. He walked over and picked up the phone.

"This is Deputy Birch. I am not authorized to speak with you. If you represent Tim Spellman, please appear at our offices on First Street and inform us as to same."

Jack Spellman screamed into the phone: "Now listen up, you have no goddamned right—" and Deputy Birch dropped the handset into its cradle, ending the call.

Birch turned to Tim and said, "your attorney will need to appear here. Until then, why don't we have a seat in the room."

"I want something to eat. And this is the last thing I am saying."

The two walked back into the interrogation room. The photos of Chad Johnson were gone, as were the still shots, and the TV/VCR.

Birch: "Sarge, he says he is hungry and isn't talking anymore."

Sgt. Schaefer relented on the food: "We will get you a sandwich and a soda. Didn't think this would go so long. And you aren't talking?"

Tim sat.

"Well, that is too bad. As I see it now, you have something to hide. Maybe you hit Chad Johnson and didn't know it. Maybe you thought it was a deer or something. No harm no foul. Now is the time to tell me that.

"If you wait for daddy, for your attorney I mean, well, then it is out of my hands. Then the kid gloves come off, Tim. And I do mean kid gloves. You are an adult now. And this is a felony, and you will be prosecuted as an adult, and then sent off to Marion until you are an old man. Unless you help me now."

Tim closed his eyes, but he couldn't help but listen as Sgt. Schaefer kept at him:

"Tim. Are you a religious man? Are you? Well, I am. And I believe in a merciful God. And I am a merciful man. Now, I am going to write down here on this pad, watch me:

'I, Tim Spellman, a man of 18 years of age, do hereby admit to driving my vehicle, a 1993 Ford Explorer, Red, into Chad Johnson on or about the evening of October 8-9, 1993, while driving on 59th Street. I further admit to failing to stay at the scene of said accident, fleeing same, and failing to report the accident. Further, affiant sayeth not.'"

Sgt. Schaefer dated the top of the page, and spun it around for Tim to read. "That sounds about right, doesn't it? Now, I'll go get you that sandwich. But if you just sign right there, well, then we are done."

The sheriff departed, leaving Tim alone in the room. It was nearly 11 p.m. and the written confession sat unsigned.

11

JACK SPELLMAN PARKED IN FRONT of the St. Clair County Sheriff's Department headquarters. He sat for a moment to collect himself. He had arrived an hour earlier at the airport, and sped through St. Louis, across the bridge into Illinois and to downtown Belleville to retrieve his son.

Tim had called only his father. He had tracked Jack down in Florida, where he was participating in depositions of another railroad case. The call between the two had been brief, but the substance was nonetheless clear—Tim was the apparent target of an investigation into a hit-and-run death.

Tim was a smart boy, Jack thought, and hopefully he was smart enough to not try and talk his way out of whatever trouble he was in. That this might not be the case, however, prompted Jack out of his car and up the short sidewalk to the Sheriff's Department entrance.

Inside, a deputy sat behind safety glass, a locked entry door to her left. "Mr. Spellman?" she surmised, knowing Tim Spellman was in interrogation and they were awaiting the appearance of his father and counsel.

The deputy pushed together the papers on her desk, slid off her chair and walked over to open the secured door to let Jack enter.

Jack was wearing a wrinkled gray suit, a white spread collar shirt, and no tie. He looked weary, but color returned to his face as he was escorted down the center hall, past chest-high counters of evidence control and processing, into what he assumed would be the interrogation room holding his son. In fact, it was a room looking through a two-way mirror into the interrogation room where he saw Tim asleep with his head on the table.

"Please have a seat," the deputy said, pointing to one of the chairs.

"I want to see my son."

"In-a minute."

"Not in a minute; I am his father, and his attorney, and I demand to see him now."

Before Jack had to push the matter with the desk officer, the door opened and a sergeant stood between Jack and the door.

"Sgt. Cliff Schaefer. Mr. Spellman, right?"

"Yes."

"Tim Spellman is your son."

"Correct."

"Do you know why your son is here tonight, sir?"

Jack glared at the sheriff.

"Coupla months ago," Sgt. Schaefer began, "there was a high school kid, from West, who was found dead in a field off 59th Street. You might remember reading about it in the paper. Chad Johnson? He played on the football team; his dad owns that big transmission shop?"

Jack had heard Tim say the name on their call a few hours earlier. It had taken him a moment to remember the name, but he recalled the story in the News-Democrat. Jack also remembered Tim having to speak at a memorial for the boy. But in any event, he didn't know much more than that, and offered only a nod of his head.

"You don't recall that?"

"Sergeant, let me see to my son."

"Well, just hold on a minute, I am trying to talk to you."

"Let me see Tim. As I told your deputy, he is also my client."

"I understand that. But…you should know that Tim has confessed to hitting the boy with his vehicle and leaving the scene of the crime." Sgt. Schaefer pulled out the yellow page, already encased in plastic sheathing, bearing the signature of Timothy J. Spellman.

Jack pushed the paper, and the sheriff's hand away, "Impossible. Let me see Tim."

Sgt. Schaefer led Jack from the anteroom into the interrogation room. Tim awoke, but didn't stand, when his dad entered. He met his father's eyes. He looked tired, Jack thought, and old.

Turning back to the sheriff, Jack asked: "What has Tim been charged with?"

"Well, now that you are here, we can proceed with that. We only received the written confession a little while ago."

"Son, please stand," Sgt. Schaefer said to Tim as he reached for the boy's arm.

"He is no son of yours," Jack growled, realizing this son of his was about to be charged with a serious crime.

Tim stood and Sgt. Schaefer spoke to him directly: "Timothy Spellman, you are under the arrest for the failure to stop at the scene of an accident, failure to report an accident, and for the vehicular manslaughter death of Chad Johnson. You have the right to remain silent. Anything you say can, and will, be used against you in a court of law. You have a right to an attorney. If you cannot afford one, one may be appointed for you by the court. Do you understand these rights?"

Tim nodded.

"Good. OK, now, Tim, we are going to lead you down the hall for a photograph and fingerprinting. We will bring you back here to see your father when we are finished."

Jack watched from the doorway of the interrogation room as Tim was handcuffed and led down the hall. He was anxious to talk with Tim; but first, Jack wanted to figure out how to minimize his son's time in the county jail. Then, he needed to get the charges reduced, or dismissed. Jack walked the interrogation room in small circles, thinking through the next steps of this new case of his. Jack was no criminal lawyer, but he knew enough to know the actions he took over the next several hours could well save his son—and himself—from ridicule and embarrassment.

First, he wanted to know how his son—who had told him explicitly on the phone that he did not do this—had somehow signed a confession.

Second, Jack considered the issue of getting bail set, and paid, before Tim ever had to spend a night in jail. That would take the assistance of his law partners, he knew.

As Jack was drafting a checklist in his head, Tim returned.

"Tim." Jack put his hands on his son's shoulders and scanned the boy's eyes, trying to figure out what had happened in the hours since they had talked on the phone. Tim looked back, scared and unsure of what would happen next.

Jack wanted to hear his son out, but not there and then. "Tim, you need to listen to me. Do not talk to me now about this. Do not talk to anyone. Do not sign anything else. I am going to work on getting a bail hearing set for the first thing this morning, and then get you out of here. They are going to take you to a holding cell right now. I will make sure you are alone in there. I need to get things arranged, so I will probably be out in my car on the phone, or down at Hayes House. But I will be back in an hour or two. Do you understand?" Tim nodded, and his head sank. "Ok, good. Stay strong, bud."

Tim nodded his head again, his eyes now swollen with tears in contemplation of his father leaving and his walk to a jail cell. The two Spellmans hugged, and Tim whispered in his dad's ear, "I'm sorry dad. Please help me."

Jack grasped his son by the arms, looked down into his eyes and nodded. He felt his throat seize, and his eyes start to well. He turned and left, as a deputy came in to lead Tim to his cell.

Jack walked back down the hallway and out the security door to the entry of the sheriff's department. It was close to 4 a.m. as he looked for his black book of phone numbers in his glove box. He decided to start with one of his associates, Matt Becker, and wait a little before calling his partner Nelson Bleaker.

Jack's call rang to the answering machine, "Matt. This is Jack. If you are around, pick up." He waited, "Something has come up, I need your assistance as soon as you get this mess-"

"Hey, it's Matt. What's up?"

"Listen, do you mind coming to Hayes House? I know its early, but I have a criminal case I need you for. Can you get up here?"

"Yeah, yeah. Give me an hour."

Jack thanked his associate, then called the firm's accountant to get a sense of how much cash the firm had on hand to use for bail.

By 5 a.m., he felt comfortable calling Nelson Bleaker:

"Nelson, Jack."

"Good morning, Jack. At it a little early for a Saturday, eh? I suppose Florida is an hour ahead, though."

"No, I'm here in town. Listen, I need your help ASAP on something. Are you free for the next couple of hours? I'll swing by your house if it helps."

"Sure, I don't have any plans until around 10, and I would love to avoid that shopping excursion with my daughters. Why don't you head over here?"

"Great. Thanks. Get some coffee up, if you could, and maybe something to eat. See you in a few."

The streets of Belleville were dark as Jack headed towards Nelson's condo in the west end. He called his associate and asked him to head instead to Nelson Bleaker's home.

Jack darted down back roads towards his partner's home. He thought about Tim sitting in a jail cell, then thought about the confession. It all angered and upset him. He resigned himself to dig into the issues as if they were presented in any other case of his. He tried to focus on that role, the zealous advocate, and not on the competing role of being the scared and disappointed parent. He contemplated calling his wife, but decided to get things under better control before ruining her morning on her weekend away with their daughter.

Jack rang the doorbell to Nelson's townhouse. It was still mostly dark outside, and Nelson switched on the porch lights. He showed Jack to a seat at the glass breakfast nook table, where a cup of coffee awaited him.

In an old pair of sweatpants and a new Stanford sweatshirt from his daughters, Nelson moved about the small kitchen. Within minutes, he had the coffee up, the toast down, and the eggs and sausage just about scrambled together.

Jack sat, feeling for the first time a slight release of tension, as he sipped the coffee, staring out on the golf course in the first morning light.

"So, what brings you here today in yesterday's clothes, Jack?"

"It's Tim. He's been arrested for hit and run, in the death of that high school kid."

"Shit."

"Yeah, shit is right."

"What do you need me to do?"

"I need you to get an arraignment set first thing this morning, get bail down, and see about getting the manslaughter charge left off. I'm here to help in whatever way I can. And I have Matt coming by too."

"Good. The more the merrier. OK. Well, I think we start with getting the arraignment called for this morning. Let's call State's Attorney Wolfe, shall we?"

"You have her number?" Jack asked. Nelson nodded.

While Jack ate, Nelson headed into the living room and returned with his speaker phone attached to a long cord. He dialed the State's Attorney, who was used to fielding early morning calls and took this one.

"This is Gina," came the answer to the call.

"State's Attorney Wolfe, thank you for answering your phone so early on this Saturday morning. Do you recognize my voice?"

"Sure I do Judge. How are you? You caught me on my way to the gym."

"Well, I won't keep you too long. I am doing well. Listen, the county sheriff has arrested a boy in connection with that hit and run a few months ago. The Johnson kid."

"I hadn't heard that yet."

"Well, it just happened, apparently. And the boy in custody is the son of my partner, Jack Spellman. His name is Tim Spellman."

"OK. I know Jack. He's a good guy from what I know of him."

"Yes he is. And Tim too. Good. Well, the two favors if you don't mind."

"I'm listening."

"First off, this kid cannot sit in jail until Monday awaiting an arraignment. Would your office agree to an arraignment this morning?"

"Depending on what the other favor is, I would think so."

"Thank you so much. You are a gem. The other thing, as I understand it, is that the boy was arrested and the sheriff noted a manslaughter charge. To me, that seems premature."

"Hard to say, Judge. Neither of us has seen the evidence," Gina said.

"I agree. But the charges for hit and run, and for failure to report—those are not charges that need to keep him in jail, or at a high bail, anyway."

"True."

"And there is nothing stopping you from adding that charge later, if it gets to that," Nelson argued. "But right now, we have what seems to—at worst, if the State's case is to be believed—what seems to me a kid making a bad call, not a kid committing a serious crime."

"But he sat on this, presumably, for months, right? If he's our guy, and he kept this quiet? I don't know how we don't lead with the manslaughter charge."

"Without knowing the evidence, I agree. But that is even more reason you can't tar this kid—he's the student body president at West, for God's sake—with that kind of charge until you know those facts."

"Let me think about that. But either way, I will have my office ready for a 9 a.m. arraignment. 9 a.m. today, okay? Now, I don't know what judge we will get."

"I know you will do your best to find a fair jurist, like I was."

"Of course judge. Of course."

"Will you be appearing in court yourself?"

"Not likely. After this workout, the boys have basketball practice, then they are off to my mom's so I can get my Christmas shopping done."

"I have the same task ahead of me today. If I don't see you in court, perhaps we will run into one another at the mall."

"I look forward to it, judge."

"Ha! Now you are blowing smoke up my ass. So, 9 a.m., and a 'maybe' on leaving off the man. charge until you know more."

"Right. Nice to hear from you."

"The pleasure is mine," Nelson said.

Jack managed a half-smile as Nelson pushed the off button on the speakerphone. "Thanks Nelson, that was great. I came to the right place."

"Of course. How do you like these eggs? They were my ex-wife's recipe."

"Very good."

The doorbell announced the presence of Matt Becker, who cracked the door and walked in. He found two of his bosses eating breakfast.

"Matt, have a seat," Nelson offered, "do you want some eggs?"

"No, but that coffee smells good. Can I get a cup of that?"

"Sure, sure," Nelson said.

Jack told the two lawyers what he knew about the case against Tim. Matt had been hired by Jack and Nelson at Nelson's request. Nelson had seen Matt in the courthouse, where Matt was an assistant state's attorney. Nelson had been impressed by Matt in several criminal cases the young attorney had before him and thought he would be a good, aggressive attorney for the firm as it grew.

The men agreed that they needed to hear more from their client, who at this moment was likely sitting very scared in a jail cell, waiting on the return of his father. The three agreed that Nelson and Matt would head to court, and Jack would go to the jail in advance of the 9 a.m. arraignment. They would then reconvene at Hayes House.

For the moment, receiving a low bail and keeping the charges to a misdemeanor were agreed to be the goals of the hearing. The men knew this would be front page news in the paper regardless of the charges, but for the time being, and for Tim's future, they agreed that minimizing the publicized charges remained important.

Jack returned to his home, only a few blocks from the judge's condo. He showered, and wandered the upstairs as he dressed. He looked in on Tim's room as he tied his tie, looking around for he didn't know what.

Jack headed back down the stairs and out to his car.

As he drove back to the county jail, Jack considered the extent to which he believed his son had committed this crime. He thought about the hit and run. He wondered whether it would have been possible for Tim to have hit the boy, and not know it. He doubted it. He remembered hitting a deer years ago on a country road, and that was a frightening and jarring hit. A human, he figured, had to feel about the same.

Jack then wondered if Tim's truck had shown any damage, and he didn't recall seeing any. That led him to consider what kind of damage a Ford Explorer would sustain when it hit a human. Would the airbag deploy? Would the bumper bend? He had no idea. He also could not recall the last time he'd looked closely at Tim's truck, typically parked out in the driveway under the basketball hoop.

A honk from behind reminded Jack to continue forward. He was lost in thoughts about what might have transpired that night in October. At worst, he decided to himself, Tim made a mistake, had an accident, panicked and left the scene. Certainly, there would be prosecutors—and lord knows jurors—who would want Tim to pay for that. He could see the headlines of the student body president on trial for killing a star of the football team.

By 9 a.m., the principal players were in their places at the county jail and the county courthouse. Jack and Tim stood before a closed-circuit camera at the jail, while at the courthouse, in the courtroom of Judge Alicia Briggs, Nelson Bleaker and Matt Becker stood at the defense table. Assistant State's Attorney Monica Peterson recited for the court the charges against Tim Spellman. They included, notably, a count for manslaughter.

Nelson rose to object. "Your honor. What we have heard today, is alleged evidence of a mistake, of an accident, and of a failure to report that accident. There is nothing in the evidence before this court that indicates any of the requisite elements of vehicular homicide, or manslaughter."

Monica disagreed, "your honor, the defendant hid this crime for over two months. If it had been a mistake, he would have turned his car around, would have helped the victim. Would have reported it. Would have done something. That callous indifference is part and parcel of this charge, and we expect that prior to trial the State will meet its burden on this and all other counts."

"Judge Briggs, you know, as well as I do, that the State is free to add charges at any time as evidence and the grand jury dictates, up to the time of trial."

"And your honor, we are also free to make these preliminary charges now, and to drop those charges as we deem fit, up to and even during a trial."

She had overreached.

"Did you hear that judge?" Nelson asked. "Might as well throw it all at the boy, I guess? Why not add on a murder charge, maybe a couple other counts to pad your stats, Ms. Peterson? This is a clear attempt to garner headlines where there is no foundation. If, as the State claims, the young man failed to report his accident, it was, perhaps, because he did not know he had hit a person, or was, I submit, simply scared. I beg this court: do not start down the homicidal path, not without something more."

"Judge Briggs. We have a signed confession that—"

Nelson interrupted: "—the defense will be challenging, and which shows nothing other than the facts of the alleged hit and run—not vehicular homicide. Not manslaughter."

"OK. Enough," Judge Briggs interjected, looking at the television monitor in the courtroom, "counsel at the jail, please identify yourself and tell me, do you have anything to add?"

"Jack Spellman, your honor. I am Tim's father and counsel, though Judge Bleaker is his lead counsel. I will let Nelson do the talking. Thank you."

"Alright. What I have before me is evidence of a hit and run. Two misdemeanor charges flow naturally from the facts before us. Absent here is any evidence of criminal negligence, such as evidence that Mr. Spellman—Tim Spellman, let me make that clear, Tim Spellman—was under the influence of alcohol at the moment of the alleged collision."

"But judge—"

"I know, Ms. Peterson, that you are going to point to the photos of the boy vomiting. I've seen those before, it turns out, and I did not believe then, and I do not believe now, that those pictures and videos show anything other than a driver of a car getting sick. I assume there is a plea?" the judge asked.

"Not guilty," Tim said, prompted by his father.

"Fine. I will allow at this point the misdemeanor charges only. Bail is set for $50,000."

"Your honor, the State requests a higher bail in light of the financial wherewithal of—"

"—of his father, of his family? Denied. This is an appropriate bail based upon the extant charges. If you show cause later to add a claim for homicide, we will reconsider bail. Anything else? No? I will set a status for this case in 30 days. Happy Saturday everyone. Merry Christmas."

The bailiff called for the parties to rise, though no one had been seated. Judge Briggs exited into the corridor and entered her chambers.

Nelson approached the prosecutor to introduce himself, but she recalled him from his days on the bench.

"It's good to see you Judge," Monica said. "I had no idea you were practicing criminal law these days."

"A special, one time case, I assure you. Dear to my heart. Anyway, fun to be back in these courtrooms and dealing with this law. I kind of missed it. You know Matt, I'm sure." Matt Becker stepped forward and shook the hand of his former colleague.

As the attorneys spoke of their holiday plans, the television with Tim and Jack Spellman went dark. The bailiff looked keen on locking the courtroom and the lawyers exited into the hallway.

"So, you went for the man. charge?" Nelson asked.

"Had to. I mean, look at the optics of this thing. Look at what the facts seem to be telling us. Nobody, connected or not, is getting off of this thing easy."

"All you have is a mistake, at this point."

"And a confession."

Nelson ignored that remark. "Anyway, Ms. Peterson, let me thank you for getting this set up so fast, and for appearing here on your Saturday."

"Sure. Saturdays are work days for me anyway. You know the drill."

"I sure do. Merry Christmas."

"Same to you. And if I don't see you, Happy New Year."

Nelson Bleaker smiled at the young prosecutor and nodded. He turned down the hall and headed for the elevators.

12

"FINALLY," XAVIER HOLDEN SAID TO HIMSELF, "a goddamned break. Merry Christmas to me."

Xavier was seated in a carrel at the field office of the FBI, which was located a few blocks from the Southern District courthouse and was empty on Christmas Eve. He pulled off his headphones and stared at the cubicle wall, thinking about what he had just heard on the tapes of recorded conversations from the phones of the lawyers of Spellman, Bleaker & Rock. He'd listened to hundreds of hours to this point, and had come to dread the hours of wasted time listening to the mechanics of a class action law firm at work.

Aside from the tapes, though, Xavier had continued to pile the bricks he needed to seek an indictment of Chief Judge William Flood and Jack Spellman. He had acquired in the past weeks evidence that the judge's $300,000 home loan had been paid. He had information that the judge had not completed the papers necessary to retain senior status with the Southern District. All signs pointed to the judge leaving the bench at year end, and joining the Spellman firm in the new year. Yet, Xavier knew that nothing about the judge's retirement and new employment was, in and of itself, improper. None of it appeared to be illegal.

But where, Xavier wondered, was the money coming from— $160,000 to pay off a bookie, another $300,000 to pay off the mortgage on his home. That money had to have come, Xavier concluded, from the Spellman firm that had a history of improving the finances of its new partners. But there was nothing in the firm's bank accounts that indicated a half million dollars in payments to the judge.

The reference on the recording blew by and Xavier almost missed it. It was a tape from 4 a.m. the previous Saturday morning, from the car phone of Jack Spellman, to his firm's finance officer, Blake Lucido.

—

Lucido: Hello, this is Blake.

Spellman: Blake. Jack. Yeah, listen, sorry for the hour. But I need you to get down to Hayes House and pull $50,000 for me right now, maybe $100,000.

Lucido: Jack, what time is it?

Spellman: Like 4, can you head down there?

Lucido: Is this for the…flood?

Spellman: What? This is for…this is for Tim. My son Tim. He's been arrested, and I need to get ready to post bail and get him out of the county jail later this morning. (pause). Sorry, I know this isn't part of your normal duties, but I really need your help. I've got to get over to Nelson's, get in touch with the state's attorney, get cleaned up, and I need you, bud.

Lucido: Alright. Sure, don't sweat it. I don't know that we have $100,000 liquid. But we have $75,000. Will that work?

Spellman: I hope so.

Lucido: Then I'll get the $75,000 and what, head to the county jail?

Spellman: I hope to have an arraignment by 9 a.m. set up. I've got Bleaker on that. It will be via video from the jail to the courthouse. So yeah, head to the jail. Get the paperwork started if they allow it.

Lucido: Sure. See you in an hour or so.

Spellman: Listen. Thanks. This is a goddamned mess.

—

It wasn't perfect, Xavier thought, but it was certainly damning. Spellman was asked by his money man if the cash he needs is for "the… flood." There was no rain in recent days; so there was presumably no "flood." But there was, certainly, "Flood."

And it was enough, Xavier thought, to seek a warrant to search the law firm for its accounting books and files. Xavier walked back towards the courthouse, and headed up to his office to modify his existing draft request for a warrant for the firm. He found Judge Randolph eating lunch at his desk, but nonetheless happy to see him.

"Mr. Holden. Good to see you. Just finishing my lunch, and heading home soon after that. What brings you here on Christmas Eve?"

"Your honor, I have a request for a warrant here. But let me be blunt—if you will recall this case, you will know it is a very confidential case, involving a public figure—a judge, in fact. And once that identity is out, your honor, we believe our fact-finding will be truncated. So—"

"So you are seeking another warrant with the identity of the target still not stated?" the Judge asked.

"In part, yes. But when I was here last, you indicated that if our wiretaps produced some evidence, to come back, and you would help our case move forward."

"Yes, I recall. What do you have?"

"We have a recording, which I have transcribed in our request, where Jack Spellman asks his accountant to pull from a firm safe up to $100,000. And the accountant asks whether the money is needed for the target—this unnamed judge."

"Well, that is something isn't it. And your request seeks, what?"

"The books, files and computers of the firm, Spellman, Bleaker & Rock."

"Alright. I will grant that."

"Thank you judge."

"Certainly. You keep me apprised of this case as it moves forward. I won't sleep wondering about the identity of this unnamed judge. It isn't me, is it?"

"Ha! No Judge Randolph, it isn't you. You have a Merry Christmas. Have a good one."

"Same to you counselor."

13

JACK SAT AT THE EDGE OF THE BED, removing his dress shoes. He enjoyed attending the late Christmas Eve mass each year, but on this night he was exhausted. He flopped back onto the bed, waiting for his wife to finish up in their bathroom.

He caught a glimpse of Kathy's flush face and red eyes as she walked by him to her side of the bed. She sat, her back to her husband.

He opted for a diversionary tactic.

"I thought mass was nice. Fr. O'Rourke's homily was nice—and short. Even the incense didn't bother—"

"He did it, didn't he?"

Jack paused, measuring his words. He didn't know if their son Tim was to blame for the hit-and-run death or not.

"I don't know, Kathy. I just don't."

"I think he did it."

"I know you do."

"And you don't? I mean, gosh, he called you in Florida to come get him from jail."

"You were in Chicago and--"

"I know, but he didn't even try to call me. He called you."

"Sometimes when boys think they are in trouble, they think their dads will get them out of it—I guess."

"Jack, please. Tim's a smart boy. Smarter than us. He called you because he needed a lawyer. And then, second, he needed his dad."

"I see it the same way."

"And you don't think he did it?"

"I don't know. I have trouble getting past his confession. But you know, they had him there for hours, no food, nothing to drink, he was trapped in there. And he got scared and tried a way to get out."

"So you think he lied on that? Or is he lying to us now?"

"I don't know."

"I stared at him all through church. I watched him, looking for any sign. He won't talk to me about it. He just changes the subject."

"Me too. He's an 18-year old kid."

"Well, no, he told you he didn't do it? Right?"

"That's right."

"And do you believe that?"

"Kathy, you can ask me that question a hundred times, and I still won't know."

"Well, I watched him in church. I did. And I've never seen him close his eyes so much. He was praying, Jack. And I think we know why."

"I was praying too."

The two pulled back the sheets and laid down. Jack turned out the lamp next to him. He reached for his wife's hand.

"You're cold," he noted.

"I'm upset. My hands always get cold when I am upset. And I guess I'm anxious about all of this," Kathy said, the emotion rising in her voice.

"Me too. Do you think you can sleep, or do you want to go down and set up some presents for the kids, like the old days?"

"I can't even think about that. Opening presents in a few hours. Our son. Jesus. My heavens." Kathy started to cry.

"Honey, we can beat this," Jack said. "We will beat this."

Kathy sat up in bed, looking through the dim light at Jack: "I don't know that I want him to beat this. Not if he did it."

"Really? Do you mean that?" Jack asked.

"I do."

"I don't."

"Obviously. You seem willing to defend him."

"Well, as his lawyer, yes I do. And as his father, I guess I do too. I can conceive of how this was an accident. How he could have accidentally hit something, and didn't know what it was. And when the police recreated it for him, it seemed plausible. And he didn't know the consequences."

"Or he could have been drunk driving, Jack. Have you thought of that? You know those boys he travels in circles with; they drink."

"And he probably does too. I did at his age."

"That doesn't excuse it." She pulled her hand out of her husband's grasp and slumped onto her pillow.

"Kathy, calm down. I didn't say that. What I said was maybe he made a mistake. At worst, maybe that was what it was. And I don't think he needs to be charged with manslaughter or go to jail for that—to learn that lesson."

"I guess I agree with that. I just wish he would tell us the truth. I just want to know. I don't know what I'd do with that information, but I want to know it. Am I crazy for thinking that? Would it be better to not know the truth? This is all such a mess. And on Christmas too." She wiped tears from her eyes.

"If he did it, he's scared as all hell right now, Kathy. He's got college coming up, he's got his—I don't know what you call it—his popularity to think about, his girlfriend. All of that goes away if he admits to this stuff. And he probably thinks he would lose our love too. So you can see why he is staying silent, even to us."

"But I don't have to like it."

"No, you don't have to like it."

"Jack, let me ask you one more thing."

"Sure."

"If you find out that Tim did do this, are you okay with getting him off? In defending him knowing he was guilty? And knowing that he could walk way, and not atone for any of it?"

Jack considered the question. He had thought about it a dozen times in his law office, but had never discussed it with Kathy.

"Yeah, I am. Where I come out is, well, it is this: I think this was at most a mistake. If he did it, I see no reason why he would have wanted to hit and kill this kid. And if it was me, knowing that truth for the rest of my life—that's plenty of punishment. He doesn't need to go to jail, or miss his senior year, or lose out on college at UVA, to learn that lesson."

"I wish I had that," she said, falling back onto the bed.

"Had what?"

"That certainty of yours. That clarity. I can't wrap my head around that. I think I would want him to pay for it, somehow. But I wouldn't want to ruin his life over it. I guess I can't have it both ways."

"No, I guess not. Listen, Kathy, we will get through this. All of us.

However it comes out. Tim is a good kid—we've always thought that. And I won't let this dim that view I have of him."

Jack could hear the sound of Kathy's head rocking on her pillow as she nodded in agreement. He waited on her to fall asleep, and she did. The clock read 12:05, it was Christmas.

14

THE OFFICES OF SPELLMAN, BLEAKER & ROCK were open on New Year's Eve just long enough for the staff to receive their generous year-end bonuses and to share a communal toast to the success of the firm.

Into this lunchtime revelry walked four FBI agents, who arrived in an unmarked white van now parked in front of Hayes House. Special Agent Ralph Ruggieri walked through the front door of the firm and scanned the crowd gathered in the dining room for someone to hand the warrant papers.

"Jack Spellman," he announced.

Jack sidestepped two associates to enter the lobby and sized up the unexpected visitor.

"I am Jack Spellman. And you are?"

"Mr. Spellman, I hereby deliver to you a copy of a warrant from the United States District Court for the Southern District of Illinois demanding the list of items found in Exhibit A be turned over to us. Do you have any questions?" He handed Jack the warrant.

"What the hell is this all about?"

"It is all there in the warrant, sir."

Jack scanned the warrant, unable to read the lines of boilerplate language as his face grew flush and his eyes bulged in his head. He flipped to the attachment, which listed virtually every file and all of the computers in the building. Under no circumstance, he thought, would he allow these agents to remove the very workings of his firm without a fight.

"Hold on. Don't touch anything yet. Please give me five minutes,"

Jack asked. He motioned to his partner, Nelson Bleaker, and the two retreated upstairs. The agents began to walk around, sizing up their task.

"So, what the fuck is this Nelson?" Jack asked.

"No clue. I mean, it is what it is—a search and seizure of our law office. We are apparently caught up in something on the federal side."

"'On the federal side?' Such as what, taxes?"

"Could be taxes, but I think we would have heard from the IRS before the FBI, for crying out loud." Panic spread across Nelson's face as he considered why the FBI was now upon the firm.

"Well, what now?" Jack was unable to put together a clear action plan.

"Well, now we call Walt," Nelson suggested.

Jack and Nelson had just seen Walter McDonnell a few nights earlier at a political action committee fundraiser in their office. They had learned he had been ousted from his role as the second in command to the U.S. Attorney and had set up shop down the street in an office on the Square.

"But he's pretty new to the defense game," Jack speculated.

"Who cares, at this point. He is down the street, he likely knows these agents, and he certainly knows his way around that U.S. Attorney's office."

"Right. The U.S. Attorney. Jesus. Ruth Whittaker, right, from AgriFarm. What the hell, is she screwing with us over our case against them? Alright I'll call."

Jack retrieved Walter's business card and dialed the offices of the McDonnell Law Group.

"This is Walter," came the response.

"Walt. Jack Spellman. Listen, I need to retain you. Can you get down to Hayes House? Right now. I mean right fucking now. I have a bunch of FBI agents swarming this place, boxing up documents, files, everything. It is insane."

"I'll be right over."

"Thanks. And if you don't mind, block their fucking van in the driveway with your car."

"Done."

Jack stayed in his office and peered out onto the street, as he saw Walter arrive in his truck. Walter parked directly behind the unmarked van in front of Hayes House, bringing his elevated bumper to rest against the back of the van.

Walter walked into Hayes House, confident in his new skin as a defense attorney.

"Agent in charge?" he yelled. No response. The receptionist offered him the intercom.

His voice boomed: "Would the agent in charge please appear at the receptionist's desk? Counsel for Spellman, Bleaker & Rock demands to see the warrant." He turned then to the receptionist: "Lock the doors. I don't want anything coming in or out right now." Shirley turned the key in the double-cylinder lock and secreted the key into the pocket inside her skirt.

Soon enough, Agent Ruggieri appeared. He knew Walter, but hadn't realized he worked the other side now: "Walter. Uh, how are you? I didn't think this was your case. Where is the defense attorney I heard yelling through the speakers?"

"Ralph, nice to see you. Turns out I am the defense attorney."

"No shit?"

"No shit. You have the warrant?"

"Yeah, here it is."

Walter read through the contents of the warrant, and of the exhibit listing the items for seizure. It was by the book, he thought. But he reconsidered that view in light of his new role.

"This is not going forward Ralph. No way. We will be challenging every item on this list. And there is no way we can have you take this crap out of here and essentially take this firm out of business on this goose chase being pushed by a, where was the name, 'Xavier Holden.' Whomever that is."

"We have a warrant."

"You have a warrant, but what I am telling you is this: we are contesting the warrant, and unless you want this whole investigation, whatever the hell it is, to fall apart right now, then you had better tell your men to stop what they are doing."

"Walter, you know we work the warrant. End of story."

"Ralph, we go way back. Right? Look, I am going to get on the horn with this Holden fellow and tell him I plan to quash this whole damn thing. So just give me 15 minutes to do that. We will get some coffee going for your guys—they can hang out in that room there with the food—looks pretty nice."

"OK, 15 minutes, starting now."

"Thanks, and another thing, nothing leaves."

"Right, sure."

Walter dialed his old extension and Xavier, who was sitting vigil at Walter's old desk waiting for word from the FBI as to the success of the seizure, answered the phone. It wasn't the call Xavier had expected.

"Mr. Holden, Walter McDonnell. You may—"

"I know who you are. I'm sitting in your old office right now."

"Well, then. What you might not know is that I am counsel to the Spellman law firm and am in receipt of your subpoena. I plan to quash the entirety of the document."

"On what grounds?"

"You will find that out soon enough. I don't know your background, Mr. Holden, but in this situation I always have been willing to grant to counsel some leeway in challenging a seizure of this magnitude. A seizure that would literally gut this firm and obliterate its ability to do business."

"Please. We are not taking client files, and it is the holiday."

"Mr. Holden, holiday or not, in the world of civil litigation, cases move forward, motions are due. There are cases in this office in the millions of dollars that hang in the balance and rely upon the documents found in the very computers your agents are ham-handedly boxing up while we speak." Indeed, Jack had due after the new year a lengthy response to a motion to dismiss the class action he had filed against AgriFarm.

"So you expect me to send these agents home? I cannot do that," Xavier said. "I will not do that. The allegations here, they are considerable. The warrant is good."

"Fine. I am a reasonable man. Are you willing to be reasonable?" Walter asked, not waiting for a response: "I suggest this. Your agents can box up whatever they want, but those boxes will stay in this office, taped, and signed across their tape by me in permanent marker. They will be numbered and cataloged as to their contents. Then—"

"That will take all day. These agents are not there to categorize, they are there to take the items listed on the warrant."

"For the love of God. Where did you--? Mr. Holden, this is exactly what these men are trained to do. I will let the search go forward. All I ask is that the seizure be left in this office, boxed and sealed. Then, as I was saying, I will appear before, who was this—oh my, Judge Randolph, where did you dig him up from—to move to quash. I expect I can get before him on January 2. We will agree to shut this firm down until then."

"Close on a holiday? How generous of you."

"Mr. Holden, what I am asking for is not novel."

"It is to me. It is to this office under U.S. Attorney Whittaker. Things are run a little tighter than when you were here, Walter. But I understand your concerns. But under no circumstance can I let those agents leave the boxes in the offices of that law firm. So I will meet you halfway. The boxes are filled, taped, and signed by you. But we take them and house them, awaiting a decision on your motion to quash."

"Will you agree to a hearing on January 2?"

"Yes."

"Alright, you have yourself a deal."

15

THE INVESTIGATION OF TIM SPELLMAN EXPANDED to the West campus after the New Year. When school resumed, the sheriff's office returned to the high school campus and began in earnest in-depth interviews with students who had been at the Stupes farm on the night Chad died.

The rather obvious plan of the sheriff's office, it seemed to everyone who was interviewed, was to turn up evidence that Tim was drunk at the time he allegedly ran into Chad Johnson. That information, even the students understood, would serve to solidify a felony charge for manslaughter, as opposed to a lesser charge for hit-and-run.

Although a notebook full of testimony was developed over the course of a day, from students who clearly established that Tim was drinking at the Stupes farm, no one saw him leave the party, and no one knew if he left alone, or with others. The speculation was, however, that he left drunk and with his girlfriend.

Assistant Illinois State's Attorney Monica Peterson told Sgt. Schaefer that she planned to interview Kate Shaw on her own. She had nothing against him, or the other sheriff's deputies, she told him, but she thought she could elicit the sensitive, turn-your-back-on-your-boyfriend information she needed to build her manslaughter case.

Thus, she waited outside the girl's gymnasium, where she learned Kate was completing an early-evening workout in preparation for the approaching cross-country season.

Monica had been told what Kate looked like—tall and pale, with long blonde hair. Kate emerged from the gym, planning a quick run in the cold from the door across campus to her car.

"Kate Shaw?" Monica queried.

"Yeah?" Kate said, wearing running shorts and a UVA sweatshirt.

"I'm from the State's Attorney's office. I need to speak with you for a couple of minutes. Do you mind?"

"OK. But this door just locked behind me, and I can't stand out here in the cold." Her hair was still wet with sweat and she shivered as she pulled up the hood on her sweatshirt.

"Maybe the main gym is open?"

The two walked up the steps and into the main gym. They walked towards the basketball court, and sat on a set of risers. The gym was empty and the dim court lights cast a warm glow on the court. As the prosecutor began to speak, Kate stared at the golden brick walls across the court, lost in her thoughts.

Kate tried, for the hundredth time, to piece together in her mind what she remembered about her ride home from the Stupes farm on that October night. It wasn't much. She remembered the farm house, the walk, the talk, and the rain. But from that point where Tim decided to drive away from Stupes, and she had passed out in the car, she didn't recall anything with any specificity.

More importantly, she thought, was the fact that Tim had professed his innocence to her as many times as she had asked. And she believed him. When Kate told Tim that she thought he had told her that night he had hit an animal, he told her that wasn't the case. When she asked him about the video the paper had reported of two people in a Ford Explorer, he told her it was just a bad coincidence of timing for them driving down that road and stopping at that gas station. Had he never gotten out to throw up, no one would have ever noticed, he said.

Kate also had lingering concerns about Tim's confession at the sheriff's department. But Tim had told her that he was tired and had done that just so he could leave—that he had no idea it would mean they would be seeking manslaughter charges and prison time against him.

At worst, Kate thought, maybe Tim had accidentally hit Chad Johnson, and she thought that a mistake like that could have happened to her. Tim had been drinking, she recalled, and quite a lot. But some of that, she thought, was her fault anyway. She had angered him with the truth about her past with Chad Johnson, and her refusals in the farm house. And hadn't she been drinking too? Certainly she had, and she was in no better shape to drive than he was. He had gotten her home safely, as he always did, and that meant the most to her.

She had no room in her heart for Chad Johnson, but had plenty for Tim, and so long as this would all go away, she expected that would only grow.

Monica could tell that her words were being ignored. "I know you don't have to talk to me, Kate. But I'm hoping you will listen." Monica reached out and placed her hand gently on Kate's knee.

Kate flinched and reacted with disgust: "To what? To you telling me Tim is a murderer? I don't believe that." Kate was red-faced from her workout, and now sweating again. She studied the face and clothes of the prosecutor and now watched her with an equal mix of attention and suspicion.

"I know you don't, and I don't believe he is a murderer, either. But I believe he made a mistake."

"I know you do. But I don't."

"Kate, we have you on videotape, in Tim's Explorer, slumped against the window. We have Tim admitting he did this."

"Tim tells me that isn't true."

"Kate, I can show it to you. I can show you the tape. OK? Sorry, let's start over. I know you like Tim."

"You don't know me, or Tim, or anything. You want to ruin our lives."

"I don't. I do not. I want to figure out what happened that night in October. That's all."

"Then why do you need to talk to me? If you believe that confession, then what else is there?"

"Well, maybe you can tell me. You and Tim left Stupes Farm together that night, right? Lots of people saw you."

Kate knew no one had seen them leave, after their walk in the field, and the rain began. She knew everyone was occupied by the beat down of Jason Flowers.

She stared at the prosecutor.

"I understood you dated Chad Johnson," Monica asked.

"Briefly."

"Okay, you dated briefly. But you had to be sad to see him go? It's hard to see anyone that young die, right?"

"Yeah, sure."

"Then don't you want to see justice done here?"

"I am done talking to you. All you want from me is some confession that Tim did this, and I don't have that to give to you."

"Kate. I understand. This is all still so fresh and new. This relationship, okay? But in five years, or ten years, or whatever, you will look back on this and think about whether you did everything you could to see the right thing be done."

"Are we finished? Because I need to go," Kate said, standing to leave.

"Yeah, sure," Monica said, reaching into her briefcase. "Here is your grand jury subpoena. I wish we could have talked some more about what went on, but I guess we can before the grand jury." Kate took the envelope and watched as the attorney maneuvered the bleachers in her business skirt and heels.

Kate sat back down and looked at the subpoena. Tim had told her a grand jury hearing was set, and had told her he would not be testifying. But she had not considered that perhaps she would have to testify. She ran her hands through her wet hair, pulling at the roots. She closed her eyes and thought about all of it all over again.

16

ILLINOIS LAW REQUIRED ANY FELONY INDICTMENT to be secured through a grand jury. This being Assistant Illinois State's Attorney Peterson's biggest case to date, she had assembled the makings of an elaborate presentation for the grand jury to consider in deciding whether to hand up an indictment of Tim Spellman on manslaughter charges.

Her presentation included video, photos, and other hard evidence. Sgt. Schaefer appeared first and explained his investigation of the crime scene. He presented the gas station footage and discussed his interview with Tim Spellman.

The coroner spoke of the cause of death and the plastic piece from a Ford truck found in the body.

In the afternoon, five students spoke to Tim Spellman being present at the Stupes Farm. Each testified to having seen Tim with a different beverage. Included was Tara Dobson, Kate's best friend, who appeared to be the last person to see Tim at the farm, save for his girl-friend.

Kate watched from the hallway as Tara entered the grand jury room. She knew every student that had walked in, and gave each the same exasperated look. Kate had not known Tara was to be a witness.

Tara was on the stand for fifteen minutes. As she exited the grand jury room, Kate came up to her, whispering: "Tara, what the fuck?"

"Kate. Sorry, it was a subpoena. I had to come, same as you."

"What did you tell them?"

"Not a lot, right? I mean, they just asked me when was the last time I had seen Tim that night at Stupes and if—." She was interrupted by an aging bailiff in his light blue uniform, who had appeared to bring forth the State's final witness:

"Miss Shaw, please enter the grand jury room."

As Kate walked into the grand jury room, Tara mouthed, "I'm sorry." Kate wondered what Tara could have said to the grand jury that would have merited an apology. Kate's knees shook as she stepped up onto the witness stand.

She swept the large, dark grand jury room with her eyes. The grand jury was seated in the front of the room, with a witness stand set off to one side. The lectern was directly in front of the grand jury, in the center of the room.

An easel in view of the jury and the witness stand displayed enlarged, gruesome photos of a dead Chad Johnson—the first Kate had seen. On another easel were the grainy images of the Explorer, of Tim looking at the front bumper, Tim vomiting, and of a person sleeping against the front passenger window. Kate knew the photos showed Tim, even though she didn't recall all of the events of that night. And she knew the last photo pictured her. But she already knew from Tim and his dad, who had helped her prepare the night before, that the pho-to was nearly impossible to decipher. Don't make that leap for them, she recalled Jack Spellman telling her.

Kate had a general sense of the purpose of a grand jury, but Jack also explained that it was the grand jury's determination, alone, that would settle whether the manslaughter charge could be brought against Tim. Tim wasn't called, Jack Spellman explained, because he wouldn't testify to anything. He explained that was typical. Her testimony, he said, was the prize for the prosecution—and the manslaughter charge was the lynchpin of the State's case. Or, as he had in fact said, "It is up to you, Kate, whether this all goes away for Tim or not."

This weighed on her. She brought her father with her to the courthouse, but he was not allowed in the courtroom. She was alone as she looked away from the easels and towards the prosecutor.

Kate took an oath to tell the whole truth and she waited for the questions to come. But Monica delayed, explaining first to Kate the legal role of the grand jury, and going out of her way to thank them for their diligent service. Monica summarized the witnesses who already had offered testimony—a clear signal to Kate that she was expected to go along with this long list for purposes of the state's prosecution of the case.

Gone from the prosecutor's demeanor was the big sister vibe she had tried to pass off on Kate at the West gymnasium. Now, it seemed, Monica's goal was to intimidate Kate into giving the testimony the state needed for its case.

"Please state your full name."

"Kate Angelica Shaw."

"What is your date of birth."

"January 10, 1976."

"Happy Birthday, then. 18."

"Yes. Thanks."

"Miss Shaw, were you present at the property known as Stupes Farm on the night of October 8, 1993?"

"Yes."

"What time did you arrive at Stupes Farm?"

"I don't know."

"Was it light out, or dark?"

"Dark," Kate recalled.

"How did you arrive at the Stupes Farm?"

"I road with Tim. Um, Tim Spellman."

"He was, at the time, your boyfriend, correct."

"Yes." All things, Kate figured, everyone knew.

"Is that still the case?"

"Yes."

"What did you do at Stupes Farm?"

"What do you mean, 'what did I do'? There was a party out there."

"Were you and Tim intimate there?"

"No." Kate thought to herself it was amazing what others, apparently, were willing to tell this prosecutor.

"Did Tim have an interest in that?"

"In what? In having sex?"

"Yes."

"I guess. I mean, he's a guy, right?" Laughter came from the grand jury. None emanated from the prosecutor.

"But on this night, Miss Shaw?"

"Sure. Yes."

"But you rejected his advances, is that correct?"

"Yes."

"And was he angry about that?"

"He was disappointed, but he understood why I didn't want to," Kate said, as she looked down at her hands.

"Why was he disappointed?" Monica asked, tilting her head as she asked the question.

"I don't see how that is your business," Kate stated with a glare and a shake of her head.

Monica changed her approach: "You said Tim was disappointed. How did he show that disappointment?"

"How did he show it? I don't know what you mean. I mean, he was upset about it, but we talked about it, and he got over it. We were both disappointed, but agreed it was the right outcome. The right time. Or the wrong time. Or whatever, you know what I mean."

"Did you spend the rest of the evening with Tim?"

"No."

"Where did you go?"

"I went to talk with other friends, he went to talk with other friends."

"And was that the last you saw of him that night?"

"No."

"So, the two of you met up again?"

"Right."

"Were you talking to Tara Dobson at that point?"

"I guess so."

"Please answer 'yes' or 'no.'"

"Yes."

"And then what happened?"

"Tim and I talked, it started to rain, we got in his truck and left."

"That would be his red Ford Explorer SUV?"

"Right. Yes."

"And where did you go?"

"He drove me home."

"What route home did Tim take?"

"I don't know. I feel asleep about the time we left the farm."

"What time was that?"

"I have no idea."

"After midnight, before midnight?"

"I don't know. There aren't clocks at the farm. I don't recall looking at my watch."

"Did you have to be home by curfew?"

"Not really. On game nights, as long as I was with Tim, my parents were okay with me getting home at any reasonable hour."

"What is a reasonable hour?"

"Like midnight, one. Like that. Not dawn or anything."

"Were your parents awake when you returned home?"

"I don't recall. I don't think so."

"At what point on your trip home did you wake up?"

"Probably when we got to my house."

"And do you recall what time that was?"

"No."

"Did you stop on your trip home at the gas station on 59th Street? Do you recall that?" Monica asked.

"Not really."

"No, or 'not really'?"

"I mean, no. I see those photos you have up there, and I don't know if that is me or not, but I don't remember stopping there or anything."

"When you were at the farm, Stupes Farm, were you drinking alcohol?"

"I don't think I can answer that."

"Why is that?"

"I am underage. If I would admit to that, it would be a crime, right?"

"Fair enough. Was Tim Spellman drinking at Stupes Farm?"

"I suppose just about everyone had something to drink. It was a party."

"A high school party?"

"Yeah."

"And how many drinks—beers, shots, alcohol—did Tim imbibe in your presence?"

"I don't know. One?"

"Did you feel comfortable in his driving you home?"

"Sure. Yes. I wouldn't have gotten in his truck otherwise. I'm not dumb."

"No one suggested you were. Now, Miss Shaw, as you are aware, this grand jury assembled before you has heard a full day of testimony from students, police, the coroner—all about the death of Chad Johnson. Did you know Chad Johnson?"

"You know I did. I told you that. Yes, I knew him, and to answer your next question, we dated very briefly."

"Was Tim Spellman aware of that fact, that you and Chad Johnson dated?"

"The whole school was aware of that fact."

"That is a 'yes'?"

"That is a yes." Kate was tiring of this process. She had gotten past her fear, past her nerves, and now she was engaged in the back and forth.

"And was Tim angry that night about your relationship with Chad Johnson?"

Jesus, Kate thought, thanks Tara.

"No."

"No? Miss Shaw, this grand jury has heard sworn testimony today from your friend, Tara Dobson, that this was a matter of dispute between the two of you at Stupes Farm. Do you disagree with that?"

"You can disagree with that. What I am saying is, Tim was upset about what went on between the two of us in that farmhouse. That was what made him angry. He threw the fact that I dated Chad onto that. He didn't really care about that, I don't think."

"But why would he have brought Chad Johnson up at all?"

"I don't know."

"Surely, you've dated other boys. Did he bring those other boys up?"

"I hadn't really dated others, not to any real extent. Tim was, Tim is pretty much, um, my only what I call true boyfriend, like ever."

"So, it is fair to say that Tim was upset, and had been drinking, and that he was also upset with Chad Johnson."

"No, I don't think that is fair to say. He was upset with me, not Chad. He had probably had a drink—which I don't think is the same thing as saying," Kate brought up her hands to form air quotes, "that he 'had been drinking.'"

"We've heard from plenty of your peers today, Miss Shaw, who have testified, let's see—I have a list here—of Tim having been seen drinking: a can of beer, a bottle of beer, a shot of flavored rum, a hit of whiskey, a second can of beer, a beverage in a blue plastic cup. By my count, that is six or more drinks in the time you and Tim were at the party."

Kate interrupted: "You know, I don't know. I don't know if that is accurate. I don't know what those people saw. I don't know how much of any of those drinks he finished, or whatever. And like I said, we went our separate ways for most of the night."

"You went with Tara. He went drinking. Right? You don't need to answer that. No further questions for you Miss Shaw. Thank you for your appearance today."

"Tim didn't do anything wrong."

"Thank you; you are no longer needed before this panel."

Kate rose from the witness chair. She ignored the grand jury and the prosecutor, opting to keep her eyes on her feet as she left the grand jury room. She found Tara in the hall waiting for her.

"Kate, how did it go? I am so sorry that I didn't tell you about the subpoena, it said not to talk about it with anyone and to appear and my dad said to take it very seriously. And I did, but I don't really know anything. And I am just so sorry, okay, for all of this."

"Yeah, I know. It sucks, huh? I mean, I don't really know anything either. They just want to put this on Tim and be done with it, but I mean, it could have just been an accident, right? Tim, or anybody, an accident."

"Is that what you told them?"

"No, they never asked about that. She asked all kinds of crap, but not that."

"Yeah, me too. Mostly about what I saw Tim drinking. Like he was the only one at Stupes drinking. Anyway, sorry."

"It's ok. It's not like you had a choice, right? Like I had a choice? Not at all."

The two girls stopped talking as their fathers approached them. The four stood in the hall, looking out the windows towards the fountain on the Square, still decorated for the holiday and capped for winter.

A few minutes later, the bailiff exited the grand jury room and locked its doors, indicating that the prosecutor had completed her presentation and the grand jury had been sent to its deliberations.

The closing argument put forth by the Assistant Illinois State's Attorney was brief, but compelling. She succinctly requested that the grand jury hand up an indictment for manslaughter based upon the evidence of Tim's drinking that night at Stupes Farm, coupled with his confession to the hit-and-run. There was no evidence, she conceded, as to the driver's blood alcohol level, but that was because he didn't stop after his accident, and the state could not be penalized for his cowardly decision to run and hide.

The grand jury acted swiftly, deliberating for only an hour. The determination was issued to the State's Attorney's office, and then to counsel for the defendant.

Kate did not learn of their decision until the next morning, when she sat down to the front page of the News-Democrat that her father had left atop the kitchen table. It announced: "Indictment! West Student Body Pres. to Face Manslaughter Trial for Killing Football Star." Kate batted the paper off the table, and ran outside to the sanctuary of her car. The paper noted that trial was set for March.

17

At ten before noon on the Friday of Martin Luther King weekend, Nelson Bleaker closed the doors to the chambers of Chief Judge Flood. Judge Flood's retirement luncheon was set for noon, and it was to be attended by a lengthy list of the judge's friends, former clerks, and current court employees.

The chief turned from the window when he heard the door close and watched as Nelson turned up the volume on the radio.

"What the hell are you doing?" Chief Judge Flood asked Nelson as the music blared. Nelson leaned into the ear of his friend.

"They served a warrant on the firm, Bill. I don't know how, but they know some of what has gone on." The judge pulled back, but Nelson pulled him back. "Just listen. This place might be bugged, so just listen. You know I helped you out of a jam. You know that. And that was all it was. I paid off that debt. The 160. You know that. And that was all it was. I did it as a friend helping a friend. That's what I do. I help people. But the timing, Bill. It came right when the class action certification came out. And—"

Flood pulled away, and glared at his friend, shaking his head. "That had nothing to do with that, and you know it!"

"Shhhhh. Jesus, Bill. Come here." The two embraced again. "You know that, Bill. I know that. We had a good case. You saw that." The chief was nodding his head. "But it is what it is. And you know this new prosecutor, she is out for blood from the plaintiff's bar. That's what this warrant is about, Bill. And then, you know, the mortgage."

The chief pulled away, pointing at his friend. "That was you," he mouthed to Nelson. Nelson nodded.

The two men rejoined and Nelson continued: "I was so damned excited about you coming on board. I wanted to give you what the firm gave me—a new beginning. But I'll be damned if it didn't get messed up by our accounting, and by a bank that was all too willing to get the loan off its books before the end of the year. Never, in a million years, did I think we would get that paid off before you were off the bench. But you are 100% right. That is my fault. But what I am saying to you, Bill, is be careful. They've gotten a look at our books and computers and found nothing. But they are on a rampage. I am so damn sorry for all of this."

The chief whispered back into Nelson's ear, "Damned gambling debts. I should be the one who is sorry. I needed you, and you helped me. What does Jack know of all of this?"

"Nothing. He has no idea there was a payoff of that gambling debt. He knew we would eventually pay off your mortgage—everyone gets something when they join—but he has no clue I mucked that up too. And he certainly would be crushed even by the appearance that there was a link between my helping you with that bookie and him winning certification in your court."

"There wasn't," the chief growled. "You tell him that."

"I will. I will," Nelson said.

The two men settled onto the sofa in the chambers. They were tired and had nothing left to say. They each looked out the window and waited for the clock to strike noon.

18

Tim planned to surprise Kate with a private pre-Valentine's Day dinner at Hayes House. The office was closed for the weekend, and he had requisitioned from a local Italian restaurant Kate's favorite meal, which was staying warm in the oven. He raided the liquor cabinet of the firm's conference room for a bottle of red wine, and set the table for two.

He traversed town to pick Kate up and was now heading back across town with her to the office, claiming he needed to stop by to retrieve his wallet before they headed out for dinner and a movie.

Tim pulled into the driveway of the office. The dining room chandelier blazed.

"Who's working on a Saturday night?" Kate wondered.

"I don't know. I'll guess we'll find out."

"Huh? Oh, I can wait in the car while you grab your wallet."

Tim pondered how he was going to get his girlfriend inside. "It's cold. Why don't you come inside and help me look for it? I can't remember if I left it up in my dad's office or in the library."

"Just leave it running so I don't freeze. I'll be fine."

"Did I tell you I found the key to the liquor cabinet the other day?" Tim tried.

"I'm coming in!" Kate joked, only half kidding.

Once inside, the scene played out for her. The flowers, the music, the set table. She smiled, "You cooked. I didn't know you could cook. Does this place even have a stove?"

"Yeah, it does. But well, okay, I didn't cook, but there is really good food. Chicken marsala, toasted ravioli, and I think I mentioned the wine?" Tim smiled. The two had stopped going out to local restaurants as Tim's face had been in the paper enough of late that they thought—real or not—that everyone stared at them.

"I'm starving. Is the food ready to eat?" she asked excitedly.

"It is, have a seat." Tim pulled out the chair at the end of the table for her and poured her a glass of wine.

"Mmm. This is good," she whispered between sips, as if someone were in the building.

"You don't have to whisper. Everyone is gone. Let's eat."

Tim shifted the food from the oven to the plates and presented them to Kate, who responded with a kiss as he leaned over to place a plate in front of her.

He tried to keep the conversation light, which had been a challenge of late.

"So, you ready for cross country season to start?"

"Um, yeah. I mean, my times are already better than last year and the season doesn't even start for a couple of weeks. I think I can make it to sectionals if I keep at it."

"That's great," Tim offered.

The two sat in silence listening to the mix of music Tim had arranged for the meal. "I forgot the salads," he said, and returned to the kitchen. "Oh, and there's dessert too—tiramisu."

The wine flowed, and the two finished the first bottle before dessert.

"You think you will try out at U of I?" Tim asked.

"I don't think so. I mean, that's got to be a lot of time. And if I stick with engineering, there's really no way. I'll just have to keep up with my running to stay in shape."

"So, I know I promised you dinner and a movie, right? Well, I hope you liked dinner."

"I did. It was awesome."

"I thought we could watch a movie up in my dad's office. There's a big TV up there and a couch and I brought some tapes.

"Um, yeah. That sounds good. But let's clean up first in case anyone comes in."

"I got it. And I'll grab dessert. I'll meet you up there. Get settled."

Kate headed up the center stairs of the mansion, looking for lights at the top before proceeding down to Jack's office, where a lamp already was lit. Downstairs, Tim busied himself with leftovers and dishes. He opened another bottle of wine, grabbed the empty glasses and dessert.

Kate opened the doors of the cabinet that contained the TV/VCR and inadvertently bumped the protruding tape back into its slot, starting the machine. The video ran.

The footage was shaky, but the image was clear. She watched for a few minutes, seeing herself walk into a family planning clinic. The camera then zoomed in on the license plate of her car. She shut the TV off and walked to the window, crying.

Tim bounded up the steps, gripping the wine bottle and glasses in one hand, the dessert in the other. He saw Kate staring out the window. He set down the dessert and wine and walked over, bringing his arms around her. He learned quickly that she was upset.

"What's wrong?" he asked.

"Nothing," Kate responded.

"Well, that can't be true. You are crying."

She turned around and faced him, her face streaked from a steady stream of tears, "I told you not to tell anybody."

"Tell anybody what?" Tim asked.

"You know what."

"I don't."

Kate pounded on Tim's chest with her fists. "Don't you fucking lie to me! How could you?" she yelled.

"Kate, I don't know what the hell you are talking about? Talk to me! Why are you so upset?" Tim asked, his hands holding Kate's wrists.

"Let go of me!" she said, breaking away and walking across the room to the television. From that distance, she said, "I can't believe I trusted you."

"Trusted me to do what? Kate, what the hell?"

"This," she said, pointing to the TV. She looked for the play button and started the videotape, rewinding it for a moment. "How could you?"

Tim approached the television. "I don't know where this came from."

"You are so full of shit," she said, hitting him again.

"I'm not! Stop hitting me for Christ sake. I mean, what is this?

Where would it come from? You told me about this after the fact—it's not like I recorded you months before we dated going into the clinic. I hardly even knew you then."

"Well then what the hell is this?" Kate realized that Tim likely knew as little about this as she did.

"I don't know. What is this video?" Tim ejected the video. They read the label, which stated the video was recorded by a right-to-life group that picketed the abortion clinic daily and videotaped those coming and going.

"Holy shit," Tim said. "I can't believe they are videotaping this stuff. I can't imagine that is legal. Is it?"

"How would I know, Tim? It is what it is, but I want to know this: how is it here in your dad's office?"

"I don't know."

"You don't? How else would your dad have known to go down this path without you telling him?"

"Kate, Jesus. I am telling you I didn't have anything to do with this." He looked around, pulling open drawers in the cabinet, looking in boxes on the floor. "Look," he said pointing, "there are boxes and boxes of stuff from a private investigator. My dad uses a guy on lots of his cases. And look here: 'Tara Dobson', 'Tyreese Jackson,' 'Jason Flowers,' there are files on everyone."

"And you know nothing about this?"

"I swear to God I don't. It looks like my dad has background on every potential witness in my trial. And here's one on the coroner, and one on the sheriff that interrogated me."

"So your dad got this—dug this dirt up on me?"

"Well, I mean, I guess someone did it at his direction, but he would have had no way of knowing about what would come of it—about the clinic. I swear, Kate, I haven't told anyone about that."

"You are full of shit, Tim. All of it."

"What do you mean, 'all of it'?" Tim asked.

"You know what I mean. I think you are a liar. I think you hit Chad, and I think you knew it when you did it. I think the confession was real, and I think you told your dad anything and everything you could to help your defense. And that included my secret."

Kate was sobbing. Tim protested: "Kate that isn't true. I didn't tell my dad anything. His p.i. just found this stuff out—I've never talked to the guy or anything. I swear."

"I'm done, Tim. With you, with your dad, and your family."

"With my family? What the hell is that supposed to mean?"

"I read the paper Tim. And my dad tells me what they say your dad is being investigated for. That office across the hall. That judge. All that money you have now. All of this—is total bullshit," she said, spitting as she yelled through her cries. "All of it Tim. I'm done."

"Kate, I wish I could explain this to you better. But those allegations against my dad—those are total bullshit. The prosecutor is out for him because he sued her old company. That's all it is."

"You've got an answer for everything, Tim, but I don't believe it anymore."

"But I—"

"And I'm tired of this. Of our hiding out, of our avoiding parties and our friends. You are a, um, a pariah Tim, and I feel like one too for defending you. So I'm done. I love you. Or I think I do, but I can't keep doing this to myself. I don't trust you and I don't trust your dad."

"But you like my dad."

"Not this man, I don't, who is reviewing videos of all my friends and me. That's crap, Tim. Total crap."

"I agree. I do. I had no idea about this. I am telling you."

"Just take me home. I—I can't—I don't have anything else to say."

"So, you are breaking up with me?"

"Yes, Tim. Isn't that fucking obvious?"

"Fuck. I don't know what else I can say. My dad didn't videotape you. Someone else did. But yeah, I guess someone he hired found that tape. But that isn't my fault. He is just trying to defend me. Still, I'm sorry."

"I just can't believe you anymore, Tim. I know your dad is doing what is best for you. But that isn't what's best for me. So, please take me home. I want to go." She pushed past Tim and headed down the stairs to the front door.

Over five miles of Main Street, the two sat in silence as Tim drove Kate home. He pulled into her driveway as he had done a hundred times before. Kate instinctively turned to give him a kiss. But she stopped herself, instead dropping her head in front of him. Tim kissed her forehead. She turned and exited. She walked up her driveway to her front door and didn't look back.

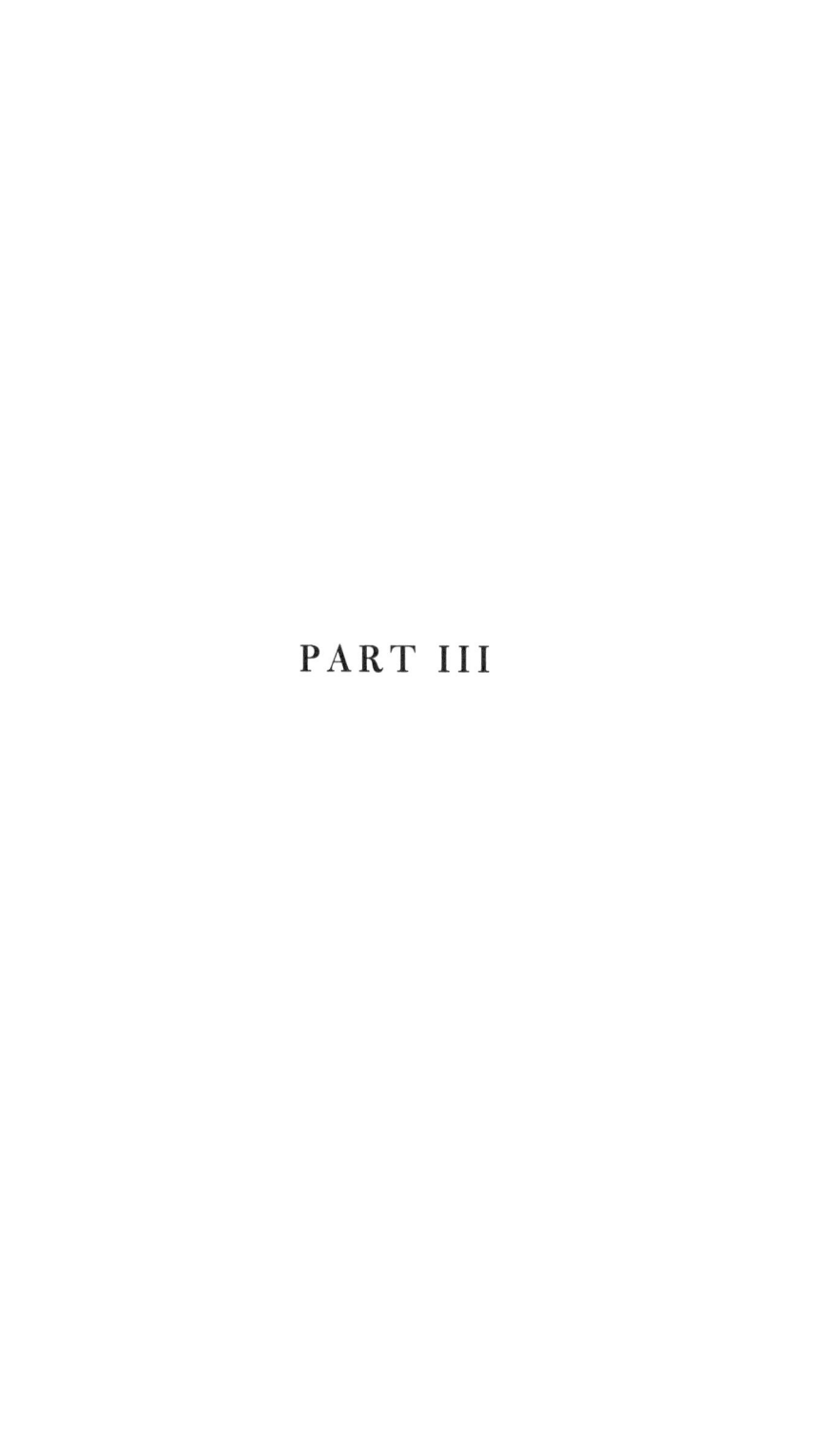

PART III

1

Spring, 1994

THE FIRST JURY WEEK OF MARCH was a busy one. Judge Alicia Briggs had asked the circuit clerk to put out a call for double the number of potential jurors. Thus, almost two hundred men and women culled from across the East Side milled about the jury room wearing juror stickers and waiting to find out if their number would be called to one of the various civil or criminal courtrooms seating juries for the week.

The courtroom of Judge Briggs would receive its first panel of jurors in the afternoon for selection in the People v. Spellman manslaughter trial. Judge Briggs expected, thanks in no small part to the recent coverage in the paper, including crime scene photos and a frame-by-frame reconstruction of the accident, a fair number of potential jurors to know too much about the manslaughter case. Thus, she asked for a large pool hoping to seat a jury not already prejudiced one way or another to the case against Tim Spellman.

Prior to the beginning of jury selection, however, Judge Briggs had before her several motions to resolve—all filed by attorneys for the defense. Indeed, Spellman, Bleaker & Rock had blanketed the State's Attorney with numerous, lengthy and well-researched motions the previous week. Some the State had anticipated, including a motion to exclude the Illinois State Police forensic report as being without scientific merit. Judge Briggs denied the motion outright, without hearing argument.

The Spellman lawyers also challenged the finding of a drowning in the coroner's written report. They claimed that the passage of time was too great—and that the crime scene had been violated by the farmer, the ambulance crew, and potentially others in the hours between the accident and the securing of the crime scene by the Sheriff's Department—to reach that conclusion. Introducing that claim, the defense argued, would so prejudice the jury as to be inadmissible. Judge Briggs denied that motion without argument, as well, ruling that the defense was free to call those issues to the attention of the jury and to offer its own expert testimony challenging the coroner's findings.

One defense motion, however, received the full attention of Judge Briggs. The defense had challenged the constitutionality of the events leading up to the signed confession by Tim to the fatal hit-and-run. They wanted the confession thrown out.

"Finally, we reach defense motion 15 regarding the exclusion of a signed confession by the defendant. Judge Bleaker, this is your motion. Let me hear you on it," Judge Briggs said.

"Thank you, your honor. Preliminary defense exhibit 12 is the signature of Tim Spellman located above a paragraph written by a sheriff, which purports to be a confession to a hit-and-run." He handed up to Judge Briggs a copy of the letter. Judge Briggs reviewed the paragraph, noting the signature, then looked up at counsel indicating he should continue.

"Viewed in a vacuum, your honor, it appears nearly identical to hundreds each of us has seen on the bench. And we do not challenge that the signature on the sheet is Tim's. Defense stipulates to that.

"The issue, as you are aware from our briefs, is one of custodial interrogation and a failure by the state to apprise my client of his Miranda rights. The defense has reviewed the audio recordings from an almost nine hour period of interrogation of Tim Spellman. Almost immediately in his interview with the sheriff's department, Tim made it clear to the sheriffs that he wanted to leave. He repeated this request numerous times over several hours—including a request for counsel. Yet, in no uncertain terms the sheriff's office made it clear that Tim was not allowed to leave.

"It is clear, from the various statements we have highlighted in the record, that Tim not only was under the belief that he was unable to leave, he was in fact unable to leave. On several occasions, the sheriff's office took lengthy breaks—never telling Tim he could leave, and when specifically asked, never allowing Tim to leave. Tim was, in a word, in custody.

"Further, it is equally clear that Tim was the focus of the sheriff's investigation into the Chad Johnson death, both prior to and at the time he was in the custody of the sheriff. The sheriff's office had been investigating Tim for weeks, including visits to his high school campus to photograph his vehicle and to talk to students about Tim.

"In light of those factors—that Tim was in custody and was being interrogated regarding his alleged part in the death of Chad Johnson— the sheriff's department had the legal obligation to alert him as to his Miranda rights. And yet, at NO time did the sheriff's office advise Tim that he had been charged with a crime, or that he had a right to remain silent. In fact, they did the opposite. They ignored his requests, told him he could not leave, avoided his request for counsel. They even told him they thought he committed the crime. And still, no Miranda.

"I submit, your honor, that this is textbook custodial interrogation. The sheriff's office was required to read Tim his rights. Because it did not, Tim's written confession and any reference thereto must be excluded from this trial."

"Ms. Peterson, your response on behalf of the state?"

"Thank you judge," Monica said. "Obviously, the state takes a different view. The sheriff's office followed its standard, legal protocols. They visited the defendant on a neutral site, at the high school, and the defendant agreed to travel to the sheriff's office for an interview. He went there in his own vehicle, of his own volition.

"The state further supports the interview process. Mr. Spellman was subjected to standard—and authorized—police tactics including, unquestionably, some delay, belittling, berating and that sort of thing. But Mr. Spellman could have left at any time, or called for a parent, or called for his lawyer—both of which he eventually did in calling his father. And it was after that, I might add, that he confessed. The state should not be penalized in prosecuting this action because of a little dumb luck."

"Judge Bleaker?"

"Even now, Judge Briggs, the state perpetuates this lie that this was somehow police work as usual. It wasn't—and it began weeks before the actual interrogation. The state already had determined Tim was the owner of a vehicle they believed was involved. They could have moved on him at any time around Thanksgiving. In fact, you refused a warrant for Tim's vehicle at that time—see our exhibit 5 to this motion."

"I recall that, yes," Judge Briggs said, as she flipped to the tabbed exhibits.

"Yet, they did nothing. And do you know why, judge? Because soon after Thanksgiving, Tim reached the age of majority. That meant they could swoop in and talk to him—anywhere—without the need for his parents to be involved.

"The delay in this case was extreme. The statements speak for themselves: Tim says: 'Can I go?' and Sgt. Schaefer says, 'Well, no, not just yet.' Hours later, Tim says: 'Can I go? I've been here for hours and don't have anything else to tell you.' The response? From the sheriff: 'Not just yet. A couple more questions.' Hours go by again, Tim begs, 'I am ready to go. Can I leave?' Answer: nothing. His request is ignored. Later, he asks to make a phone call, or to leave. He is granted the right to make a call, but not allowed to leave.

"And finally judge, the sheriffs appeared at Tim's school—at a time when his peers were around him, but after hours when school administrators—who already told the sheriff's office that all requests for interviews of students on campus go through them—were nowhere to be found. From beginning to end, judge, from the very beginning up to the confession, the sheriff's department—"

"I've heard enough," interrupted Judge Briggs. "This investigation, from the get go, Ms. Peterson, has been a rush job by the sheriff's office. They had no right to go tow that vehicle, I recall. Then they waited until the defendant reached 18, and then decided to corner the defendant at school, in front of his fellow students. Of course he went with them.

"The evidence is clear that the state knew they were interested in Mr. Spellman as a suspect in the death of Chad Johnson. They should have informed him of that fact at the outset of the interview. They didn't. He asked to leave—several times—and was denied.

"I find, therefore, that at the time of his written confession, Tim

Spellman was in the custody of the sheriff's department as its chief suspect and target in the homicide of Chad Johnson. Accordingly, Mr. Spellman should have been provided the standard constitutional protections afforded to him by law, including those provided under Miranda. The sheriff's failure to take these clear and necessary steps, which are not new or onerous, makes the written confession submitted by Tim Spellman inadmissible at trial. Both parties are prohibited from making any reference to the confession itself, or to the physical process of Sgt. Schaefer having rendered it, or Mr. Spellman having signed it. Further, and I am not aware of any such evidence—and the defense presents none—any evidence that was unearthed because of—and only due to—the confession is similarly prohibited."

"Judge Briggs," Monica opted to interrupt the judge before things got any worse, or before Nelson wedged in. She paused, searching for the words for what she wanted to do next. Her case was harmed considerably by the loss of the confession, and she pondered whether to move forward. "In light of the court's decision, the state would request an additional thirty days to proceed with trial."

"Judge, can I be heard—" Nelson asked.

"No need, counsel. State's request for a delay is denied. Jury selection begins this afternoon, unless there is a plea arrangement, which I suggest both sides consider. Anything else?"

Bleaker: "No judge. Thank you."

Peterson: "No."

Judge Briggs: "Court is adjourned until 1 p.m., when voir dire begins."

2

RUTH SAT ALONE ON THE HIGH-BACKED SOFA, flanked on all sides by businessmen of importance in St. Louis and the East Side. She listed patiently to the men, who surrounded her in the parlor of the private dining room of the St. Louis Athletic Club.

First came an earful from SL&SP Railway's Guy Sampson: "mayors, councilmen, aldermen, mailmen...I don't care about any of them. You need to shut down these damned plaintiffs lawyers that are ruining this country, and this town. That, Ruth, that is where you need to be focusing." Sampson was still smarting from the multimillion dollar thrashing his company had taken at the hands of Jack Spellman. He continued: "You've been in this position for what, six months? And you have been doing a great job. Really, we all think that."

Sampson paused, looking around to see the nods of his corporate brethren. "And I think everyone agrees that you have taken on not just the violent crime, but all this other shit we know is going on over there." Sampson motioned generally to the East. "But I think there needs to be a focus, a laser focus, on what is really killing business, killing our livelihoods. And that is those goddamned trial lawyers over there," he said, waving his hand from the top of his head.

"I second what Guy has to say, Ruth," added the chief executive for Arch Coal. "You are just the person for this role. I used to think our bottom line was damaged the most by the unions, the regulations, all of that. But Guy is right, it is the lawsuits and the insurance we have to carry that is killing us. Look, you were in-house counsel not that long ago. You know what I am talking about."

"I do."

"Damn right," Ruth's former boss at AgriFarm, J. David Meirs, began in earnest, "and Ruth knows, guys, that it is only getting worse. AgriFarm's under fire now. We just got served with a $500 million suit from Spellman. A national class action, filed over there in your building Ruth. It will cost the company tens of millions to defend, even if we win. Ridiculous. Think about that."

"I don't have to, Dave. Our case for the SL&SP started at that same amount and we spent $8 million before deciding to pay out. Spellman is a goddamned monster," added Sampson, "and everyone knows it."

The youngest in the room by a decade or more, brewery-head Matthew Lambreth, offered a more conciliatory approach: "Ruth, we are just here to see how you are doing and to let you know that we hope you can do more. And to see if there is anything we can do to help. And, well, I think that's it."

But Sydney Driscol was having none of it: "Hells bells, Matt. That is fine for you. Where's the liability in your beer? My company makes bullets and guns—that are intended to kill people and—you know what—do kill people! Meirs, hell, he's got antitrust issues, napalm, and Frankenseed that, combined, pretty much piss off the whole world. And the railroad, well, they've been getting raked over the coals for a century.

"Ruth, my concern isn't with my guns, their beer or your—their seeds. It is with this region, and our way of life here. We used to make everything around here. You know that. Stoves, shoes, baby carriages, you name it. Now, what is left is threatened by these snakes, these sharks, these, I-don't-know-whats. And you've got one of them in your grasp, and yet, we've yet to see anything come of it."

Guy Sampson reclaimed the conversation: "Ruth, why don't we start there. We all heard about the raid on the Spellman firm. We heard that Judge Flood's name is on court documents alleging impropriety. But the last I heard, he's joined that firm. This is the judge, I don't have to tell you but I will, this is the judge that granted class certification against us—and now he joined that firm! Where is the justice in that? That has to be illegal, right? Total crap. Look, if you had to start somewhere to address what it is we are talking about, this seems to be the place. Right?"

"Gentlemen. Can we sit down to lunch? You eat, I'll talk." Ruth motioned the men over the table, which was set with salads and iced teas. The men did as they were asked, giving her the head seat at the table.

"First, thank you for inviting me to be here today at your monthly lunch. I know that you all had a lot to do with my being here in this capacity. And I am thankful for that and I am mindful of your concerns. I am.

"As you mentioned Guy, yes, it's not been that long since I took over the position of U.S. Attorney for the Southern District. And yes, in that time, we have instituted a Good Government unit that prosecutes government corruption wherever it is found in our district. We have netted—and there is nothing confidential about this—a dozen convictions of government officials already, and another 30 or so are in the works. The word is out across the East Side that we are watching and we are taking action—"

"But—" Driscoll interrupted, without success.

"Let me continue, Sydney. Thank you. While this has been going on, we have continued to investigate others, including the men you mentioned. As was reported in the local papers, and as some of you may know from other sources, we have an active investigation underway against the Spellman firm with regard to activity between the firm and the judge."

SL&SP's Sampson: "And does that include the fact that he handed them tens of millions of dollars, and then went to work there?"

"Everything," Ruth explained, "is on the table. Certainly, from a legal ethics vantage, and from our criminal probe, the timing of the judge's decision in your case, and his later decision to retire to that firm, is a concern. But we are working to find out if it was criminal—on his part or the law firm's. And that takes time, especially now that so much is known about the prosecution."

"But you had their files, you had their computers. I mean, there were pictures in the paper of the boxed-up materials in front of that mansion of theirs. What came of that? Why aren't these guys in jail right now?" Guy Sampson asked.

"Guy, I appreciate your vigor. I do. But don't you think that if we found the smoking gun in those boxes, in those computers, that we wouldn't be having this conversation? That you would see the indictment—and hopefully the conviction—in the papers?"

"So, they hid it all from y'all?"

"The facts speak for themselves, Guy."

The beer baron was growing uncomfortable with the conversation, "Ruth, thank you for that. I think that answers our questions. How have you been enjoying the transition to the public sector?"

"Hold on Matt. If you don't like this, you can leave," Sydney Driscoll snarled. "I, for one, want to know that our concerns are being taken seriously, and that Ruth understands what it is that we want. I, for one, haven't heard that yet."

"I'm not comfortable with that, Sydney, and I don't think anyone else is either," Lambreth said. "Are you, David? I don't think we are here to tell Ruth her job. She knows her job and I think she is doing a hell of a job so far."

David Meirs tried to calm the room. "Matt, I agree with you. Sydney, I hear what you are saying. We all had a hand in supporting Ruth for this position. And I think it is right and appropriate that we be able to meet with her, as she allows, to express our frustrations and to inquire of how her office's initiatives are progressing. We support those initiatives. But I don't think it is right, I'm sorry, I don't think it is right to dictate to her what we want." In fact, he had been doing just that.

"And I'll just add," Matt Lambreth said, "that she damn-well knows where it is we are all coming from. She fought these people for years. She knows as well as any of us do how the plaintiff-bench relationship works in these counties in Illinois. She knows that. Everyone knows that. We just want to see something done about that, and I think we all understand that this takes time."

"It does," Ruth added. "I took this job as a four year commitment, perhaps more. I am not delusional. I do not believe that we can re-craft the judicial system in this part of the country in six months, or perhaps even four years. But we can make a move in that direction. And I believe we are."

Sampson was not finished: "That all sounds good, Ruth, Matt, David. It does. But this is what would sound better: 'we plan to indict Jack Spellman and Bill Flood tomorrow.' That sounds good to me. The rest of it, to me, doesn't amount to shit. Pardon my French, Ruth. But you know. I mean, hell, do I care that the mayor of Dupo is in jail? Not one bit. Would I care if a signal was sent across the bow of the plaintiff's bar and the bench that this shit between local judges and trial lawyers ends now? Yeah, yeah I would."

"I don't disagree with you," Ruth said. "I just don't think it works as easily or as quickly as you might think. We aren't in the business of getting quick indictments only to lose at trial. We work hard on building a case that we know is a winner. And that is what we are doing. We have a good team in place, including Xavier Holden—"

"Xavier is a great lawyer," David Meirs offered to the group. "He worked for us for years. Smart, tough."

"Thank you, yes. He came from Chicago for this role, and replaced a career political appointee in the top slot," Ruth added. "Guy, I hear you," she continued, "I do. And I can tell you this, I wake up every day thinking about things in much the same way you do. And I will say this, too. You will be hearing major things very soon from this office. Not 'mayor of Dupo' stuff, but things that make you sit up and notice. Things that, if I am lucky enough to be invited before you again in a month, you wouldn't have anything but good things to say."

"Well shit, Ruth," Guy offered with a smile, "why didn't you just tell me to shut the hell up, then?"

"My thought all along," Matt offered as steaks descended onto the table from a team of waiters. "Thanks, Ruth, for coming to lunch. You are welcome to join us anytime."

3

THE JURY BOX HELD FOURTEEN JURORS, including two alternates. Voir dire had taken six hours the day before. The state had attempted to exclude young jurors, it appeared, especially younger black male jurors. The defense, meanwhile, appeared keen on selecting those with an apparent intellect, but a lack of knowledge about the press coverage of the case.

The seated jury was mostly white: six of the jurors were older white men, four were middle-aged white women, two were young black women, and two were older black men.

The State entered trial with three counts: vehicular manslaughter, leaving the scene of an accident involving a fatality, and failing to report an accident.

"Good morning, ladies and gentlemen. Thank you for responding to jury duty. The State thanks you for your service in this important case. I am Assistant State's Attorney Monica Peterson. My office represents the State in prosecutions like this one. We prosecute crimes. We speak for the dead. That is what we do. But we need your help.

"In this case, the deceased is Chad Johnson, a rising football star at Belleville West High School, killed one night after a game in a hit-and-run. The State will show that the defendant, sitting there, Tim Spellman, operated the SUV that hit Chad, and that Mr. Spellman's failure to return to the scene led directly to Chad's death." Monica summarized the report from the coroner, and the investigation of the sheriff's office.

"Further, the State will show that, before getting into that SUV, Mr. Spellman had in the course of only a few hours almost a dozen alcoholic beverages." Monica ran through the drinks Tim was alleged to have consumed, elevating her voice after each: "and a rum, then a beer, then another beer, and another, and still another."

Then she dropped her voice: "under the law in Illinois, those drinks, and that decision to drink and drive, well, that makes what could have been a mere accident into a criminally negligent one. It makes it manslaughter."

Monica feigned to her seat, then spun back towards the jury. "And one last thing. This was no accident. It may have been coincidence, or fatally bad timing, but there was no coincidence that the SUV of Tim Spellman hit Chad Johnson. For, as witnesses will tell you, Tim was jealous of the deceased and angry at him for having dated and broken things off with his girlfriend.

"Alcohol, hate, and a brand new SUV barreling down a small country road aimed like a bullet at the deceased. That is what you will have before you, ladies and gentlemen. And, at the end of the week, after the defense has tried to muddle these clear facts, we believe you will find that, beyond a reasonable doubt, Tim Spellman is responsible for the death of Chad Johnson and should be found guilty on all counts."

Monica sat as counsel for the defense, Nelson Bleaker, stood. He had not argued a criminal case in decades, but he knew the drill and he knew his way around a courtroom. He opted against greetings or good mornings so typical of defense attorneys in their efforts to cozy up with the jury. He had no need for that and proceeded with his opening.

"I've known this boy since he was this tall," Nelson began, leveling his hand at his waist. "I've watched him receive his first communion, and his confirmation. I've watched him rise to be an excellent student, a student leader, a standout athlete. I've watched him unload boxes upon boxes of canned goods for the poor, and I've seen him counsel young children against drugs and alcohol. I know Tim Spellman, and I know he did not do the things the State claims he did.

"For a long time, I was a judge in this courthouse. I adjudicated criminal cases involving adults, and also cases involving kids like Tim. I know how prosecutors like Miss Peterson work, and I know the difference between those times when they have their man, and when they are barking up the wrong tree.

"They are barking up that wrong tree." Nelson paused to let his comment sink into the rapt jurors. He surveyed the seating in the back of the courtroom, recognizing a few reporters, noting a courtroom artist he had seen in past cases. He saw Tim's mother, but not his sister. At the defense counsel table sat Tim, in a simple blue suit, with a red tie. His dad sat next to him, in a charcoal gray suit, busily taking notes.

"We all know that a boy died here. And we are saddened by his loss. Belleville is a big small town, I always say, and we feel the loss of Chad Johnson deeply. And so did Tim. At a memorial service for Chad, it was Tim who spoke in memory of Chad, and it was Tim who organized the memorial plaque to Chad at Township Stadium.

"Chad's death is tragic. But it is made more so by the State's wrongful and contrived prosecution of Tim Spellman, who had absolutely nothing to do with it. Yet, from nearly day one, the state has focused on pinning this on Tim—and without any clear evidence of his guilt.

"Somewhere, someone sits nervous with the knowledge that they collided with Chad Johnson, and that he may have died as a result of that collision. But that person is not Tim.

"Now, Miss Peterson speaks about facts. Don't be fooled. There may be evidence, there may be statements, there may be pieces of a puzzle. But stay alert, and pay attention, because the puzzle pieces don't fit together. The dots don't connect. The state has bricks, but they don't make a wall. You get my point. For the next few days, the State will throw these so-called 'facts' at you. But when you turn to deliberating the future of this young man—who was still a boy on the date in question—remember what Judge Bleaker—that's me—remember what old Judge Bleaker said to you: the State is barking up the wrong tree."

"The State calls Sgt. Cliff Schaefer," Monica declared before Nelson had even left the side of the jury box. She wasn't going to let his show endure a moment longer.

Monica walked Sgt. Schaefer chronologically through his investigation. He discussed his review of the crime scene. He played for the jury the videos from the gas station, and shared with them the photos of the red Ford Explorer. Sgt. Schaefer showed exemplars of the student parking permits that were on the SUV in the video, and compared those to photos of similar stickers on Tim Spellman's SUV.

After a lunch break, Nelson Bleaker had his opportunity to question the sheriff.

"Sgt. Schaefer, can you describe for me the crime scene when you arrived?"

"It was an open field, as I described."

"Where was the body?" Nelson asked, looking towards the jury box.

"Gone to the morgue."

"To the hospital, you mean?"

"Right, to the hospital, and ultimately, to the morgue."

"So, no body at the scene?" Nelson raised his hands up to accent his mocking question.

"No."

"Any physical evidence?"

"We collected bags of evidence."

"And have you tied any of it to Mr. Spellman?"

"The coroner's office—"

"I'm sorry, Sgt. Schaefer, we will hear from the coroner later today. Of the evidence your office collected—the physical evidence—have you tied any of it to Tim?"

"No."

"Bags of evidence. And, yet, nothing."

"Well, a lot of it was garbage and—"

"Yes. Garbage. Exactly. Thank you. Now, had the perimeter of the crime scene been secured prior to your arrival?"

"No." Sgt. Schaefer started to lean forward, his displeasure with this process becoming quite clear.

"The road was open?"

"Yes."

"The field was open?"

"Yes."

"And in fact, was being plowed prior to the discovery of the body, correct?"

"Yes."

"And tell me about the field itself," Nelson said. "Any other tracks besides the tractor?"

"Yes. The ambulance."

"The ambulance drove through the crime scene?"

Sgt. Schaefer knew this would be raised: "Yes, but my investigation indicated the ambulance crew, the EMS, that they were not aware it was a crime scene when they arrived and were simply getting as close to the victim as possible for purposes of attempting to save his life."

"So, an open scene, with no body, and tracks from various vehicles, and bags of garbage. OK. Now, you interviewed, what did you say 'dozens' of students during the course of your investigation?"

"Correct."

"Did a single witness see the alleged hit and run?"

"No. Except Mr. Spellman obvi—"

"Thank you. No one is on record in this case as having witnessed the accident, isn't that right?"

"Well," the officer looked to the judge, knowing of the confession, but having been warned not to discuss it.

"Answer, sergeant."

"No. No one on record."

Nelson continued: "That's right. Now, Sgt. Schaefer, were you able to find any video surveillance of the scene of the crime?"

"No. Just the after minutes from the gas station."

"So, that's also a 'no.' No video of the crime scene," he said straight to the jury. "But let's talk about that video you just showed us. Any positive ID on the person or persons in that video?"

"No, but we believe—"

"Oh, we know what you believe, sir. We are concerned in this court of law with what you can prove," Nelson scolded the sheriff. "Any positive ID on the truck in that video?"

"No, but again—"

"Right, you believe you know what truck it is, you just can't prove it. Now, Sgt. Schaefer, I want to take you back to Thanksgiving of this past year."

"OK?"

"Were you able to celebrate that holiday, or did you have to work that day?"

"Yes, I was. My wife and me, we had our sons and their wives over. I did not work that day."

"Then why, may I ask, were you hanging out at the home of Tim Spellman?"

"I don't recall that."

"Well, that is interesting," Nelson said, as he walked over to the defense counsel's table. He lifted a VHS tape from his first trial box and placed it into the VCR. "This, Sgt. Schaefer, is video surveillance of the Spellman home. It—"

Peterson: "Objection, your honor, this was not on the defense list of exhibits. We were not apprised of its contents."

Bleaker: "Your honor, this is rebuttal evidence, and we were under no compulsion to offer it to the State."

Briggs: "Objection denied."

Bleaker: "As I was saying, officer, Sergeant, this is video—very high quality color video, I might add, from the Spellman home. Before I hit play, you ever been there?"

"I may have driven by."

"Well, indeed you are right! And on Thanksgiving no less. See, here you are, slowly driving by. And let's watch this together. Here you are, sitting in your truck for several minutes glimpsing back at the Spellman house. But you weren't working that day, right?"

"Well, no. But I had left to get some air, and decided to drive by the Spellman house. They live only a few miles away."

"Had you interviewed my client at this point in your investigation?"

"No, I don't believe so."

"Did you see him when you arrived at the Spellman house?"

"Yes."

"Then, why not stop and talk to Tim then?"

"It wasn't the time."

"Because he was a minor at that time?"

"Objection. Relevance?" yelled Monica.

Judge Briggs asked Nelson, "Counsel, where are we headed here?"

"Just that Sgt. Schaefer was not telling the truth about his whereabouts on Thanksgiving, and that he was stalking my client. That is all."

"I think you've made that point. Shut off the machine. Objection sustained."

"OK, Sgt. Schaefer. You testified earlier that you narrowed down the field of suspects in light of the Illinois State Police report that stated that a piece of orange turn signal light plastic was found in Chad Johnson. That orange plastic piece, the report claims, is unique to Ford trucks. Is that right?"

"Correct."

"Thank you. Now, did you impound any other Ford trucks?"

"No. We focused on the ones we saw in the video."

"Did you find any of those other vehicles from the video?"

"No."

"Right, so you focused on this one Ford SUV. And you photographed that, correct?"

"Yes."

"And you did a plain view inspection of that vehicle in the West parking lot, and again at your headquarters a month or more later."

"Yes."

"And did you find any evidence of a turn signal light having been broken on Tim Spellman's SUV?"

"Well, no. But he could have replaced that."

"'Could have?' Did you find evidence that the signal had been replaced?"

"No."

"No receipts from a credit card showing a repair of the Ford SUV, or the purchase of an auto part?"

"No."

"No testimony from a service shop as to having replaced a Ford signal light?"

"No."

"Again, no evidence. I sense a trend here. That is all. No more questions for this witness."

Monica declined to rehabilitate her first witness, deciding instead to move forward with the coroner, who would offer striking testimony regarding how Chad had died.

The coroner, Fred Donovan, made a good witness. He had been the coroner in St. Clair County for nearly twenty years, and had testified in hundreds of trials. He spoke with an infallibility that was difficult for most criminal defense attorneys to crack.

The coroner discussed the process of the autopsy, the contents of his report, and most importantly, his finding that Chad had not been killed by the immediate impact with an automobile.

"So, Dr. Donovan, can you please explain your finding that the cause of death was drowning?" the prosecutor asked.

"Certainly. First, there is no question in my mind that the impact Chad Johnson sustained could have been enough to kill him. It did, in fact, break his neck, and other bones in his upper body.

"But in a case like that, with a broken neck, a major trauma, death would have been evidenced by some level of massive internal bleeding. And we did not have that here, amazingly enough. Instead, what we found in our autopsy was the presence of water—dirty water, in fact—in the deceased's lungs. The victim, we believe, was hit by a vehicle driving upwards of 70 miles per hour, which broke his neck and sent him into the ditch. Unable to move, and very possibly unconscious, he drowned in a shallow ditch, filled with water from the hard rains that day."

"Thank you. In light of your findings, would you agree with me—"

"Objection. Leading."

"Sustained."

"Dr. Donovan, did Chad Johnson die from a broken neck?"

"No. It is my opinion based upon the autopsy and other factors that I discussed that he could have survived that."

"How long would it have taken for Chad Johnson to drown?"

"In this situation, probably a matter of minutes, not seconds. It takes time to take in that water, likely try and involuntarily expel it, and fail. And even after that, there would be time to perform CPR."

"Then, if I am following you, had Tim Spellman stopped and attempted to help Chad Johnson, Chad could have survived?"

"Objection: leading, calls for speculation," Nelson yelled.

"Sustained."

"How could Chad Johnson have survived?"

"Well, had he fallen into the field face up, he could have survived. Or had his neck not been broken, and had he not been unconscious, obviously he could have moved his head away from the water. And of course, had someone been there to lift his head up and out of the water, that would have avoided the drowning."

"Thank you doctor."

"Sure. You are welcome."

Judge Briggs turned to the defense: "Your witness."

Nelson Bleaker stayed seated. "Doctor, just a few questions. The plastic piece. Where on Chad Johnson did you find that?"

"It was found lodged in his torso, on the right side of his chest."

"Are you aware of whether that plastic was deposited into Chad because of the collision, or because of his landing?"

"I don't follow."

"Sgt. Schaefer testified previously that his department collected bags of trash, including various plastic parts, from along the road and surrounding farmland. My question is this: are you aware of whether the piece of plastic you found, whether it was placed in the deceased from a truck that hit him, or from him falling on a piece of plastic?"

"Objection to form."

"Overruled."

"Can I answer? Ok. No, I do not know how that plastic got there. It is consistent with a car hitting the victim, but I suppose it is possible—if unlikely—that he could have bludgeoned himself on it somehow."

"So, you don't know if the plastic came from the truck that hit Chad Johnson, or from somewhere else, do you?"

"No. There really is no way to confirm that from an autopsy table."

"Right. Now, Dr. Donovan, your report places the time of death sometime between 11 p.m. and 5 a.m., is that correct?"

"It is, yes."

"Why the large spread of time?"

"When you are dealing with a drowning, and the cold, wet conditions, it is very difficult to narrow that time period. The water in the stomach, in the lungs, that hinders our ability to determine time based, for example, on the contents of the stomach. The cold and the wet, that makes determinations based upon body temperature and rigor harder."

"Could the window even be wider?"

"I suppose it could, but not by much. We know what time the call came in, and the condition of the body when we arrived. So the 5 a.m.

figure is a pretty firm number. The same is true on the other end since we were aware of the deceased's whereabouts prior to that time."

"Tell me about the contents of Chad Johnson's stomach."

"As I said, dirty water. Some food, probably pasta. Alcohol."

"Did you measure the type or amount of alcohol?"

"No, with the potential length of time passed, and the water in the stomach, there was no way to do that with any level of accuracy."

"And did you test the blood of the victim?"

"Yes, of course."

"And you found evidence of a heightened blood-alcohol, and of marijuana, is that correct?"

"Objection."

"It goes to the potentiality that the victim may have been under the influence, your honor, and potentially dangerously in the street."

"Overruled. Please answer."

"Yes, that is correct. Chad had a heightened blood-alcohol level, and the presence of marijuana was noted in his system."

"And that is consistent, isn't it doctor, with the diagram provided in this case as to how the deceased may have fallen in front of the car or truck that hit him?"

"What is consistent?"

"That Chad Johnson was outside of his car, and fell because he was drunk."

"Objection!"

"Sustained."

"There is no way to know that."

"Is there a way to know if Chad Johnson had vomited prior to death?"

"Certainly, and he had. But that likely was related to—and a part of, in fact—his drowning. I cannot say one way or the other if the traces of vomit we found were from some prior vomiting incident, or not."

"Either way, though, doctor, you are telling us Chad Johnson was drunk."

"Objection!"

"Withdrawn. Nothing more for this witness."

4

THE GOVERNMENT CRIMES GROUP of the U.S. Attorney's office was bringing considerable notoriety to Ruth Whittaker. The St. Louis Post-Dispatch had dubbed her early as a "Sorely Needed Elliott Ness for the East Side."

Indeed, in less than a year, her office had pushed through speedy trials, and even speedier pleas, with nine mayors, twenty aldermen, and another dozen government employees. The one glaring exception from that list, however, was the prosecution of the highest flying plaintiff's lawyer on the East Side, Jack Spellman.

That investigation was faltering. The decision to raid the Spellman firm had closed every apparent source of information to fuel Ruth's investigation. Worse, it had started to turn the press and the public against her mission.

The law firm had responded to the unfruitful search of its firm's offices with a juggernaut of positive good works in and around the community, including cash donations to major charities. The firm portrayed itself as innocent victims of a prosecutor's office hell-bent on destroying the culture of the East Side, which always had served proudly as a bastion of trial lawyers standing at the ready to take the battle to the corporate lawyers across the river in St. Louis.

In Illinois, the letters to the editorial pages called Ruth "a crusader without a clue," and a prosecutor "uninterested in stopping real crime."

Ruth decided it was time to double-down on her prosecution of Jack Spellman. She considered her options as she road in the back of a black sedan, which travelled over the Martin Luther King Jr. bridge into downtown St. Louis. She was meeting Xavier Holden for lunch in the city after he completed some meetings he said he had with law enforcement there.

The two prosecutors had agreed to meet at a soul food dive just east of the campus of Saint Louis University in Midtown. Ruth arrived before the lunch crowd and commandeered one of the tables away from what would become a loud and busy lunch counter.

Ruth ordered sweet tea and flipped through a month's worth of reports on the investigation into Judge Flood and the Spellman firm.

Xavier arrived promptly at 11:30, as the restaurant was starting to fill up with a mixed crowd of young and old, black and white. He spied Ruth and took a seat across from her. "What's good here?" he asked, looking flustered.

"Good morning to you. How was the meeting?"

"Ah sorry. Yes, good morning to you. I didn't have breakfast. The meeting was, um, it was good," Xavier said.

"Good, good. There's a paper menu over there, and up on the board is pretty much everything. I like the fish sandwich." Two fish sandwiches, and another tea, were ordered. While they waited for their food, Ruth and Xavier got down to the business of William Flood and Jack Spellman.

"Xavier, I've been thinking about this case a lot. And I know you have been as well. Where do you see this headed?" Ruth asked.

"It hasn't gone the way we planned. But it is going, and there is something there. We know that. But I've seen the same reports you have that there is nothing new coming out. I think there is enough there for indictments against the judge. We have him on the campaign finance violations, the illegal gambling, and we have a decent case on the conspiracy and bribery. And of course he is working at the Spellman firm now, which certainly won't be lost on a jury."

"So, you would say we have a decent case against the judge."

"I think a good case."

"OK. And as to Jack Spellman and his partners?"

"Not enough, I don't think. No case," Xavier said.

"Unless," Ruth started.

"Unless what?"

"Unless we bring in Judge Flood and show him what we have, and see if we can flip him onto the others."

"And offer immunity?" Xavier questioned.

"He gets the benefit of his years on the bench," Ruth offered.

"But he would have to testify and soil his reputation anyway."

"Right, I know. But he gets to walk away. And he gives us the lawyers." Ruth nodded at her own idea.

"But is that we are about? I mean, we started this unit to find and prosecute governmental corruption—and we have that here in spades—and you are talking about letting that go to bring down lawyers who, it seems to me, have done something somewhat less galling."

"I get that. I do. But we go after the corruption where we find it. And Jack Spellman has made a career of hiring former judges, under questionable circumstances, and then leveraging them to millions of dollars in verdicts. The railroad case, with Judge Flood, is just the latest and most blatant example. And one, I might add, that could be overturned in the event of a conviction on either side of this."

"Really? At this point, who is crying for a few million dollars out of the railroad's pockets? I'm not."

"I'm not really, either. But it is tied together, Xavier, and you know that." Ruth lowered her head and leaned in, above the plates of food they had yet to touch. "You know that the two go hand-in-hand, the judiciary and the trial lawyers. So maybe on this one, we get the lawyers."

"I simply don't have the case against Spellman. I have somewhat of a case against Bleaker. But there's no evidence other than that tape where Spellman said he needed money for his kid to get out of jail. If that evidence even made it into a trial, I would be surprised."

"And that is why you need to flip Judge Flood."

"No, that is why I need to go indict Judge Flood, and forget about the rest of those clowns."

"I fundamentally disagree," Ruth said.

"So, you would rather try and fabricate—well, no, not fabricate, but certainly create a case—where there is none, and offer immunity for the conspirator against whom we have a case? That makes no sense to me." Xavier said, biting into his sandwich.

"If our case was stronger, I'd go after both of the men at the same time. But it isn't." Ruth was adamant.

"I agree, and so, the question is, who gets flipped. And I don't see how you flip the guy with all the bad conduct against the guy with none apparent. That makes no sense to me. If you want to set an example, we set it with the mayors, with the judges and especially the chief judges. We don't set it with the trial lawyers, who are a dime a dozen over there."

"Spellman is unique. I believe that. He has the skills, and the capacity, to take down company after company in this country, to the benefit of no one, other than himself. Do you think those class plaintiffs, who get $10 off their next phone bill, or get a coupon for free corn seed, that they are beneficiaries of this system? Spellman is the problem here. Not a judge who got caught up in some gambling debt and looked for a way out."

"Jesus, Ruth. Are you kidding me? The judge was caught up, sure, but he appears to have flipped the case for a monumental class action settlement. Sure, the Spellman firm was a beneficiary of that—and I think complicit in that—but how do you excuse the man who took the oath to be a judge? How do you just let him walk away, as you said? Are you crazy?"

Ruth hadn't finished her bite, and so she sat eating, letting Xavier's last comment hang in the air. She knew that Xavier had no inkling of the extent to which she felt beholden to the powerful men in local industry that had placed her into her position. She also figured that he had not seen the fall in AgriFarm's stock price since the Spellman-fueled class action against it was filed.

Moreover, Ruth understood, her failure to act on the trial bar on the East Side would tank her future plans—whatever they were. She would receive little backing for an additional term without movement on this front, and she certainly would receive no support for a seat on the federal appellate bench, or a run for federal office.

She knew that not all of this hung on Spellman, but his was the largest active investigation in her office and she wanted badly for it to succeed. Quite simply, Ruth thought, she needed Spellman's head above her mantel. Her convictions of local mayors and councilmen abounded—and that satisfied and preoccupied the media. Now, she needed a trial lawyer, and these days, there was none bigger than Jack Spellman.

"No, Xavier, I'm not crazy. But I do set the direction for this office." This was her first pulling of rank on Xavier she could recall. "The lack of evidence against Jack Spellman does not convince me that he is not worthy of our prosecution. Rather, I believe he is complicit, and we need to develop the evidence necessary to convict him.

"Therefore, I want you to summon Judge Flood to my office. I want you to make him queen for a day. Lay out all of our cards against him—the gambling, the illegal campaign solicitation, the conspiracy, the class action verdict. You give him the years under the sentencing guidelines, which he will already be calculating in his head while you talk. You give him those years, and then I will tell him that it doesn't have to be this way.

"I will tell him that he made mistakes, and out of fear in most cases broke these laws. And that we understand this, but that he has to give us Spellman. Otherwise, we are going after him."

"And if he declines? Will we go after the judge?"

"He won't decline. He is an old, wise man. He doesn't want to be in a plaintiff's law firm. He wants to be retired in Arizona playing golf. We give him that chance to remove this cloud, and to walk away."

"He will never agree he flipped that verdict. At best, Ruth, I think we can get him to agree to the little stuff. And then you still have nothing against the law firm."

"Maybe you are right. Maybe not. But we have nothing else left in our quiver. So unless you can come up with something better—and I will not agree that a prosecution of the judge, alone, is better—then this is what we are left with. Call Flood in."

Xavier, more shaken than he was when he walked in the door, simply nodded.

5

JACK AND TIM SPELLMAN BUCKLED THEMSELVES IN to Jack's car for the trip to Hayes House, and then to court. Each morning of Tim's trial, Jack used the trip downtown to go over what would occur during the day. It was as much for Tim's education as it was to calm Jack's nerves.

"So, from the witness list, the prosecution is going to call on all those students, each of whom will claim you had something to drink. Our plan is to short-circuit that and just stipulate that you had been drinking that night. The state won't go for that, but the judge might. And these kids—you know them all?" Jack recited the names he recalled from the witness list.

"Yeah, most of them, at least a little."

"And do you think they were drinking too?"

"Yeah, I mean, of course. Just about everyone drinks at Stupes. I mean, I can name on one hand the people that I know that go out there and don't drink. And most of them are too busy doing pot."

"Jesus, Tim. Okay. Well, we might go ahead and let them testify and drag them down into this too. We'll see what Nelson has to say."

"Okay."

"And then, their last witness is Kate. I don't think there is anything there to worry about, since she told us what she testified to at the grand jury."

"Yeah, but you know, right? You know we broke up, like a month ago?"

Jack's eyes widened. He pulled the car into the driveway of the country club and stopped. He looked at Tim: "you what?"

"We broke up. I told you that."

"I don't recall that conversation. And your mother certainly would have told me if she had known."

"Okay, well, whatever, we broke up. Have you even seen Kate around the house in the last few weeks?"

"Tim, I don't know. But honestly, now? At this point, you break up with the girlfriend who drove home with you that night? Damn it,

Tim! And now what is she going to say?"

"Dad, you still think I did this. I did not do this. And she knows that."

"But she knows you stopped the car, right? And got out and checked the front of the car? And threw up? Yes, I know she does. And she knew you had been drinking. She knew you did not care for the fact that she had dated Chad Johnson. Right? And what else?"

"I don't know."

"Son, you damn-well better think. This is crucial. Goddamn it, how could you let this happen?"

"She broke up with me, Dad. I mean, she had enough of it, of me. Of this. The kids at school mock me, you know, and they mock her. They say she is dating a murderer, and saying she knows the truth. We can't go anywhere but school. No one wants us at parties. It is embarrassing for her, and for me. And maybe I didn't tell you, I don't know. But you could have noticed. Or asked. Or whatever. Geez."

"Alright," Jack said, trying to calm himself. "But Tim, you understand this: Kate Shaw is the State's most crucial witness. She is the one who can tell the truth if you aren't—or confirm the truth if you are. So don't lie to me, Tim. Don't lie. This is the last time I will ask: what else do I need to know to protect you? Tell me now Tim."

"Nothing, Dad, I swear. But I will talk to Kate."

"But she testifies today! When were you planning to break this to us—when she took the stand? We need to defend you, Tim."

"I'll try and talk to her before she testifies."

Jack circled around the parking lot and headed back onto the road. "And if you don't reach her?"

"I will Dad. Anyway, I don't think she would lie about anything. It will be okay."

Jack doubted that very much, but drove in silence. He figured it very likely that Kate had no longer believed in Tim's innocence, and could no longer continue to date him. But what, Jack pondered to himself, would Tim possibly say to his ex-girlfriend at this stage that would make an ounce of difference?

When the Spellmans entered Hayes House, they found Nelson scribbling final outlines of his cross-examinations for the day. He noted Jack's demeanor, but did not inquire as to its cause. "Jack," he said. "I think we let all of those kids testify. They had to have been drinking, and they likely don't know much of anything. Let's just let more witnesses with nothing to say clog up the State's case."

"I agree, Nelson. Tim and I were just talking about that. They were all drinking too. But we appear to have a bigger issue."

"And that is?"

"Kate Shaw. She broke up with Tim a few weeks ago. I had no idea. Though Tim says he told me. Anyway, she could be a real problem."

"Oh my," Nelson said, considering the repercussions of this new fact. "Well, we know what she said before the grand jury. And if she contradicts that, well, we use that against her. She can't have it both ways. But, I guess that raises the question of what she really knew. And whether she will be willing to confess that she was lying before the grand jury because she was protecting her boyfriend. Wow. Bad timing, Tim. I'm sorry."

"Thanks." Tim could see now how this could all play out badly for him. He had pretty much let Kate walk away, and had not fought for her. Now, he knew, he should have fought, or should have at least tried to salvage the relationship through the end of his trial.

So, while his father and lawyer discussed the morning's testimony, Tim considered what it was Kate knew, and all of it was bad. He grew sick to his stomach. He headed into the restroom and looked at himself in the mirror. He looked ill. And then he was, vomiting into the toilet.

6

JUDGE FLOOD AGREED TO MEET with Ruth Whittaker and Xavier Holden, but the location of the meeting took some negotiation. He refused to re-enter the courthouse where he had worked for decades, now that he was under a cloud of suspicion with regard to his joining the Spellman firm. Meanwhile, Ruth and Xavier refused to meet with him on his new turf at Hayes House.

Ultimately, Ruth charmed the old judge with an invitation to her home for breakfast. So, as his partners were getting ready to head to court for the on-going trial of Jack Spellman's son, Judge Flood headed to the far west end of Belleville and the glass-clad manse of the U.S. Attorney.

The judge arrived on time and parked his aging maroon Buick behind the gleaming German cars of the prosecutors. He hoped the meeting was an announcement of an end to the investigation, and the backing off of the U.S. Attorney's office. He knew it was as likely, however, that it could go the other way.

Judge Flood exited his car and pulled the lapels of his overcoat up around his neck as he made the walk up the driveway.

Ruth answered the door with a warm greeting, "Come in, come in out of the cold, Judge. Good to see you."

"Thank you. Nice place, Ms. Whittaker. AgriFarm treated you well, I see."

"I suppose so, yes. Thank you. And please, call me Ruth."

"Well, until I know why I'm here, I'll keep it to Ms. Whittaker. And you," he said, turning to Xavier, "I know to be Xavier Holden. Good morning."

"Same to you judge. Thank you for agreeing to meet with us."

"But before that, Judge, please," she directed him towards the dining room table, "have a seat. I've got fruit salad and some breads and pastries. Anything else I can get for you?"

"A cup of black coffee, perhaps?"

"Already in a carafe, on the table. Please have a seat."

Judge Flood took the head seat at the table, glimpsing the impressive early glow of the St. Louis skyline out the windows. He poured himself coffee and pulled a chocolate croissant from the pastry tray. "Where did you find these around here?" he asked.

"Made them myself, actually," Ruth said.

"Goodness, very good. And warm."

Ruth sat down to the judge's left, and Xavier sat to his right. The judge considered how the East Side had changed, as evidenced by the fact that he was facing down two black federal prosecutors in a lavish west end Belleville home. "What can I do for you?" he offered.

Ruth began softly, with compassion in her voice. "Judge, you know that my office has investigated—and is investigating—issues in relation to your retiring from the bench and joining the law firm of Spellman, Bleaker & Rock."

"Yes. I do, and can I say—"

"Let me finish. Please," Ruth asked.

"Certainly. Go ahead."

"Thank you. You know that you, Jack Spellman, and Nelson Bleaker are targets of our investigation. We believe that there may have been impropriety with regard to contacting you prior to your retirement, and while you were adjudicating a class action brought by that firm.

"What you do not know, however, is that my office also has evidence of other impropriety." The judge placed his croissant down on his plate. He wiped his hands together and sat back in his chair, prepared to listen. He fixed his eyes on Ruth, who continued: "we are aware, for example, of your gambling and gambling debts. We are aware of your use of your federal office to solicit campaign funds. These actions are violations of the criminal code, judge. There is no other way to put this. They are criminal, and worse, they served to deprive the public of your honest services, which also is a violation of federal law," Ruth said.

"With what we know now, Judge," Xavier Holden chimed in, "we are in a position to move against your lifetime pension, to charge you with no fewer than twelve felonies, and to seek a prison sentence of up to 96 months."

"Well," the judge began calmly, "what a bunch of horseshit. Where in the hell did the two of you come up with all of this? My gambling? There is a goddamned casino spitting distance from your office. And soliciting campaign funds? What kind of piss-ant do you take me for? Did you shake down my secretary for that?" he asked. "So I did some of that from my chambers," he conceded. "Well, of course I did, you fools. I spent my life in those chambers. I worked twelve-hour days, and the only way to fit in those calls was to make them from my office. What was I supposed to do? Go home in the middle of a court day to call donors?

"And what else did you say? Oh, right, honest services. That's a load of crap. Look at my record. Look at it. The fewest overturned decisions of anyone in the Southern District, and one of the lowest percentages of anyone in the whole Seventh Circuit. My career was ironclad. This is unbelievable. Unbelievable," he trailed off in a mutter.

"Judge, you can defend yourself to these charges," Ruth began anew, "and I know you will. And in truth, we have known about the gambling, and the campaign finance, for months. And you deserve to know that we have not made that a part of any further investigation. But Judge, it is the malfeasance with regard to your leaving and joining the Spellman firm that causes my office the most concern."

"Your office? It causes your office concern? Because after three decades on the bench, I'm still driving an old Buick instead of a damn Mercedes or whatever I saw out in that driveway? I'll bet had I joined one of those silk-stocking firms across the river, like Jones Reed, we wouldn't be having this conversation. And do you know what? They recruited me. They recruited me just as much as Spellman and those boys did.

"But I didn't pick the big corporate firm. You wouldn't understand that choice, from what I know of your career, Ms. Whittaker. Corporate, corporate, corporate. God forbid, old Judge Flood start to make a dime with the trial lawyers.

"Let me tell you something. That is a hard working firm. Good lawyers. They bring good cases. Hell, you know as well as I do that their last big case, against the railroad, was a hell of case. Upheld by the Seventh Circuit on appeal—"

"And now you are going to cash in on that, right?" Xavier asked.

"I don't know what you are talking about. That I will earn a good wage in private practice? Or that the Spellman firm happens to be doing well? Would we be talking if the firm hadn't been successful, or if, Ms. Whittaker, it did not now have a very good case against AgriFarm on file? I say, enough of this. What your office needs to do—"

"I won't be hearing any of that, Judge Flood. What my office needs to do is at my discretion. Not yours." Ruth sensed there would be no niceties from here out, and so she looked to Xavier to begin to lay out their case.

Xavier leaned in: "Judge, I don't think you understand what we are saying. We are ready with an indictment on the honest services, gambling, and campaign finance charges. We are ready on that. Today. Those are easy convictions for us to get, no matter what you contend. The law is clear on those counts.

"And we believe that you were subjected, innocently or not, to ovations from the Spellman firm, to woo you to their employment, in exchange for assistance in the certification of their class action. And we have voicemails from your law clerk, and documents from the federal court computer system, that back that up.

"Finally, we have reason to believe that they may have induced you to this result by extinguishing your considerable gambling debts, and relieving you of the mortgage on your home," Xavier said.

Ruth continued, "Judge Flood. We can show all of this. Conspiracy, the bribe, all of it."

"Then why the hell are you calling me here?" he asked.

"Because, for one, Xavier and I believe you are owed a chance to be heard. Second, we want to figure out how to make this right for you. For you to retire, with your pension, in peace."

"By helping you do what? Bring down Jack Spellman and Nelson Bleaker? I won't do that. Those are good men," Judge Flood said.

"Good men who have a habit of playing it over the line," Xavier added.

"Judge," Ruth said, "I am offering you an out here, a one-time only chance to speak with us candidly and to work out an accommodation that works for you. And us."

"You want me to confirm that what you say is true, and testify to it. And that if I do, then I get immunity as to all of this shit, and I get to retire and keep my pension."

"Essentially, yes," said Ruth.

"What you fail to understand, Ms. Whittaker, is that I spent the better part of my life building and cultivating a reputation as a lawyer and judge that is above reproach. If all the things you say are true--and I am not going to sit here today and tell you that they are--if all those things are true, and I confirmed that, with immunity or not, then that reputation that I built is gone. Gone, like that," he said, snapping his fingers.

Xavier had heard enough and was ready to push the line: "but judge, what I think you are failing to appreciate is the position you are in. Your reputation is gone either way. If you go along with this, and help us bring a successful prosecution against the Spellman firm, then you walk away. It might not be under the terms you had hoped, but you walk away to Florida, a pension in hand. If you don't, the wheels begin to spin on the prosecution of these other crimes and, win or lose, your reputation is lost. And if we prevail, your pension is gone too. And there could be prison time."

"They don't give prison time for that kind of crap."

"Judge, come on. You know the federal sentencing guidelines as well as anyone. You know it is a possibility, and I am telling you, we would seek it," Xavier said.

"So you are screwing me either way. That is what you are doing. Either I give you dirt on Jack and Nelson and the firm, or you proceed to trash my reputation on these bogus little charges."

"And," Ruth piled on, "we will eventually bring the charges on all of the rest of it—the bribes, the conspiracy, all of it—and that includes you too."

The judge leaned back in his chair and stared out the window towards the Arch in the background. He remembered it being built, and waiting for months for it to fall, though it never did.

Judge Flood contemplated his next move. The truth, of course, was that he and Nelson Bleaker were old friends. It was Nelson who had offered the job to him. It was Nelson who had resolved the gambling debt when the judge so badly needed help.

The judge knew that, at some level, in light of the help Nelson had given him, he did look anew at his firm's class action case. He had been biased in previous years against such cases, and he was inclined to rule against the class certification at first. But as he looked at the briefs again, he found that, in reality, the case was good enough to certify as a class action. He never imagined the railroad would settle for a hundred million dollars, but that was out of his hands. Not to mention, he considered, the Seventh Circuit had backed him by upholding his certification.

Judge Flood took measure of himself to determine whether he had it in him to turn against his friend. He decided he couldn't. Jack Spellman, however, he thought was another story. He knew nothing of Jack's participation in clearing the judge of his debts—and in fact had been told by Nelson that Jack had had played no part. Still, the U.S. Attorney wouldn't know that, and at trial, Judge Flood knew that it would be his word and stellar reputation against a trial lawyer's—and he knew he would get the better of that match.

Xavier and Ruth repeatedly glanced at one another while the judge sat thinking. Neither prosecutor planned to speak until the judge had spoken. Nearly twenty minutes later, Judge Flood stood and walked to the window, speaking into the glass and avoiding the gaze of the prosecutors.

"Here is what I want. First, I want the small shit to go away. I'm talking about the gambling and the campaign finance stuff. If you thought any of that was important, you would have gone after me while I was still on the bench, and you didn't. No mention of that. No charges. Nothing that this is a part of an immunity deal. Nothing.

"Second, I will not allow you to go after Nelson Bleaker with my help. He is a boyhood friend of mine, and a good man, and he has done nothing materially wrong."

"Third, I will not be a part of any prosecution that casts doubt on my class certification. That was a decision I reached in my review of the facts of that case and the application of the relevant law to those facts. It is, as the Seventh Circuit affirmed, a logical and well-supported finding.

"Fourth, I will give you Jack Spellman. I know he is who you want. I will tell you that his firm, presumably at his direction, paid off my debts to incentivize me to join his firm. His firm also paid off my mortgage as a signing bonus, which accidentally was paid prior to my retirement from the bench. This had nothing to do with the class certification, I hasten to add."

"Fifth, I want it to be made clear that this prosecution was at my behest. That I helped you come after Jack Spellman once I realized what was going on. Does that work? Because that removes the cloud over my head." The judge turned around and looked to see the response from Ruth and Xavier.

"Well, judge, that is interesting," Xavier said, wondering mainly if any of it was true. Ruth motioned for the judge to sit. He sat, staring at his plate.

"Judge," Ruth said, "I think you missed your true calling as a criminal defense attorney. You are asking for a lot. And I don't know at this moment whether it is enough for the prosecution we had in mind. But I think I am going to have to give some thought to all of this."

The judge stood, and claimed his coat. He headed for the door: "Good. But know this, I either come out in the clear, with my pension and reputation intact, or I will fight with my firm against every charge you throw our way. They've got the resources not only to win this, but to drag this out until a Democrat gets back in the White House and you all are sent back to corporate America. Good day."

"We will be in touch," Ruth said, with a smile on her face, as she closed the door behind the judge.

With the door closed, Ruth and Xavier watched from the window as the judge got in his car, struggled to turn over its engine, and then retreated down the driveway.

"I guess," Xavier offered, "you don't get to become chief judge, and to be in control of your domain for nearly 30 years, without having a very clear sense of how to manipulate time, people and events."

"Or put another way," Ruth said, "that old bastard is a force to be reckoned with."

7

ASSISTANT ILLINOIS STATE'S ATTORNEY MONICA PETERSON lined up her case on the second day of trial with a battery of high school students, some under subpoena, who would testify that they saw Tim Spellman drink a dozen alcoholic beverages at Stupes Farm on the night Chad Johnson died.

In a gentle cross-examination, Nelson Bleaker asked each student whether he, or she, also had been drinking that night. Each had.

He asked each student if he, or she, had seen Tim Spellman consume the entire beverage in each particular bottle or cup. Each said they had not.

Nelson asked each student if he, or she, had seen Tim leave the party. No one had.

Over objections, which were overruled on the defense theory that Chad Johnson's own drunkenness had contributed to the accident that killed him, Nelson also asked the students to recount the beverages Chad Johnson had consumed. That list, it turned out, was far greater than Tim's.

One witness, Tyreese Jackson, also conceded that Chad was borderline drunk when Chad had driven the two of them home. "Yeah, he probably was. And I should have driven, but it was Millstadt, man. And I drive through there, I get stopped. You know?"

Nelson was content with his brief cross-examination of the students. He believed their cumulative testimony showed, at most, that a couple of drunk kids collided by accident in the night.

The prosecution asked for a lunch break, opting to slot Kate Shaw as the final State's witness after the recess. Judge Briggs ordered the parties and jurors back for a 1:30 p.m. start.

Monica headed down the stairwell and through the back entrance to the State's Attorney's office. In a conference room awaited Kate and her father.

"Hi Kate, thanks for coming early."

"Sure."

"So, your dad told me on the phone that you have more to tell me than you did before the grand jury. Is that right?"

Kate looked away from the prosecutor. Her dad patted her on her leg, whispering in her ear that it would be okay; that she was doing the right thing.

Through tears, she said: "I do. A little. I didn't lie to you before. I swear. But now I, um, I recall some more about that night."

"The night that Chad Johnson was killed."

"Yeah."

"OK. Let's hear it."

"Well. For one. Gosh, I don't know where to start."

"Start from the beginning, like you did with me," her father instructed.

"Right. Okay. So, I was drunk too. Right? And Tim wasn't as drunk as me. But he had definitely been drinking. And he and I had been fighting. About me having dated Chad, which he didn't like.

"And, so we left when it started to rain. Left the farm. And he drove because he is a better buzzed driver than I am. And it was his new truck, and he never let me drive it anyway. But, see, I passed out—fell asleep. Right when we got off the bumpy field and on the road, I was out. Gone.

"But I woke up at the gas station, under the lights, okay? That's me on the camera. That's Tim on the camera. That was us.

"And I think I remember a bump on the ride. But I can't be sure. But I do remember seeing Tim checking the bumper of the truck, like in the video, right? Yeah, and I remember asking him, like, what was up. And he was, like, he said, 'I hit a dog,' or maybe a deer. But he said he had, um, hit something, but the bumper was fine. And then that was it."

"And did he tell you anything else that night?"

"No."

"And subsequently, did he tell you he had hit Chad Johnson that night?"

"No, he always denied it."

"And you are willing to testify to all of this?"

"Yes."

"And why the change?"

"What change?"

"Why are you coming forth now?"

"It's the right thing to do, I guess. I mean, that's what my dad says. And me too. Plus, you know, Tim and I broke up and I don't see the need to, um, protect him anymore."

"Ah, I see. Okay. Well, my main concern is that you might look vindictive. You might look like you are changing your testimony a little now because you are angry at him regarding the break up and looking to get back at him."

"Yeah. But I broke up with him, right? And what I am saying isn't made up—it's just what I remember."

"And," Kate's father offered, "it just confirms the very same things you already know to be true. That's how I see it."

"Right, thank you. But Kate, you have to expect that Tim's lawyers are going to state just that. They are going to come after you."

"OK. But I can handle that, right?" she asked the prosecutor.

"Sure you can, so long as you are telling the truth. Anything else you can think of to tell me?" Monica inquired.

"No."

"Alright. Thank you. You made the right decision, Kate. I need to head to my office to write up my examination of you in light of all of this. But you stay and try and have some lunch. We don't need you fainting on the stand. You could be up there a while."

"Okay."

8

TIM WATCHED AS THE COURTHOUSE ELEVATOR OPENED and Kate Shaw emerged with her father. He contemplated how to get to Kate, who was heading for the restroom, while avoiding her father. He quickened his pace to reach her before she went inside. "Kate," he whispered, but his voice reverberated along the glass atrium. Kate's father heard Kate's name, as did she.

Mr. Shaw walked towards Tim, yelling: "Tim, this is not the time. You stay away from her." He headed towards his daughter and Tim, holding his arm out in a futile attempt from such a distance to keep Tim away.

"Dad, it's okay. Tim, he's right; I don't have anything to say to you."

Tim hugged Kate, saying aloud for the benefit of Mr. Shaw: "I'm sorry."

Kate resisted the embrace, but Tim leaned forward, holding her tightly. He buried his face into her hair, searching with his mouth for her ear. "Change your story, and my lawyer will ask about it. Everyone, Kate, will know." Tim stepped away, watching the fear rise in her eyes, as Mr. Shaw pulled on his arm.

Kate's complexion paled; tears welled in her eyes. Her father noted all of it. "Tim, get the hell away from my daughter." Tim pulled out of Mr. Shaw's hand, and flicked out his arm to straighten his suit coat.

Kate returned to the restroom. When she emerged, she avoided her father's eye and his questions. Kate simply assured him that she was okay, was ready to testify, and wanted to get it all over with.

They waited in a witness anteroom. Once the jury was seated, the bailiff ordered the courtroom audience to stand, and Judge Briggs entered. She called upon the state to resume its case.

"The State calls Katherine Shaw." The bailiff retrieved Kate from the anteroom, and escorted her through the courtroom to the witness stand. Kate remained standing, placed her hand on the Bible and swore to tell the entire truth. As she sat, Kate looked out in the courtroom and saw Tim, his father, and his lawyer, all staring at her. The jury was staring at her too—and they were much closer than the grand jury had been.

Kate noticed students from school, and men with steno pads taking notes—reporters, she figured. Her dad stood in the back, his back against the wall, slowly nodding his head in encouragement.

Monica Peterson stood and approached the witness stand. She took Kate through her name, address, and date of birth. She asked her what school Kate attended, and what her plans were for after graduation. She asked Kate if she knew Tim Spellman, and she answered, "Yes, I do."

"How do you know Mr. Spellman?"

"Um, we go to West together. We have had classes together in the past. Spanish, I think. We also dated."

"For what period of time did you date?"

"Maybe late summer of last year, 1993, until just a few weeks ago."

"And who ended that relationship?"

"I did."

"Why?"

"Objection, your honor, what possible relevance does this have?"

"Overruled, you can answer," Judge Briggs decided, looking to Kate to continue.

"Well, I guess this whole trial, it just sort of made it hard to be ourselves anymore. And we were both going away next year. Tim's going to Charlottesville, I'm going to the U of I. And there aren't even planes between those places. So we thought, I thought, might as well break up, you know?"

"Okay. And when was the last time you talked to Tim Spellman?"

"Objection. Relevance."

"Overruled."

"I talked to him a few weeks ago, when I ended things."

"Kate, I want to take you back to the night of October 8, 1993. Were you and Tim dating at that time?"

"Yes. Like I said, we had started dating late that previous Summer."

"And did the two of you head to the property known as Stupes Farm on that night?"

"Yes, we did."

"What time did you head there?"

"Maybe around 9 p.m. We got there early."

"Why?"

"Tim wanted to be there early, so we could have some time alone. With school and our parents, and stuff, we didn't get a lot of time alone."

"And did the two of you have sexual intercourse that night?"

"No."

"And did Tim tell you he was upset about that fact?"

"Objection: leading," Nelson declared. His objection was denied.

"Sure. Yes. I guess we were both disappointed, but agreed the time was not right."

"Then what happened?"

"We decided to go our separate ways for a while. He went out and found a couple of his friends, and I left him to go look for some of mine."

"Did the two of you reunite that night?"

"Yes."

"When?"

"A few hours later, probably. He came to find me, I think."

"And then what occurred?"

"We talked. It started to rain. We left."

"And at the time Tim had come to see you, was he drinking?"

"No, not at that time. He had come to pee in the field, actually. And he didn't have anything in his hand."

"Were you aware that he had been drinking?"

"Sure. Pretty much everyone was drinking. It was a party."

"Was Tim still angry when he saw you?"

"Yes."

"Why?"

"He was still upset about the farmhouse, and to some extent, about the fact that I used to date Chad."

"Were you aware of Tim's relationship with Chad?"

"Um, yes?"

"And what was their relationship?"

"Not much. I mean, they didn't really know each other. Chad played football. Tim played soccer. They didn't have classes together or anything. But Tim didn't like all that much that I had dated Chad briefly, like I said."

"Alright. Now you previously stated that the two of you spoke in that field. Then it began to rain and you left."

"Right."

"When you decided to leave, did Tim Spellman appear capable of driving?" Kate paused, looking down at her lap. Monica leaned in, hoping to coax Kate's eyes back to her.

Nelson considered an objection; Kate was not qualified to answer that. But he knew she had answered this question in her grand jury testimony to Tim's favor, and so he waited to see if her story would change.

"I wouldn't have gotten in the car with him if I thought he was drunk," Kate testified.

Monica was stunned at Kate's reversal. With her back to the jury, she glared at her most crucial witness. She raised her eyebrows and widened her eyes in hope of extracting a different answer from Kate. But the look was not lost on Judge Briggs. "Is there a question pending, Ms. Peterson? Or are you finished with this witness?"

"No, judge. I mean, yes, there is a question pending. One moment please." Monica walked to her counsel table, taking a drink of water to buy herself time to collect her thoughts. She noted out of the corner of her eye that her boss, State's Attorney Gina Wolfe, was in the back of the gallery. Great, Monica thought, just in time to watch her key witness flake out. She decided to give Kate one more chance to get her story right.

"Kate. You have just testified that Tim drove the two of you away from Stupes Farm. Where did you head?"

"Well, he was taking me home, but I fell asleep pretty much after we got on the main road."

"And what time was that?"

"I really don't remember."

"At what point did you wake from your sleep?"

"When we got to my house, Tim woke me up."

Kate had again recanted. "Sidebar your honor?" Monica requested. "Granted."

Nelson joined Monica at the side of the judge's bench, out of earshot of the jury, and with the microphones muted.

"What do we have here, counselor?" Judge Briggs inquired.

"Judge, not an hour ago, Kate Shaw sat in my office and told me that she recalled her trip home that night. She recalled a bump on the way. She remembered stopping at the gas station, and hearing Mr. Spellman tell her he had hit a dog or a deer. She recalls him inspecting his bumper at the filling station. But we are now back down the road of her not remembering anything."

"Sounds like an unhelpful witness, your honor." Nelson added. "But I should note for the court that this testimony of Ms. Shaw's is completely consistent with her prior testimony to the grand jury."

"Ms. Peterson, what are you requesting here?"

"I would like a recess to speak with this witness."

"We would object to that, your honor. Now is the time, here is the testimony, which is entirely consistent with her prior testimony."

"But not with the truth, judge. She knows what happened."

"Well, then get it out of her counselor, consistent with the rules of this court. Request for recess is denied."

"Judge, I may have to treat this witness as hostile. And I'll put that on the record."

"Fine. I will grant that. I presume you have no objection to that, Judge Bleaker?"

"No your honor. But I would ask that the court keep an eye on the questions and make sure Ms. Peterson doesn't testify herself."

Nelson returned to his table and whispered into Jack's ear that the State would now beat up on Kate in an effort to extract a very different story she apparently had told the prosecutor hours earlier. Jack whispered the same information to his son.

Monica began again: "Kate. I thank you for testifying today. I know this isn't easy." Kate watched as Tim wrote a note on his legal pad, sliding it over—past his father—to Nelson. Nelson read the note and did what it said: he gave Tim a look, a raised eyebrow, and then nodded his head.

Monica again tried to connect with her witness: "Please look at me, Kate. Ms. Shaw, as I was saying, I thank you for coming here today and telling the truth under oath. It takes a lot of courage to do that.

"Now, before we took that break for a moment, I was asking you about your trip home on the night of October 8, 1993. Do you recall that?"

"Yes."

"And you stated that you fell asleep upon leaving the Stupes Farm, and did not wake until you were home. Now, previously, you informed me that—"

"Objection. Ms. Peterson can't testify to what may or may not have been said to her previously."

"Objection sustained. Ms. Peterson, you are on the edge here. And I am watching."

"Permission to treat this witness as hostile, your honor?"

"Granted. But as I said, I'm watching."

Monica opted to wheel out the VCR, and play the footage of the Explorer entering the gas station. She slowed the video, which captured grainy images of a passenger in an Explorer rising, then later slumping against the window.

"Ms. Shaw, that is you in that car, correct?"

"I don't know."

"Don't you? You don't recall waking up at any point in your trip home?"

"No, not really."

"Not really? You don't recall the Explorer hitting something on its trip down 59th Street?"

"Obj—"

"Sustained! Watch it," Judge Briggs cautioned the prosecutor.

"And you don't recall stopping at the gas station on this video?"

"Without foundation, judge! Asked and answered," Nelson objected.

"Overruled. The witness will answer."

"Like I said, I don't recall that. I fell asleep. I mean, I was passed out."

"And you don't recall Tim Spellman checking his vehicle for damage, getting back in and talking to you?"

"I don't, sorry."

"I don't need an apology, Ms. Shaw, I need you to answer truthfully. Were you in my office earlier today?"

"Yes."

"And is this the version of events you recalled at that time?"

"Objection."

"Overruled."

"Mostly, yes. But some of it, I don't know if I really remembered, or if, you know, this proceeding, and the photos, and the newspaper, and my imagination, and breaking up with Tim," she was now in tears, "if I wanted to remember things differently. But, you know, walking in here, I couldn't be so sure, and swearing on the Bible. And I told you months ago that I didn't know, and then I still didn't know in front of that other jury—" Kate sobbed.

"Alright, calm down Kate. Calm down. And slow down. Our court reporter here is having a hard time catching all of this. Now, I understand what you are saying. Did you talk to anyone between the time we met, earlier today, and when you testified here?"

"No." Kate looked for the first time at her father, who was rubbing his beard with his hand, a pained expression on his face. She could tell, lies or not, he wanted this to be over for her. And she did too.

"Ms. Shaw. You took an oath today to tell the truth. And that is what I expected and required by law. I am saddened—"

"Objection. She is testifying here, Judge. Is there a question?"

"I agree. Ms. Peterson, let's move this along."

"No more questions at this time. Your witness."

Nelson stepped to the witness stand, offering Kate his handkerchief, an act that received a swift objection from a miffed prosecutor. "You are objecting to my helping her dry the tears that you caused?"

Nelson asked.

"Enough. Start your cross, counselor," Judge Briggs cautioned.

Nelson considered his original line of questions, similar to those he had asked of the other students who had been at the party. But neither he nor his client wanted to see Kate taken through that.

"Kate. You felt Tim Spellman was competent to drive the two of you home from Stupes farm, correct?"

"Yes."

"And it is your testimony that you fell asleep upon leaving Stupes and did not wake until you were at home?"

"Yes."

"And you don't recall anything else during that time?"

"No."

"And you are not convinced that this video here, that that is you and Tim on the tape?"

"Right. I don't know if that is Tim or me."

"Kate, I am sorry you have had to go through all of this. Thank you for testifying here today. Good luck next year at U of I."

"Thanks," Kate said to Nelson, offering back his handkerchief, which he waved off. She noted his initials on it, and turned to the judge, "Thank you. Am I done?"

"That is for Ms. Peterson to decide? Re-direct, counsel?"

"No," Monica responded, without rising from her seat. "At this time the state rests."

Kate descended the witness stand and walked with her father into the hall, wherein she collapsed onto a bench in tears. "I couldn't do it, dad. I couldn't do that to Tim. I am not sure what I believe. I just don't know. I am so sorry I was drinking, and that I got caught up in this, and that even now I don't know…" she buried her head into his chest.

Inside the courtroom, Judge Briggs instructed the defense that its case would be allowed to begin in the morning.

"Your honor," Nelson stated, looking to Jack for a confirmation of what they considered doing at this point. Jack nodded. Nelson rose to his feet and addressed the court, "your honor, may it please the court, the defense does not intend to call any witnesses. We rest our case and are prepared to offer closing arguments in the morning without delay."

The courtroom spectators, who had sat quietly through the testimony of Kate Shaw, now began to stir. The jurors looked at one another as well, calculating that their service would be shorter than they had thought, all thanks to the defense.

"Ms. Peterson, I presume the State is prepared to close tomorrow as well?"

"We are your honor."

"Well, then, we are in recess until tomorrow at 9:00 a.m. Jurors, you are excused for the day. Thank you for another good day of your service." Judge Briggs stood, and the bailiff called upon those in the courtroom to do the same.

Jack put his arm around his son and whispered in his ear, "that's a good girl you let go." Tim nodded and turned with his father to leave.

9

"A BOY HAS DIED," Nelson Bleaker said softly as he began his closing argument. Judge Briggs's courtroom was filled to capacity and the crowd spilled into the hallway. "A boy has died, and we grieve for the loss."

Nelson addressed the entire courtroom, half-turned towards the jury. He rubbed his eyes, and smoothed his hands along his face, showing the jury that these words and events mattered to him.

"And when a boy dies, we search for answers. We want to know how this happened. We want to know who was responsible, and we want those people to be held to account for their crimes.

"But, sometimes, no matter how hard we want answers, they do not always come. Tim Spellman is not the answer.

"As much as we want vengeance on the driver of the vehicle that hit and killed Chad Johnson, Tim was not that driver. It will hurt, it will pain us, to not have closure. To not chalk this one up to Tim, and to not be able to just move along in our minds that a crime was solved here today.

"But punishing Tim unjustly will only cause more grief for this boy and his family. This would not be closure. It would be the opening of a new set of wounds."

Nelson turned back towards the jury. "The prosecution has charged Tim with manslaughter, which carries with it a considerable prison term. The prosecution is charged with proving, beyond a reasonable doubt, that Tim committed the crimes of manslaughter, hit-and-run, and failing to report an accident.

"Now, 'beyond a reasonable doubt' is a high standard. It is, in fact, the highest standard of proof in our court system. It is a serious standard and it means that if you have any reasonable doubt that Tim committed these crimes, then you cannot vote to convict him."

As Nelson spoke, Jack pulled out three large whiteboards that would summarize for the jury the State's case. He propped them backwards on an easel in view of the jury and the entire courtroom.

Nelson turned to the easel and flipped the first board around to be in view. It was a list of the State's witnesses. "Now, the prosecution called a lot of witnesses. Twelve, by my count. You will be tasked with considering their testimony, and any exhibits they offered.

"You should ask yourself, what has the government shown? And that is a good question.

"They have shown that Chad Johnson died from a horrible hit and run. That is what the autopsy shows, and what you heard from the coroner. Chad died sometime between 11 p.m. and 5 a.m. A large, six-hour window, when possibly hundreds of cars and trucks passed by on the busy two lane road that leads to Route 15. The autopsy and the coroner also tell us that there was a high level of alcohol in Chad's system. And the autopsy and coroner tell us that a piece of plastic was found lodged in the deceased.

"We heard from a sheriff, Sgt. Schaefer. We heard him talk about a botched crime scene, full of plenty of vehicle tracks and trash, but no body. We heard about, and watched, a videotape of someone throwing up. We heard that the piece of plastic was traced to a Ford truck, and that the truck in the video was a Ford.

"And then we heard from a lot of kids that saw Tim drink alcohol out in the country the night Chad died. Those kids, each of them, they were drinking too. Everyone, it seemed, was drinking out there. Even Chad.

"And finally, we heard from Tim's girlfriend at the time, who was with him at the farm, and who headed home with him that night. She is no longer his girlfriend. She remembers nothing remarkable about her trip home that night, including no recollection of any collision. She does not believe she is in that video. She does not believe Tim is in that video."

"And that is all, folks." He paused, his hands up in disbelief.

"Now, here is what you didn't hear. You didn't hear from a single witness who saw the accident that killed Chad Johnson. You didn't hear of a single piece of physical evidence that ties Tim to Chad.

"And what about that piece of plastic, from a Ford truck, the Illinois State Police stated? Never corroborated. No evidence of a broken light on Tim's truck. No evidence of a repaired light on Tim's truck. No evidence that he bought a new light. No evidence. No evidence. No. Evidence.

"No evidence that puts Tim on 59th Street at all, nonetheless at the time of the accident. No evidence. No evidence. No evidence."

"Perhaps you are wondering why I didn't call a single witness, or why Tim didn't just get on up here and defend himself," Nelson said, pointing to the empty witness box. "Well, the short answer is, we didn't have to. It is not our burden to carry here, folks. It is the State's." He pointed straight at Monica Peterson. "And they didn't do it."

Nelson turned to the second whiteboard. "Here is what the State is going to tell you. They will tell you that you are smart people, and that circumstantial evidence is still evidence, and that all you need to do is connect the dots they have laid out for you.

"Well, here are the dots. Over here, Tim, like everyone else at the farm, drank some, and drove home. Like a lot of those kids—and hundreds of other drivers over the course of those six hours the coroner identified—perhaps he traversed 59th Street. No crime there.

"And Tim, like thousands of others, drives a Ford truck. No crime there. And someone driving a Ford truck, like Tim's and having stickers like Tim's truck, happened to stop at a gas station off of 59th Street. And that person checked their vehicle and threw up. No crime there.

"And that's all folks, that's all. Could someone else have driven a Ford truck down 59th Street between 11 p.m. and 5 a.m.? Well of course someone else could have. I might have. You might have. That busy road was full of Ford trucks, and that broken blinker light is probably still out there."

Nelson flipped to the final board, which read simply, "Reasonable Doubt."

"If you heard what I heard this week, you know there was no reason for me to put on a defense for Tim. The state failed utterly to establish beyond a reasonable doubt that Tim Spellman hit Chad Johnson, failed to stop or report that crime.

"We grieve for Chad's loss. I do, you do. All of the people in this courtroom do. But it is not fair, and it is not right, to convict Tim Spellman for a crime he did not commit. That criminal may be out there, and the police may yet find that person, but it is not this young man sitting here.

"Reasonable doubt. Reasonable. Doubt. There are too many dots that you cannot connect creating that reasonable doubt. Tim Spellman. Not guilty."

The courtroom observers shifted in their seats, having been rapt for the hour as Judge Bleaker brought home the case for the defense. Judge Briggs indicated she wanted a 15 minute recess before the closing statement of the prosecution. The court stood in recess.

Nelson Bleaker sat and placed his hand on Tim Spellman's leg. With a cold and sweaty hand, Tim gripped the top of Nelson's hand and slapped it a couple of times. He stared forward at the seal of Illinois behind the judge's bench.

From the row behind the defense counsel's table, Randall Cutler tapped Judge Bleaker's shoulder. "Judge, can I talk to you?" Randall had assisted Nelson throughout the trial by carrying trial boxes, exhibits and more up to the courthouse from the firm's offices. He also liked Tim and had stayed in court on this morning to hear Nelson conclude the case for the defense.

Judge Bleaker turned in his chair, recognizing the voice but nonetheless surprised by Randall approaching him in the courtroom. He stood and leaned over the railing. "Randall, surely this can wait?"

"I don't think so judge. I don't think."

"What? What is it?"

"The blinker."

"The what?"

"The blinker you were talking about. I broke that. And I fixed that."

"What on earth are you talking about?"

"Back in October, Jack brought that Explorer of his up to the house, on a Saturday. It was all muddy and I washed it."

"Yeah. OK. So what."

"Well, I used the power-sprayer, that I use for the walks, right? I used that, on the wheels and tires, and then I hit the blinker and I saw water spraying into the blinker. I broke that."

"OK. You broke the orange blinker light."

"On the passenger side."

"OK, and did you tell Jack? I don't see where this is going."

"No, he was talking to that newspaper reporter."

"From the Journal. Okay, I recall that."

"And so I drove down to AutoWorld, and got a new one and put it in myself. I threw the old one out right there in their parking lot and put the new one in. It took just but a minute. And I paid cash for it, like ten bucks. Since it was my fault, I didn't mention it to Jack."

Nelson finally understood. "And you don't think you broke it?"

"I did, until now. I thought for sure I had the sprayer setting too high, and I felt bad about that. And I left for the day before Jack ever came out. And I totally forgot about it, and I didn't know it was a part of—"

"It isn't Randall. They never found the broken light, because they had the wrong car, the wrong driver. Listen, I understand what you are saying. It is a coincidence, and a weird one. But that is all it is. I promise you. Do not worry about it."

"But that is going to trouble me."

"Randall. I see how it could. But don't let it. You have not been here this week, you have not seen this trial. There is no case here against Tim."

Nelson saw the jury room door opening. Court was returning to session. He put his hands on Randall's shoulders and looked him in the eye. "Randall. You are a good man. And I have been a judge and a lawyer for a long time. You can trust me. Like I trust you. Let this go. Tim has a bright future, and a broken light is not going to derail that. I will see to it that it doesn't. You are a good man. Let this go."

Before Randall could respond, the bailiff silenced the room: "All rise, this court is back in session. The Honorable Alicia Briggs presiding."

10

"Ms. Peterson, for the State, your final argument, please?" Judge Briggs asked.

Seated, her chin on her clenched hands, Monica began: "Criminals. They hide their crimes. That's what they do. And it makes it hard on the police, and on the coroners, and on the prosecutors, and on the jurors to do their jobs. But still we must. And to this point, we've done all that we can. The police have been through reams of evidence, hours of tape. They've interviewed hundreds of witnesses, scoured acres of fields. They've found their man and left it to our office, the office of the State's Attorney, to take it from the arrest to this point.

"Now, whether we have done enough, that is in your hands. That is your job. And I submit to you, that the police did their jobs incredibly well, and I think I did mine.

"You see, a hit-and-run is, by its very nature, tough to prove.

Tough, unless the driver comes forward and said, 'I did this. I was wrong and I made a mistake, and I did this.'

"Sometimes, a hit-and-run happens, and the driver does not know he hit a person, but thinks it was a deer, or something else. But in those cases, the drivers come forward. They don't hide.

"And in those cases, the State often is lenient, even where the accident led to a death, as it did here.

"But this case is different. You heard from several peers of the defendant, including his own girlfriend, that he had been angry that night, and had been drinking. And not just angry, but angry at Chad Johnson.

"Now, we don't know why Chad was outside his vehicle that cold, rainy October night. We know he was going to get help for his friend. Perhaps his car had stopped running. But the reason doesn't matter. For we don't blame victims," she pointed at the defense table, "though sometimes some try."

Monica walked to a map of the area, pointing to 59th Street. "I submit to you that Tim Spellman saw that Chad was ripe for the picking, and barreled down 59th Street, far in excess of the speed limit, and hit and killed Chad.

"Mr. Spellman was drunk. You heard that. You saw the video that he was on 59th street at the time of the accident. You saw him check his bumper. You saw him vomit.

"No matter what his lawyer says, these are easy dots to connect. And I know you can connect them.

"Did other cars pass down that road? Sure. Were some of them also Fords? Sure. Were some of those drivers also drunk? Maybe. Did some of those drivers have a reason to want to hurt Chad Johnson? I don't know. But we do know that all of this applies to Tim Spellman.

"The law does not require an eye witness to every crime. Indeed, few crimes would ever be solved if that were the case. The law doesn't require a confession. It doesn't require a bloody fingerprint.

"Chad Johnson was a strong kid. He could have survived the hit. His neck was broken, you heard, but that didn't kill him. It was the cowardly run that killed him. Had Tim Spellman come back, and lifted Chad's head from the ditch, Chad could have survived.

"But Tim ran, and ran and ran. And it took months for the sheriff's office to find him and his shiny new Explorer. They found him on video. They found Ford plastic in Chad Johnson. They corroborated that Tim was drunk, and that Tim drove. Don't let him run anymore.

"Now, the defense talked a lot about unconnected dots. Perhaps some of you have headed up north to Chicago to the art museum there. They have a painting by Georges Seurat. Up close, it is a bunch of dots. Thousands of dots. Maybe more. I don't know. But when you back up a couple of feet—those dots paint a very clear picture of people enjoying an afternoon on a river.

"Tim Spellman left us nothing to go on but dots. But you don't need to connect them to see the picture they paint.

"The anger. The drinking. The drunk driving. The hit. The run. The drowning. The video. The Ford plastic. These are the dots. So, when you get in that jury room, just back up a little, and you will see the very clear picture these dots paint: Tim Spellman killed Chad Johnson with a reckless indifference to Chad's young life."

11

THE JURY IN TIM SPELLMAN'S CASE had only had the case for half a day, but Jack Spellman was growing more worried as each hour passed. On this morning, he sat in his office picking at breakfast, reading the coverage of the case in the papers. The local paper had quoted Nelson's closing extensively, and Jack thought it was convincing. The consensus of so-called trial experts interviewed in the St. Louis paper seemed to be that the jurors would have to take a bit of a leap to convict, but might settle on some middle charge if they couldn't agree manslaughter was appropriate.

None of that settled well with Jack. A conviction on any charge, he felt, indicated Tim had done the crime, and he told Nelson as much:

"I'd be likely to appeal that, you know, because there was no evidence in this trial. None."

"Well, Jack. There wasn't. But there was the excluded confession, and you can be sure they will bring that up in your appeal if given the chance. And I'll tell you something else you might not want to hear."

"What? Is this going to piss me off some more?"

"Yeah, I would think so."

"Alright. Have at it."

"I spoke with Randall yesterday, in the courtroom."

"I saw that. What was that all about?"

"Do you remember last October, when you interviewed here at the office with the Journal?"

"Yeah, sure. The settlement."

"Well, you drove Tim's Explorer that day. And apparently, Randall washed it."

"And that means what?"

"Well, he used the power-washer he uses for the brick sidewalk. And he used it to clean mud off the truck and managed—he thought— to crack the orange front passenger turn light."

"Okay."

"And he went while you were interviewing and swapped it out at AutoWorld. He left the broken light in the garbage can in the parking lot. That's where the broken plastic—"

"Shit," Jack said, knowing exactly what it meant. With regard to the confession and even the videotape, he had been willing to entertain the notion that Tim was telling him the truth in his denials. But it was fact: his son had hit the kid, left him to die, and lied to everyone about it. Jack was finally sure of it. But he knew there was nothing to do with that knowledge, at least not in the context of Tim's trial. "Jesus," he said to Nelson, "and I assume nothing else was broken by the sprayer, because a sprayer doesn't just break plastic on a car."

"Right. Randall surmised this from my closing."

"And you told him what?"

"Not to worry about it. That it wasn't his fault, and to let it go.

That there were a lot of Ford trucks, and this wasn't evidence that Tim was in the accident."

"And he was okay with that?"

"Yeah. I think he was. Where is he going to go with that? What is he going to do? He knows we have been real good to him. I think he will let it go."

"God. I was so willing to believe Tim. Through all of this. His mom, she knew, from the beginning. But I thought, no, this is all a mistake."

"It still is, Jack. Tim is a good kid. He made a mistake. And if the state can't pin it on him, well, that's on them. Not him. Not you."

"I guess so. But man, a kid died. And he hasn't owned up to it—to me. To me. That's what I can't get past. I still want him to beat this thing, to go to college next year, and to move on with his life. But how he can't even tell me the truth? That just. That just. It infuriates me. Or, really, I guess, it makes me deeply, fucking sad."

"I know. I do. Kids are tough like that. They need you when they think they need you. And when they think they don't, that's probably when they need you the most," Nelson offered, placing a hand on Jack's shoulder.

"Yeah. But I mean, what now? I can't ground the kid for a homicide, right? I mean, do I live this lie with him for the rest of our years. Hell, part of me is hoping the jury dings him now on the hit and run. Give him a suspended sentence, something. Community service. I almost want some finality to this, some acknowledgement of his guilt."

"His possible guilt."

"Oh hells bells, Nelson. You know it as well as I do."

The phone on Jack's desk rang. It was his secretary, telling him the jury had reached a verdict and would report back after lunch. Jack's face turned red. For the first time since arriving at the sheriff's department months ago, he was scared for his son.

12

THE WALK TO THE COURTHOUSE WAS A SOMBER ONE. Nelson walked with Kathy, assuring her things would go their way. Jack and Tim trailed, with Jack telling Tim what would happen if they didn't.

"If it goes our way, that's it," he said. "But if not, we will ask that each juror be polled as to each count to make sure they agree with the verdict. If we lose, I have to tell you this, so you are prepared; you could be taken into custody, at least briefly, pending a determination of when sentencing will take place. Do you understand?" Jack asked his son.

"Yeah."

"Now, Tim. I think I know what happened here. And that is all I will say. I've learned more information. And I'll bet you have always wondered what happened to that broken blinker light. I now know. And I have to say, Tim, that I am sad—really sad—that you did not think you could come to me. I'm not happy about what happened here. Don't think that for a minute I am ignoring that. But accidents happen, and you need to come to me when things get bad. And that doesn't change whether you are 8 or 18."

Tim stopped. He looked up at his dad, crying. "Dad, I am so sorry about all of this. Am I going to be okay? I really fucked up. I know I did."

"Tim, win or lose today, you will be okay. You won't ever forget this. And you shouldn't. But whether you walk away or not, I love you and I'm there for you."

"Thanks Dad. Can you not tell mom?"

The Spellmans turned the corner and saw the news vans of the main network channels parked along the entrance of the courthouse. Reporters already were filling their lunch newscasts with information about the pending verdict. The Spellmans and Nelson again descended the underground parking entrance, avoiding the press.

As they exited the service elevator and headed to the courtroom, Tim saw Kate. She came up to him, alone.

"Hey. Shouldn't you be in class?" Tim asked. He stared at his feet, knowing what he had last done to his former girlfriend. He had no idea if she was present in hopes of seeing him go to jail, or to support him. He held out hope for the latter.

"Hey. Yeah, but I got a pass."

"Kate. I'm sorry about the other day. I was—I am—so scared right now. And I didn't know what you were going to say. My dad, and Nelson, they thought the whole case came down to you, and I freaked. I, I don't think you can forgive me. But, I guess, you know, I…. Well, anyway, sorry."

"Thanks. I'm scared too."

"Tim, let's go," Jack said, nodding with a faint grin towards Kate, "Hi Kate."

"Hi, Mr. Spellman. Good luck," Kate said to the two as they walked away. She wasn't sure what she wanted to happen, but either way she knew she could not stand to follow them into the courtroom for the reading of the verdict.

The courtroom was half-full, mostly with reporters waiting on the verdict. Chad Johnson's father had come again, as he had throughout the trial, and stood against the wall in the back of the courtroom. He watched Tim and Jack take their seats and then watched as they stood in unison with the rest of the courtroom upon the call of the bailiff.

Tim had not slept, and had not eaten, and he sat back in his seat, his eyes on the table in front of him.

"Has the jury reached a verdict?" Judge Briggs inquired of the jury foreman.

An older black man in a sweater vest and tie stood, clearing his throat: "We have your honor."

"Please pass it to the bailiff." The bailiff forwarded the sheet on to Judge Briggs, who checked that it had been completed correctly. She gave no inclination as to its contents. She handed it back to the bailiff, who in turn gave it to the foreman.

"The defendant will please rise," Judge Briggs instructed. Tim and his lawyers stood, facing the jury. No juror looked his way.

"Stand up straight," his Dad whispered. "This is it."

Judge Briggs: "As to the first count in the indictment of People v. Timothy Spellman—failure to stop at the scene of a motor vehicle accident resulting in the death of another, a Class 2 felony—how does the jury find?"

Foreman: "We find the defendant 'not guilty.'"

Tim darted a look at his father, who gave him a nod of the head, his lower lip pulled tight over his top lip. Jack gripped his son's hand.

"As to the second count in the indictment of People v. Timothy Spellman—failure to report an accident involving personal injury or death, a Class A misdemeanor—how does the jury find?"

"We find the defendant 'not guilty.'"

"As to the third count in the indictment of People v. Timothy Spellman—vehicular manslaughter, a Class 2 felony—how does the jury find?"

"We find the defendant 'not guilty.'"

Jack could hear his wife behind him, quietly whispering, "thank you, Jesus. Oh, thank you, Jesus." He looked back, reached over the railing and clenched hands with her. He placed his other hand on Tim's shoulder. He pulled his hand back from his wife. He leaned towards his son and whispered: "Your new life starts today, bud. Don't mess it up." Tim closed his eyes as he nodded.

As the judge thanked and dismissed the jury, Jack closed his briefcase. Once court was adjourned, he and Nelson shook hands with Monica Peterson, who left the courtroom through the rear entrance. She had been roundly defeated in a case that had started with a confession and once seemed a lock.

Jack turned to Nelson and gave his partner a hug. "I'll be damned, Nelson. You did it. Thank you. For all of the Spellmans, thank you."

"I was happy to do it Jack. Tim's a good kid, no matter what. And he has some great parents."

The two continued to grasp at each other's elbows, as Jack started to well up. "Send me your bill," he finally said, and the two laughed.

Chad Johnson's father turned to leave the courtroom. He watched as the Spellmans hugged. He folded the newspaper he had in his hand,

and put it under his arm. He felt fairly certain that Tim Spellman had
hit his son, but had never been convinced it was more than an accident,
as the prosecution had insisted. Without a word to anyone, and with
only a shake of the head towards Sgt. Cliff Schaefer at the other side
of the courtroom, he exited the courthouse and headed back to his
transmission shop.

PART IV

1

Fall, 1994

THE TWO OLD MEN SAT POOLSIDE, the Atlantic Ocean just ahead of them. It was mid-morning, and they had sat together for over an hour, mostly in silence, staring at the water.

"You fucked us, Bill," Nelson Bleaker finally said.

"You came all the way down here to tell me that? Well, you were fucked long before I came along," the former chief judge Bill Flood added, unhelpfully.

"I don't think you have any idea what has happened since you left to come down to Ft. Lauderdale. You don't get the local papers from up there down here, do you?"

"No, thank god," Bill added, "and I've not been back since I testified before that grand jury."

"Well, Bill, you've put us in a hell of a bind. The railroad has moved to overturn the class action settlement as based on fraud, and AgriFarm is trying to toss our firm as class counsel in the Frankenseed case. We are talking about sways of hundreds of millions of dollars."

"I can imagine."

"So, why?"

"Why what?"

"Why did you testify before that grand jury? Why not stay with Jack and me and fight. We could've won this thing."

"Maybe you could have. Maybe you will. But they had me dead-to-rights on a bunch of little shit, but all of that is gone now. But you should know this, Nellie, I kept you in the clear. I didn't say a damned bad thing about you."

"But Bill, what you did say; Jesus, you sold Jack out for nothing."

"It wasn't for nothing. I walked away unscathed. And look around. It's been months, and I have not missed for one minute that scene. I don't miss the cases, my courtroom, any of it. I wake up every day and smell this ocean air, and sit here at the pool and get drunk as a skunk, and I love it." The chief tipped up his cocktail as he spoke.

"I don't buy that," Nelson said. "I know you. Since we were kids, a hundred years ago, remember? I know what makes you tick. And I know you are three sheaves to the wind right now because it is tearing you up inside seeing me and dealing with what you did." Nelson stared into the judge's dark sunglasses.

"And that was what, exactly? Telling those little shits in the U.S. Attorney's office what they wanted to hear—that the hotshot plaintiff's attorney wasn't an angel? That none of us are?" Bill waved his hand across the table, as if to say the hell with all of it.

Nelson kept at him. "But you made that shit up, Bill. At the end of the day, lies set you free. And you could have stayed and fought, and maybe still have been free—and still a part of our firm. Why, Bill? I mean, why did you make me take sides here?"

"I didn't make you take sides, Nelson. This is about you too, you know. And you had a decision to make, just like me."

"That was some decision you left for me. I either take on a federal indictment supported by you and your 30-year grip on the federal court, or take on Jack—the guy who has made me richer and happier than I ever thought possible in the practice of law," Nelson said.

"So, that's it? I take it you've made your decision? That is why you are here? You are coming to tell me that you are taking me on, aren't you Nellie?"

"I came down here on a fact finding mission, Bill. To see what you have to say, and to see where things stand. I want to hear it from the horse's mouth that what you said to the grand jury was bullshit."

The chief sipped his drink, offering nothing by way of response.

"Here is what I know, Bill," Nelson continued. "You've had a gambling problem for a quarter of a century. And it finally got out of control and you needed help. I gave you some help. And there was nothing wrong in one friend helping another friend out of a situation like that. I mean, geez, you owed hundreds of thousands of dollars, Bill. You could've lost your house. It was real bad."

"I know what it was Nelson. As you say, I've lived with it forever.

Still do, in fact. Ever heard of jai-alai? It's all over the place down here. Like betting on dogs, but with people. Fascinating."

"Bill, that's funny. Ha. But I'm not laughing. You throw your money away however you want. Or, I guess, it's really my tax dollars, seeing as your pension is about all you've got, I imagine."

"Screw you, Nelson. My pension was hard earned."

"Damn right, Bill. Damn right. So why didn't you stay and fight?"

"You know how these things are, Nelson. The government claims they want you for one thing, and then every whack-job in the world who got screwed in your courtroom comes forward with some additional charge and as soon as you know it, it snowballs and you've got thirty shit claims, not one. Well, they had a couple of valid claims. I did some things wrong and I knew it. Small stuff. And I was willing to make this deal to walk away. Thirty years is a long reputation to piss down the toilet."

"So, your reputation. That's what this is about? Anyone around this pool have any idea about that reputation?" Nelson asked, receiving no response. "Of course not. No one cares about you or that reputation down here. You are just another old fucker like the rest of these people. The only people who cared about your reputation are back in the place you left. And, let me tell you, Bill, that reputation is going to be in tatters up there anyway."

"How's that?" the judge asked, sitting up slightly in his chair.

"The plaintiff's bar, they like me. And they like Jack a hell of a lot. They want to see him beat this. And you are the key witness to the government's case.

"And do you know what? You are at least half right. We talked to dozens of people who've come up and told me shit you have pulled over the years. And there is some bad stuff in there."

"Oh, of course. Let me hear this. What kind of bullshit are you digging up? And for what?" the judge asked.

"Well, the 'for what' is easy, Bill. Jack's lawyer, Walt and I—we aim to take apart the government's case. And that pretty much begins and ends with you.

"I am telling you this as a friend, Bill. Walt is going to destroy you when you take the stand. He was a former prosecutor for a long time down there and he knows about a lot of your skeletons. And I do too," Nelson said.

"I cannot even fathom the lies that weasel Walter McDonnell has made up about me," the judge said as he finished his drink and waved it towards the bar, catching the bartender's eye. "I know him; he appeared before me a hundred times over the years. I can take him on."

"To be honest, Bill, it isn't just Walt. The people came—as you said—out of the woodwork. We've got a team of investigators. And we are leaving no stone unturned." Nelson sat back to see if the judge flinched.

"I don't need to hear this."

"This is a favor, Bill; a courtesy to you. You can hear it now, or you can hear it on the stand when Walter lowers the boom. But you are going to hear it."

"Fine. So, what have you got? I was mean to someone? Fired someone who didn't deserve it? Ruled the wrong way on a case? What? Give it to me, Nelson."

"For starters, I've got three female law clerks who say you sexually harassed them, threatened their jobs, and promised to land them law firm jobs in exchange for their silence."

"That's a bunch of horseshit. Who? What are their names?"

"I've got a racial discrimination claim, too. And also a claim that you played it pretty free and loose with petty cash payments to jurors over the years."

"Oh, that old shit. I paid juries in cash on a Friday after a case settled and the clerk would be gone. No one wanted to come back down to East St. Louis to get a check for forty bucks, or whatever the hell it was, for their week of service. Please. You sound like that Ruth Whittaker—finding fault with every little goddamned thing."

"That's just a taste, Bill. You lasted a long time on that bench, but you made an awful lot of enemies."

The judge sipped on his refreshed drink, avoiding Nelson's stare and focusing instead on the ocean. He realized he had misplayed his hand. He hadn't considered that when he agreed to a deal that saved himself, and he agreed to give the U.S. Attorney the testimony she wanted, that the entire legal establishment would rush to attack him and his years of service to the profession.

He wondered if Nelson was right, that his reputation already was a shambles. "Who knows of these allegations—the harassment and all of that?"

"Just our defense team—for now."

"Nelson, you know damn, good, and well, that I cannot sit here and defend against all these claims and charges from people with vendettas against me. Hell, I can barely remember the names of my clerks from last year, nonetheless ten or twenty years ago."

"Well, they certainly remember you. And they have journals and notes and all kinds of things to back up their claims."

"Right. Of course they do. What a world…" the judge said, his voice trailing off. He began again, "So, my friend, what do you want from me? To recant my testimony to the grand jury, get Ruth Whittaker to drop her case against Jack? You know that won't happen. She will just move forward against all of us—recall it is my testimony that is keeping you in the clear. And then she will add on campaign finance charges, illegal gambling and now, I guess, perjury, against me? You know sure as shit that me changing my story is not going to happen."

"I figured as much, Bill. I know you too well to think you would recant. I am just here to tell you that what awaits you in a trial next month is far worse than anything you expected. No one will buy your story once they hear the line of impeachment to your credibility we have set to go. Your testimony against Jack is going to be shit. It really is. And you are going to be running back here with your beloved reputation in worse shape than you feel right now, four drinks before noon."

"Ah, fuck you, Nelson."

2

"MR. RAHN, I UNDERSTAND YOUR MOTION as you have explained it. I just am not inclined to grant it," Judge Randolph said from atop his bench to Tom Rahn, the general counsel for the St. Louis and St. Paul Railway. Before the judge was the railroad's motion to set aside the settlement it had made with Jack Spellman. "I am well aware of the allegations leveled against Mr. Spellman, his firm, and their interrelation with former Chief Judge Flood."

"Well then, judge, you know that Mr. Spellman influenced Chief Judge Flood, who ultimately certified this class action, which drove my client to settle for $100 million."

"Mr. Rahn," the judge said softly but sternly, "your company was sued by Mr. Spellman's law firm for $500 million, claiming that the railroad defrauded thousands—or was it tens of thousands—of land-owners over the course of many years. Judge Flood certified that class action in a decision that is a veritable tutorial on determining the bed-rock issues of a class. It was a decision your client appealed, and lost, before the very conservative Seventh Circuit.

"Your client could have tried the case. Had you taken that route, Judge Flood would have been retired by now, and that case would still be on the docket. But you settled.

"And this was no mere settlement where you offered 'go away' money. This settlement granted to your railroad a land right—a valu-able land right—to run its communications lines across those tens of thousands of miles of property, for only a few dollars per foot.

"I don't know if you have tried to buy communications corridors of late, Mr. Rahn, but your client settled because settlement was favor-able to it. And I don't see how the allegations against Mr. Spellman change any of that.

"Mr. Spellman," the judge continued, looking to the opposing counsel table, "do you have anything to say in response?"

"Not much, your honor, thank you," Jack said rising from his chair. "You have articulated well our opposition to the motion to set aside the class settlement. I would add only three points.

"First, in the eyes of the law, I—and by extension my firm—are entitled to a presumption of innocence. Thus, at most, the railroad's motion should be held in abeyance pending the outcome of my trial, which is set for next month.

"Second, the sworn testimony of Judge Flood in this regard is that he already had made up his determination as to class certification before the alleged bribe was paid to him. There is no evidence, then, that his decision was at all improper—even if you were to believe the allegations leveled against me."

"Third, and finally, if the goal of the railroad here is justice, then I will agree that, in the instance where I am found guilty of the government's charges as to these counts, I will remit to the railroad the fees paid to my firm, but the money paid to the class should remain for the reasons your honor so eloquently stated."

"How about that, Mr. Rahn? What do you think about that deal? If Mr. Spellman is found to have had some malfeasance here, he gives back his fee and the plaintiffs get to keep their awards."

"Well, your honor, but for that 'malfeasance'—as you say—the SL&SP likely would not have had a class certified against it, and likely wouldn't have settled. We simply could not have predicted this outcome. What we would call for, essentially judge, is a 'do over,' back to the pre-certification status of this case. Let a new judge look at these facts and decide whether to certify."

"A 'do over.' Interesting," the judge said, considering the idea. "Well, had your client not appealed to the playground monitor, I might agree with you. But you already got that second opinion from the Seventh Circuit on appeal. I don't see the need for upsetting this settlement, or for the delay and expense to go through it all over again. Whatever the allegations against Mr. Spellman, he could not control the facts of his case, which the Seventh Circuit gave a fresh look when you appealed—and lost.

"But Mr. Spellman, I like your offer. And the Court accepts it. You arise from your trial with no felony convictions, then this settlement stands. If you lose on any of those counts, then post appeal you return your fee. The award to the class stands in all events.

"Defendant's motion to set aside settlement is denied except to the fee paid to class counsel, which is deferred as stated. Thank you gentlemen. This Court stands in recess….I couldn't help myself there, Mr. Rahn."

3

NELSON LOOKED UPON THE U-SHAPED TABLE in the back room of Addie's Restaurant. This was his war room, which he had rented through the end of Jack's trial. On this night, it was full of local trial attorneys, who had come for a free dinner and to hear updates on the case against Jack Spellman.

Nelson and Jack agreed that they would pay any expense necessary in aid of Jack's defense. A verdict of not guilty virtually assured the firm's case against AgriFarm would remain on track and its settlement with the railroad would stand. Those two cases, nonetheless others in the pipeline, represented $50 million in revenue to the firm that would vanish with a guilty verdict.

Thus, at a brisk clip of tens of thousands of dollars per week, Nelson worked to build their defense. That included fees to their trial counsel, Walter McDonnell, as well as Nelson's army of legal assistants, paralegals and private investigators—most of them on loan from the lawyers seated for dinner in the room.

As the trial approached, and Nelson knew that Judge Flood had no intent to recant on his testimony, he needed to update them that the case would head to trial and to make sure he had their support through to the end. He walked around the room, slapping the backs and shaking the hands of many of the most legendary trial lawyers in the area.

"I want to thank everyone for coming tonight. These are interesting times," Nelson began.

"As we have dug into these charges against Jack, we know two things. First, we know that Judge Flood—and he was a close friend of mine—is not the man we thought he was. And his false testimony is the center of the case against Jack. Thanks to the assistance of many of your employees, we have uncovered incredible evidence against Judge Flood that we will use to impeach him at trial and, well, otherwise.

"Second, we know for certain what this case against Jack really is about. It is about power and politics here on this side of the river.

"You all know what is going on here. The businesses over there across the river, and their silk-stocking lawyers and big law firms, they've dubbed this a 'judicial hellhole.' They are tired of having their asses handed to them in our courts, by our juries. As if we could make up the things they do to their employees, their customers, the environment! As if those juries could never come to those verdicts without the help of corrupt judges and lawyers!

"Well, excuse me for speaking so frankly, but bullshit. And now, for the first time that I can remember, we have a U.S. Attorney who takes her marching orders from those companies and law firms—from big business.

"Would it surprise you to know that Ruth Whittaker meets monthly with the CEOs of some of the biggest companies around here? I thought not. And what do you think they talk about? Her prosecution of drug warlords?"

Nelson answered his own questions: "Of course not. It is us—you and me—that they meet about. They want a stop to what it is we do. And if they can't get changes through the appellate courts when they appeal every damned verdict, or through the legislature with their attempts at changing our venue laws, well, they are left with the executive branch—the enforcement arm. And that is Ms. Whittaker. And so here we are.

"Jack Spellman has spent his career fighting for the little guy. He's one of us. And we are now just a few weeks from his trial. And this is not just any trial, ladies and gentlemen. This is a trial on our very culture. On our way of life here. That court house down the road is where we bring justice for those who have been injured.

"The U.S. Attorney finds something scandalous about that. I wonder if that has anything to do with the fact that her former company, AgriFarm, and others like it, fear being brought to account for their wrongdoing. I submit there is no coincidence that at the same time our firm filed suit against AgriFarm, Ms. Whittaker brought this action against Jack.

"So, that's what this is. This prosecution against Jack is intended to try and stop that forward progress, and to reverse that past progress," he said, referring to the railroad case.

"We are the ones keeping this place honest and true and if Jack falls for that, well—" Nelson stopped, his voice cracking with anger and worry.

As Nelson paused to collect himself, Jack's former partner Peter Demitri stood: "Nelson, let me finish. Everyone, one of our own is on trial here. And this is a trial that goes to the root of what we all do. We litigate. We make friends. We fight for the little guy. And we are a family.

"Now, Nelson already told me that some of you have started to feel the strain of having your assistants and associates on loan for so long to Jack's case. Well, I for one will continue to offer some of our staff through Jack's trial. And I ask all of you to recommit to doing so.

"Know this: if Ruth Whittaker gets Jack's head on her mantle, she will come for yours, or yours, or mine, next," he said pointing around the room. "Ever hire a judge? Or a judge's kid as your clerk? Hired a judge's wife? Sent an attorney from your firm onto the bench, and prevailed before that attorney years later? Bought a judge a beer or played golf with a prosecutor? Raise your hand. Any of this sound wrong to you? Me neither. That is standard operating procedure. But it does to her and her anti-corruption unit.

"So, Nellie, we've got your back, my friend. I've heard the work this team is doing in here. And you are putting together a hell of a defense. One hell of a defense. Keep it up. And all of you, you keep it up too. We've got to win this thing for Jack, certainly, but our survival depends upon it too."

4

NELSON WAITED OUTSIDE, watching the sun rise over the farmer's market and the brick row houses just south of it. It was a cold but clear morning and he kept the car running, listening to a Sunday sports-talk show on AM radio.

He was parked across the street from the address he had for Xavier Holden. It was a nice, Victorian row house, three stories tall.

He saw that a yellow-sleeved newspaper still sat at the bottom of the stoop. With the Spellman trial set just one week away, Nelson figured Xavier would rise soon to retrieve it. He waited.

Fifteen minutes later, wearing glasses, a maroon sweatshirt and boxer shorts, Xavier opened the front door and descended the steps to the sidewalk to grab his paper. Nelson emerged, "Mr. Holden!"

Xavier looked up, alarmed, as his dogs started to bark in the background. He recognized the face, but couldn't quite place it. The street was empty and he shouted back, "and you are?"

"Nelson Bleaker. Spellman, Bleaker and Rock. Can I talk to you?" he asked as he crossed the narrow street.

"This is highly improper, Mr. Bleaker. You are not under indictment, but nonetheless you are a key witness in the Spellman trial and I do not believe I can or should speak with you. And this certainly is not the place."

"What I have to say, Mr. Holden, likely should not be said in your office. Please, can I come in? Or perhaps we can take a walk over to the market. I think it is open."

Xavier considered what it was Nelson could want and could not come up with anything. He deemed a brief meeting harmless. "Too cold for that. Come in."

"Have a seat," Xavier offered, "and let me get some clothes on."

Nelson sat on a chair in the front window, admiring the view through the large windows to the market. He looked around the room, noting the exposed brick, the elegant furnishings. It was a nice home, and one not normally afforded on a public salary, he knew.

Xavier returned in khakis. He rubbed his short haircut. He opted not to offer his visitor anything by way of drink or food. "What can I do for you?" he asked.

"Well, first off, thanks for agreeing to talk to me. The last time we met, we were nearly in fisticuffs."

"Right. At the courthouse up in Belleville. I remember."

"I've learned a couple of things that I wanted to talk about with you. The first is this prosecution. I understand you were the lead in putting together this case against Jack."

"That is largely correct, yes."

"And you will be the lead trial counsel, correct?"

"Yes."

"I think you should reconsider."

"Reconsider what, being lead counsel, or bringing this case?"

"All of it."

Xavier laughed. "I think I could have saved you the trip to the city, Mr. Bleaker. We are a week from trial and we are ready to go. We feel very good about our case."

"We do too. And instead of waiting until trial, I thought I would try to talk to you about what we have found. And perhaps then, you will reconsider.

"Our defense team could fill this house, Mr. Holden. We have an army of legal assistants and investigators who have investigated every lead, every witness, and every potential witness in this case."

"Good for you," Xavier said.

"Well, yes, very good for us as it turns out." Nelson reached into his briefcase and produced a series of folders. "Beginning tomorrow, and running for the remainder of the week, we intend to leak a series of affidavits, signed by several former employees and clerks of the judge who allege considerable wrongdoing by the judge over the years."

"Can I see those?" Xavier asked.

"Perhaps, but hear me out. There are allegations of sexual harassment, racial discrimination, improper use of court funds, use of federal property for soliciting campaign contributions, illegal gambling, and more.

"And when we release this information, we also will hold daily press conferences whereby these women—most of them women, anyway—will explain their stories and indicate a willingness to impeach the credibility of Judge Flood. A story per day, at least. It will lead the Belleville paper, and probably that one too," he said, pointing to the yellow-wrapped St. Louis paper.

"So, that's your plan, to try this case in the media?"

"No, not the case, just Judge Flood. And you."

"And me? What are you talking about?"

"I'll get to that later, if I must, but let me first ask you this: How do you feel about the case against Jack?"

"I feel good about it."

"That is not what I have been hearing. My understanding from various informants is that it was Ruth Whittaker that pushed for the indictment against Jack. I understand that you thought you had a good case against the chief, but not Jack. But that you were overruled. Is that true?"

"I'm not getting into—no, that is not true. I wrote the indictment, which is based on solid evidence—only part of which is the judge's testimony against Mr. Spellman. And frankly, Mr. Bleaker, I don't understand your willingness to undermine that testimony. I recall it is the only thing keeping you off the indictment."

"That is true," Nelson conceded, "but my point, I guess, is that the only indictment here should have been Flood's. And I think you agree with that."

"I am paid to do a job, Mr. Nelson, and I work for the United States Attorney. And for the next few weeks, that job is to prosecute Mr. Spellman. Judge Flood, as you know, has been or will be awarded immunity for his testimony as to his complicity in this conspiracy with you and Mr. Spellman. And that is the end of the story."

Nelson stood, feigning to leave. "And what of me, Mr. Bleaker?" Xavier asked.

"Ah, right. You, Mr. Holden. I understand you to be a very impressive trial attorney. I am aware of your c.v. and I am impressed by what

I have heard about you. I've seen the list of trials you have handled, and I've read the press accounts of your performances. Very impressive.

"I can understand why Ruth hired you and your Chicago firm back in the day. And I can only imagine the skeletons you hid for her over the years at AgriFarm. Your addition to her prosecutorial team was a stroke of genius for her. In fact, I would wager that there is no one in that office—and certainly not Ruth herself—who is as capable as you in the courtroom. The last real trial specialist they had in that office was Walter, and well, he works for us now."

Xavier sat down, wondering where this was going. Nelson sat back down as well. He reached into his bag for a manila envelope and placed it atop the coffee table.

"I think I mentioned that our defense team includes investigators?"

"Yes."

"Well, within the bounds of the law, they investigated witnesses, and they investigated prosecutors. Including you."

"What's in the envelope?"

"Just some public documents we found about you."

Xavier reached for them, but Nelson picked them up first. "Hold on," he said, "hear me out. I suppose the story goes something like this for you. Good kid moves out of the ghetto, goes away to good schools, sets up life in cosmopolitan Chicago, owning a nice condo in Boystown.

"But he leaves that life for a high profile government job near St. Louis, settling into Soulard, and looking to make friends."

"Enough, Mr. Bleaker. You can leave. This is ridiculous."

"Well, hold on, now," Nelson said, continuing his tale: "and he finds himself arrested for fraternizing the racquetball courts in Forest Park, and not for the sport of it. Then he uses his connections to get that arrest brushed under the rug."

"Unbelievable," Xavier offered.

"Only he didn't realize that the detective who did the work filed his report nonetheless, and that report included pictures leading up to the arrest."

"This is blackmail, Mr. Nelson. That is a crime. I can call the police and have you arrested right now."

"Yeah, but see, it isn't. Now, if I told you I had photos I took of you here in your house, or in a men's club in the west end, and I had taken those illegally and tried to do something with those—yeah, sure, that's perhaps blackmail.

"But what I have here is a public arrest report document, obtained lawfully, as well as the supporting file, including these photos. And I'm not asking you to do anything Mr. Holden. I'm simply telling you that I think the newspapers will find it interesting that the city police covered up an arrest of a federal prosecutor who solicited sex with other men on public property.

"I imagine they will want to see the photos, maybe run a few of the ones that aren't X-rated across the front page."

"You are a sick fuck."

"Me? I'm sick? I've seen these photos, and I don't think I am the sick one."

"You have no right delving into my private life—"

"Mr. Holden, I used to be a judge, and a prosecutor before that. You don't think I know the law? This isn't your private life. This is you going down on a guy at a public place. This is your public arrest report and your public mug shot," he said, waving it in front of him. "Here, take a look. I have copies ready to go to the papers. I imagine the state bar—not to mention your boss and her benefactors—might be interested in this too."

Xavier opened the envelope. It was as Nelson had stated—the same report file he had seen and he had been told would be destroyed. There was no way, he knew, that he could survive in the righteous office Ruth had assembled.

"So what do you want from me?" Xavier asked.

"I don't want anything. As I said, there is no blackmail here. This is public and it's going to be going more public this week—along with the Flood stuff."

"And how do I stop this?"

"I don't know that you can. That would be a quid pro quo, which you don't seem inclined to make. I don't need to be arrested here, as you threatened, when I can dismantle your case from the outside one piece at a time."

"You are unbelievable," Xavier muttered. "Fuck."

Nelson watched as Xavier thumbed through the pictures again.

"I can't drop the charges, you know that, right?" Xavier finally offered. "That's Ruth's call. And even if I fall on my sword over this," he said, holding up the spread of photos, "she is going to go forward here. You get that, right?"

"I do."

"So, what do you want?"

"Nothing."

"Well, what if I quit right now?"

"And?"

"And I quit, and Ruth takes the case forward. And if you keep this all between us, I can return to my firm in Chicago without issue."

"I think we would need a noisy exit. Something that makes clear you are parting ways with this prosecution machine of hers."

"Um, well, I'm not opposed to doing that, I guess. But in what context would that occur? I cannot conceive of me calling a press conference to announce my departure."

"True. Alright then, this: you quit, and we will leak the information to the media that the reason you were at odds with Ruth was that you did not believe there was a strong case here against Jack, but that the real case was against Flood. We can release that towards the end of the week. That gives you time to get out of Dodge."

Xavier considered this option. He could not find a better exit. "Fine. I'll quit later today, and tell her I need to get back to my firm, or back to that salary, or whatever. She already knows I didn't like this prosecution—as you apparently know. That is some operation you've got over there, Mr. Nelson."

"Why don't you call her right now?" Nelson asked, pointing to the phone. And Xavier did.

5

"WELCOME HOME!" THE SIGN READ. Bill Flood drove into the garage of his longtime Illinois home, welcomed by the banner and an affixed arrow pointing to his workshop table. It was Friday evening, and the case against Jack Spellman for which he had returned from Florida was set for Monday.

Atop the table sat a neat stack of the week's newspapers. After glimpsing the first headline, he ripped down the banner.

The names came back to him in waves, in pages upon pages of coverage, replete with photos and dates. The local paper made the story a five-day arc, starting the prior Sunday, under the heading "Benched: The Story of a Fallen Judge."

He flipped from one front page to the next, reading the captions under the pictures, remembering the names of the women and his transgressions—some of them decades ago.

The paper also delved into his gambling addiction, as well as his political fundraising dalliances. Missing from this list of wrongdoing, however, was anything having to do with Jack Spellman, his firm, or the railroad class action.

Judge Flood brought all the papers inside and spread them across his dining room table. This coverage, he decided, was far worse than anything Ruth Whittaker had brought at him. There were some half-truths, he thought, and some exaggerations, but none of it was altogether false. He had had many problems and shortcomings over the years, and had overcome or outgrown most of them. But here they were again—and now for all the world to see.

He read with some interest the success his law clerks—who now sought to destroy him—had enjoyed since they left his employ. He circled on the broadsheet the names of the lawyers who had come forward to speak against him on the record; the list was almost thirty-strong. All of them were local plaintiffs' lawyers, he noted.

The evening light was beginning to fade, and he watched from his living room window as the vans arrived outside of his home. He saw their numbers: 2, 11, 4, 5. Someone knew he had arrived this afternoon. The newspapers had had their way with him for an entire week, and now, it seemed, the networks were ready for their piece.

He considered hiding, wondering how he could possibly begin to respond to all that he had just read. But he knew that he needed to respond, and this was a quick way to do so.

The knock on the front door came with an urgency, but the chief took his time getting to the door. When he arrived, he had to push back against the cameras and microphones. "Back up," the chief barked, "back the hell up and I will give you a statement."

He walked out to the middle of his sidewalk and squinted into the lights beaming down from atop the news vans. He could hear the reporters' questions, but didn't focus on what they asked.

"I don't plan to answer your questions, ladies and gentlemen. But I am happy to provide you with a statement."

The reporters kept their microphones in place. The judge collected himself, choosing his words carefully.

"I am a retired judge. I worked on the federal bench for nearly 30 years. Never, during that time, did a single person raise a single allegation against me. Not one.

"Now, I have the misfortune of being a witness in a trial of a very influential attorney—from a very powerful firm. And in advance of that trial, they have dug up, and in some cases wholly fabricated, charges against me that—"

"Which ones?" a question came.

"Which what?" the judge asked, confused.

"Which charges do you deny and which do you admit?"

"Well, I am not getting into that. What I am saying to you is that—"

"Are you admitting these allegations, but simply believe they are old news?" another reporter interrupted.

"Yes. That is—"

"So, you admit these allegations," the reporter concluded.

"No, I was agreeing that these alleg—that this is all old news. In fact I deny—"

The reporters pounced:

"How long have you been aware of these allegations?"

"Where are you living now, judge?"

"How's your wife taking to these charges?"

"Who bought your Florida condo judge?"

"Do you still have a gambling problem, judge?"

"I am done here. That is clear to me," Judge Flood answered, waving off the questions, and turning for his door.

"Anything to say to Jack Spellman, judge?" a reporter called out as he reached the door.

The chief turned around, "Yes. I've not been charged with anything. It is his trial set for Monday. And I guess I'll see him in court."

6

RUTH WAS HOLED UP IN HER HOME, preparing for Monday's trial. It was her first trial in well over a decade, and her first criminal one ever. She knew that Walter McDonnell would have command of the criminal rules and she was doing her best to relearn a subject she had not touched since law school.

The ten o'clock news started on the television in the corner and she saw the chief, accosted by the media, unable to answer their questions. He looked confused in one clip, and turning over to another station, she heard his salvo to Jack Spellman.

Ruth was aware of the media accounts trickling out over the course of the week about the judge. But presuming she found a good jury, she was not worried about most of it. She would do her best to keep this a trial about Jack and not the retired chief judge.

"In related news tonight regarding the trial on Monday of East Side power lawyer Jack Spellman, we have a Channel 5 exclusive."

Ruth put down the rules of criminal procedure and watched the television screen.

"Several independent sources have reported that federal prosecutor, and chief federal trial counsel Xavier Holden, who abruptly quit the case and the office of the U.S. Attorney last week, did so out of concerns that his boss, U.S. Attorney Ruth Whittaker, was waging an unmerited attack on Mr. Spellman. Further, it is reported that Mr. Holden believed the allegations against Judge Flood, from whom you just heard, merited charges from the U.S. Attorney's office—and not the immunity deal the U.S. Attorney herself brokered with the former chief judge for his testimony against Spellman. We tried reaching U.S. Attorney Whittaker, but were told by her office that she was unavailable for comment. We are told Mr. Holden has returned to his Chicago criminal defense law firm and has no comment at this time. Back to you, Dick."

Ruth sunk deeper into her chair. The Spellman firm was slowly, but surely, picking apart her case from the outside. They had somehow forced Xavier out, she thought, and had marginalized the chief judge through a steady series of news reports undermining his truthfulness and character. They had done it in print and on the air, on both sides of the river. It was impressive, she thought, and she feared not only about her case, but the class action against AgriFarm, which would be Jack Spellman's next conquest if she lost her case.

What she needed, she knew, was to seat a good jury, to not succumb to Walter's superior trial skills, and to get her story told in the face of the news hurricane Spellman and his team were creating. She resolved to work around the clock, to bring in a team of assistant prosecutors over the weekend, and to gird herself for the trial of her career.

Her phone rang, and she walked over to it, expecting to get an earful from David Meirs. She answered.

"Ms. Whittaker, this is Walter McDonnell."

"You've got to be kidding me. You are calling me at home on a Friday night?"

"I've tried you at the office all day; I'm sorry."

"I doubt that. I think you just got done watching the ten o'clock news."

"Well, that is true, but there was no 'news' there for me."

"So, why the call?" she asked.

"Well, I thought we never really talked about a plea deal in this case, and now seemed like a good time. I cannot imagine you are looking forward to trying this case."

"Actually, I am. I've not gotten to try a case in a while, and I am ready to get back in there."

"Well, good for you. This is a pretty special case for me, too. It's my first since you fired me."

"You quit."

"Well, yes, I suppose that's true. And you got Mr. Holden in my place."

"Enough. Can I help you?"

"Right, yes, the plea. We would be willing to plead to the single count on the improper tax accounting charge."

"That's it? The misdemeanor count? Please. Why did you bother to call me?"

"As a courtesy, mainly. We also think it is likely you will get nothing next week. And we think you would like a conviction."

"To a petty tax charge?"

"It was good enough for Al Capone," Walt said.

"I think your client has made more money off corruption than even Capone. I'll pass," Ruth countered.

"OK, suit yourself. See you Monday."

"Good night, Walter."

7

RUTH APPROACHED THE COURTROOM'S MAHOGANY DOORS, and stared upon the nameplate attached to them: "Hon. Spencer Donahue." She questioned the neutrality of the system that allegedly had randomly assigned United States v. Spellman to this judge. There were, after all, a dozen judges in the district that could have received the case. In her view, Judge Donahue was the worst possible choice.

Judge Donahue had been a Carter appointee, and not just a liberal, but a former trial lawyer and three-time president of the Illinois Plaintiff's Attorney Association. He was now in his late-70s, well-along in his lifetime appointment, but with no plans to take senior status or retire. He was known to be a criminal defendant's judge, and to still be cozy with the plaintiff's bar.

Already, in pretrial conferences, Judge Donahue had struck pieces of evidence that were important to the prosecution, including recordings on the day Jack had bailed his son out of jail and his firm accountant had asked if the money was for a "flood" or for Judge "Flood," depending upon who was listening. Judge Donahue had found the recording vague at best, and more likely to be overly prejudicial to the defense. Thus, he refused to allow any use or mention of the tape in the trial.

Ruth's assistants had searched for grounds to disqualify him from the case, but they were unable to find any link whatsoever between Judge Donahue and Jack Spellman. The only silver lining they had found was that Judge Donahue had been a good friend of the former chief judge, who would be testifying later in the week.

Ruth had left jury selection to one of her more senior deputies with years of criminal experience. She had no sense of what kind of jury she wanted in a white collar case. She figured she didn't want anyone from Spellman's hometown, or anyone with ties to the plaintiff's bar. But beyond that, she didn't know, or really care.

Her instincts seemed about right, however, when she was told that Walter McDonnell had pressed for Bellevillians on the jury. As it turned out, neither side received quite the jury they had hoped. The jury was split in all senses, along race and gender lines, and was comprised of men and women from up the hill, and from down along the river. Ruth had reviewed the jury sheets and saw it was a decidedly low-income, blue collar crowd, and that she liked.

It was now 8:00 a.m. on Tuesday, the opening of the trial. Ruth walked into Judge Donahue's courtroom alone. She placed her trial briefcase atop the prosecutor's table and walked about the courtroom. Within the hour, a half dozen assistant prosecutors and paralegals would filter in with boxes of trial evidence. But for now, she wanted to walk herself through the paces of her opening argument in the privacy of the courtroom.

She began from the podium and moved away towards the jury box, her argument playing in her head. The courtroom was dark, save for two bands of light slicing across the floor from the pair of large windows facing onto Missouri Avenue. Judge Donahue had managed to commandeer one of the original courtrooms in the building, and aside from the chief's courtroom, it was the most imposing.

A janitor came into the courtroom to turn on the bank of lights and to power-up the microphones. Seeing Ruth walking about the courtroom with her eyes shut, he decided against it and quietly closed the door as he departed.

Ruth tried to push out of her mind how long it had been since she argued a case to a jury. She tried also not to think about Walter's statistics as a prosecutor, the number of cases he had brought through verdict, or his very favorable win-loss record. And most of all, she tried to avoid the thought that she had made him into the formidable defense attorney she was about to face.

She focused, instead, on Jack Spellman and her case against him. She had used virtually every resource of her office over the last fortnight in preparation of her case, and she was ready to bring it. Ruth was convinced of the merits of her prosecution of Jack Spellman, and always had been.

Thirty minutes later, the janitor returned through the rear door, and her assistant prosecutors began to flow through the front doors. The lights warmed the courtroom to a yellow glow. Ruth looked upon the oil mural inlaid into the wall above the jury panel. It showed the view from the banks of the river near the courthouse across the muddy river towards the green-topped dome in downtown St. Louis. In the foreground of the picture were dozens of barges—carrying the wood, furs and other commodities that had built the region on both sides—crowded along the banks of the river ready to unload their contents. Commerce, fairness, law. This was what made the region great, and this was the essence of her case.

8

THE SPELLMAN HOUSE WAS QUIET. Tim was off to college at Virginia, and Wendy was already at West for school. The drive down to the federal courthouse was perhaps a fifteen minute one, and Jack had no intention of arriving early.

So, he sat at the kitchen table talking with Kathy. Unlike in Tim's case, where Kathy, and to a lesser extent Jack, suspected their son had been complicit in something criminal, they were generally in agreement that Jack had not done anything wrong in this case.

Kathy was convinced, however, that the Spellman family could not dodge the prosecutorial bullet a second time. And that belief made her start to doubt her original position.

"A conviction will just destroy us, Jack, and especially Wendy. She's just a freshman, and she has to hear about her brother, and now her father."

"I know that. I do. But a plea, a deal, that's an admission of guilt. And it hands back millions of dollars."

"We don't need the money," Kathy protested, hoping, as she had for the last week, to avoid another trial within her family.

"We would if I lost my license and our livelihood."

"I know."

"And you know that I had nothing to do with this, right?"

"Yes. Right. I think so."

"You think so! We've been through this a million different ways. Nelson helped the judge. The judge admits, amidst other lies I recognize, that Nelson's help had nothing to do with his decision in the railroad case. That was a good case."

"I know it was. But, I mean, you and Nelson are so close. How he helped us with Tim. I just don't see how a jury won't think that you must have known something about this."

"I am not getting into this again. You saw the press coverage about Judge Flood. You know what kind of man he is. Do you think that about me?"

"No. No, I don't. But I also recall how you brought Nelson into the firm. And I know that is how it's done—to lure them off the bench. But, well, anyway…"

"Judges have a right to work once they leave the bench, and they make for great lawyers. You saw Nelson in the courtroom. If I plead to any of this, I could go to prison, or at least lose my license."

"I know. I know. I don't want that. I know. Should we go?" she asked.

Jack looked at the clock, which read 8:30, and put on his coat. He helped Kathy with hers, and then placed his arms around her.

"You know I did nothing wrong," he whispered.

She closed her eyes: "I do."

"And you know I have the best lawyers, and we have the better case."

"I do."

"And you know that whatever happens, our family will still be our family."

"Yes."

"And you know I love you."

"Yes."

She turned her head back to his. Jack wiped the tear off her cheek and whispered that it was time to go.

9

JACK WALKED TOWARDS THE DEFENSE TABLE and took his seat. He glanced over at the U.S. Attorney and noted the young bench she had assisting her. The loss of the highly capable Xavier Holden, he thought, could make all the difference in his case.

At precisely 9:00 a.m., Judge Donahue limped into his courtroom. He pulled himself up the steps to his chair and watched as the spectators and participants in the mostly empty courtroom sat. He called for the jury and delivered to them cursory preliminary instructions as to how they were to comport themselves throughout the trial and in their time away from the courthouse. He then asked if there was any plea, and hearing none, allowed Ruth to commence her opening remarks.

She asked for permission to enter the well—to move freely about the courtroom—which the judge granted. Her first words of good morning came haltingly, but in announcing her position she quickly found her voice.

"Ladies and gentlemen of the jury, I am Ruth Whittaker, the United States Attorney for the Southern District of Illinois. I've lived here, in southern Illinois, pretty much my whole life. I imagine that's the same for most of you.

"O'Fallon, Dupo, Cahokia, East St. Louis," she rattled off the towns of all of the jurors. "These are our towns. They are great places to live. But sometimes…well, sometimes it doesn't seem like it any more.

"We've lost a lot of jobs around here. And the jobs that remain, well, they don't pay what they used to."

Ruth continued on a path to someplace defense attorney Walter McDonnell could foresee. He moved forward to the edge of his seat, ready to put an end to this story of Ruth's. Nelson, though, sat next to him and backed him off. "Walt, let her take all the rope she wants. The easier for her to hang herself." Walter nodded, unconvinced.

Ruth continued: "And even if you have a job at a local company, well, you are probably paying a whole lot for your medical insurance, if you are even lucky enough to have it. And some more of you, you've seen your doctors up and leave, heading across the river to West County.

"Now, I see some of you nodding, that yes, this is what has become of life around here. And some of you are looking at me quizzically, wondering what any of this has to do with the criminal case in which you have been impaneled as a juror.

"It means everything. This case is a referendum on what has become of our neighborhoods, our cities and our towns. The defendant, Jack Spellman, is a power broker in this district. He is a lawyer. A trial lawyer. His firm, and others like it, prey upon doctors, insurers, small businesses—and big ones too—to make themselves very very rich.

"They do that through any number of means. One way they do that—and one way Mr. Spellman has done that—is to poach from our judiciary their future partners. You see at the defense table Mr. Spellman, there in the glasses and dark blue suit. Next to him? Well, that is a former chief judge from St. Clair County. He is not under indictment here, but the government alleges he is a co-conspirator of Mr. Spellman's. Mr. Nelson Bleaker—that's the judge—he is a named partner in Mr. Spellman's law firm.

"And what is it, then, that the government alleges against this man, Mr. Spellman? Well, I will tell you. The government alleges that he directed Mr. Bleaker to bribe the chief judge of this courthouse. And that is bad enough, in and of itself. But they undertook to do this while the chief judge had on his docket a $500 million class action filed by Mr. Spellman against the SL&SP Railway.

"We will show, through testimony from the chief himself, that Mr. Spellman attempted through that bribe—as well as through the inducement of future employment in his wealthy firm—to influence the judge to certify that class action to the considerable pecuniary benefit of Mr. Spellman and his firm.

"This is no small matter, as the railroad handed over to Mr. Spellman's firm tens of millions of dollars as a result of a settlement of that case.

"These kinds of cases, ladies and gentlemen, are what drive companies out of our towns. They are what give us all a bad name around the country, as a depraved place, full of corrupt judges, lawyers, and politicians," Ruth said. She paused, listening to her words reverberate in the courtroom.

"They call this place a judicial hellhole. And it is. There exists a culture of corruption, of cronyism, that pervades every courthouse in this district, including it now appears, this one.

"And I, for one, don't think it has to be that way. But we have to start naming names. We have to start cracking heads. And low and behold, through tape recordings, reams of financial documents, and witnesses—all of which will be presented to you—we have found that one of the biggest heads around here needs a cracking."

Ruth walked behind the defense table and spread her arms just wide enough to frame Jack for the jury. She continued, "Mr. Spellman directed hundreds of thousands of dollars in benefits to the former chief judge of this courthouse. He induced him into his private practice, and lavished him with a huge salary. He did this to sway the judgment in his case against the railroad. And, thanks in no small part to that railroad settlement, he could afford to pay off those bribes. Indeed, he had 25 million ways he could afford to do it.

"The government will show that Mr. Spellman conspired to bribe a federal judge; that he did bribe a federal judge, and that in so doing he violated a handful of federal conspiracy, honest service, money laundering, and other laws.

"We will show this through documents and testimony. And let me say this, there are a lot of bad actors here. We have a chief judge who probably should have known he was in over his head, and we have Mr. Spellman's law partner, who appears to have walked along the very fine line of the law. However unsavory their testimony may be, it is Mr. Spellman who is ultimately culpable here."

Ruth turned towards Jack, pointing:

"A fine example may be made of finding this man guilty. And a fine beginning too. Let's—you and I—send a message to lawyers, and judges, and to those like you and me that may have lost some faith in our system of justice. Let's send a clear message that says that justice is no longer for sale in the East Side."

The jury sat transfixed as the words of the U.S. Attorney sank in, until Walter McDonnell shook them from their stupor:

"That's crap," he yelled, catching Ruth unawares as she was returning to her seat.

"Pardon my French," he said, moving his way past an earned objection that did not materialize and avoiding the glare of Judge Donahue.

"I like it here. And I think you do too. That's why you are here. If Ms. Whittaker wants to make this case a referendum on our community, well, fine, because I think you are here for the same reason I am. I like it here.

"The world is an adversarial place. There are prosecutors, there are defense attorneys. There are lawyers who fight for the big companies, and those who fight for the little guy. It just so happens that where we live, it's where the lawyers for the little guy are found. That's what Mr. Spellman does. It's what Mr. Bleaker does too. Hell, it's even what Judge Donahue used to do, a few decades ago, before he climbed up on that bench."

"Objection, relevance," Ruth's said.

"Sustained," the judge said. "Move it along, Mr. McDonnell."

"Mr. Spellman fights for the little guy. Ms. Whittaker does not."

"Objection."

"Sustained."

"Prior to becoming our U.S. Attorney, Ms. Whittaker was the top lawyer for AgriFarm—the chemical company."

"Objection, relevance."

"Overruled."

"And do you know who Mr. Spellman currently is suing? Agri-"

"Objection!" Ruth yelled.

"Goes to overzealous prosecution, judge," Walter asserted.

"Overruled."

"AgriFarm. And he has a case, too. It is all about how the company hid the nature of its genetically modified seed from the small farmers who bought it. Now, don't you think our farmer friends in this area would like to know about that? Would like to be compensated if they were wronged by being sold some messed-up Frankenseed?

"Well, I am getting ahead of myself. There is some semblance of a case here that we need to deal with. Let's put aside that Ms. Whittaker has her own motives—like a seven figure stock package from Agri-Farm—that needs for this prosecution to succeed."

"Objection, your honor, please! Where is the relevance in all of this?" Ruth yelled.

"Sustained. Let's hear you address the actual charges in this case, or sit down, Mr. McDonnell."

"Yes, your honor. The charges. What were those again? Oh, yes. Money laundering. Conspiring to bribe a judge. Bribing the judge.

"There was no money laundering here. As he will testify, Mr. Bleaker provided his lifelong friend relief in a time of financial hardship. Nothing more, nothing less.

"The judge, after some 30 years on the bench, desired to retire. He needed to make a livable wage for once, and he wanted to hang his shingle with a reputable firm. Well, as you will hear, they do not come more reputable than Mr. Spellman's firm.

"So, the judge quit and went to work in private practice. No crime in that.

"And what of that railroad case? Well, the very judge that decided that case will himself testify that the money he received from his friend made no difference in his order that certified the class.

"Maybe Ms. Whittaker doesn't think this place is what it was when she grew up. But I think it's better than it ever was. Don't punish those who have succeeded in our time, in our place. Don't punish those who, at every turn, give back to their communities, all the while fighting for all of us.

"The charges—and the justification for those charges—are bunk."

"Objection," Ruth called out.

"Withdrawn," Walter said over his shoulder as he sat down. He winked to Jack and Nelson. He was enjoying his first run around the courtroom from the defense table.

10

RUTH BEGAN HER CASE with the financial documents that undergirded the charges against Jack. The documents were presented through subpoenaed testimony from the accountant of Spellman, Bleaker & Rock, and various bank representatives.

It was mundane and tedious work, and it showed on the faces of the jury. But from that testimony and those documents, Ruth was able to show the firm's payments to a bookie—through an intermediary—who was owed $160,000 by Judge Flood. She was able to show that additional money, nearly $300,000, also went from the firm to a bank in satisfaction of the judge's mortgage.

What she was unable to prove, however, and what defense counsel Walter McDonnell focused upon in his cross examination, was any bad act—or any act at all, he noted—by the defendant, Jack Spellman. The case would have to turn, then, on the conflicting testimony of the two unindicted coconspirators: Nelson Bleaker and William Flood. Anticipating that everything Nelson would say would be rebutted by Judge Flood, Ruth called Nelson first. She needed Nelson to testify that he conspired with Jack Spellman, and that he acted at his partner's behest. Nelson, meanwhile, needed to walk the line between defending Jack and incriminating himself.

Nelson took the stand and sat confidently forward on the wooden witness chair. He swore his oath and sat with his body positioned mostly towards the jury.

"Mr. Bleaker, if you will," Ruth asked, directing his attention back to her at the lectern.

"Anything you wish, Ms. Whittaker," he offered whimsically.

"What is your role in this case, Mr. Bleaker?" Ruth asked.

"I don't understand your question. My role?"

"Yes. You have entered an appearance as defense counsel for Mr. Spellman, is that correct?"

"It is, yes. I entered my appearance to assist in the defense. But Mr. McDonnell is an able adversary—as you know—and he has needed little assistance from me."

"And you are aware that you have been listed in the indictment in this case as an unindicted coconspirator with Mr. Spellman?"

"Yes, I am aware of that."

"And you saw no ethical conflict in defending the man whom you are also alleged to have conspired with?"

"I did not. I do not. And as far as I am aware, your office has not said 'boo' about this until this very moment—if I am to understand this line of questioning."

"And are you appearing of your own volition this morning?"

"No. You have subpoenaed me to appear here today. Thanks for that."

Ruth, turning to Judge Donahue: "Could the court please advise the witness to answer only the question asked, and avoid these extemporaneous comments?"

Judge Donahue: "So ordered. This isn't your courtroom, judge."

"Noted," Nelson said, nodding his head.

"Mr. Bleaker, I want to turn your attention to the events of the Fall, 1993."

"OK."

"We have heard testimony that your firm, the law firm of Spellman Bleaker & Rock, paid to a bookie $160,000 through an intermediary. The testimony from the bookie, Mr. Diaz, was that the money was used to pay off various gambling-related debts of Chief Judge William Flood." She looked at Nelson.

"Is there a question?" he asked.

"Yes, do you agree with that statement of events?"

"Objection to the form, your honor," Walt said, "what statement of events is she talking about?"

"Sustained."

Ruth was flustered by the objection. She stumbled in rephrasing her next question: "Did you direct money to Mr. Diaz?"

"Yes," Nelson offered.

"You did?" Ruth's eyes betrayed her cool demeanor. She had not expected such candor, but quickly realized that his ready response had just defeated her plan to draw out the testimony in a fashion that cast the evidence against Jack.

"I think I just answered that," Nelson stated.

"And this money came from your law firm, isn't that right?"

"It came from my account within my law firm."

"Your what?"

"We are each P.C.s in the firm. That is, each of us named lawyers, we are each our own private company. We are also a partnership. It is a little complicated." Ruth had not asked about such an accounting practice of the firm's accountant, and it was too late now to travel down that road, for she had no idea where it would lead.

"So, you have admitted you paid Mr. Diaz?"

"Yes."

"Was it Mr. Spellman's idea to use an intermediary?"

"No. Mr. Spellman was not aware of my payment to Mr. Diaz, or my use of a go-between."

"Why not take the money from your account and bring it to Mr. Diaz?"

"Because I have better things to do with my time than pay off a bookie for a friend."

"And how much did you pay?"

"You know the answer. We all do. $160,000."

"Who did you speak with before deciding to pay that amount?"

"I spoke with our accountant. I spoke with the go-between."

"And you spoke with Mr. Spellman," Ruth tried to confirm.

"I categorically did not."

"And Mr. Spellman was okay with your taking $160,000 out of his law firm?"

"It was out of my account. It was my money. And he had no idea."

"How much money do you make at your firm?"

"It varies from year to year."

"How much money did you make last year?"

"Objection, relevance. This is prejudicial, judge," Walter argued, rising to his feet with his arms out in feigned disbelief.

"Ms. Whittaker?" Judge Donahue inquired, "the witness testified the payment came from his account. Why do you need to know how much money he made last year?"

"I want to know how much he earned from the class action settlement in the case before Judge Flood. It goes to motive, judge."

"Then ask that," Judge Donahue answered, "objection sustained."

"Alright, Mr. Bleaker, how much did you make from the settlement in your firm's case against the SL&SP Railway?"

"Ostensibly, I was given $5 million. But I also contributed to the firm's reserves to pay for the expenses to bring the case. Still, even discounting that, I made a few million dollars."

"And was Judge Flood aware that you had paid off Mr. Diaz on his behalf?"

"You will have to ask him," Nelson said.

"But surely that was your intent?"

"What was my intent?"

"For him to be aware of the fact that you paid Mr. Diaz?"

"I suppose at some point he would have become aware, but again, you would have to ask him."

"And you paid off Mr. Diaz during the pendency of the case against the railroad, isn't that correct?" Ruth asked, over an objection from Walter that was denied.

"The judge needed help. Mr. Diaz was threatening his family, his livelihood. Bill was my friend and he needed some money. He and I go back a long, long way. I know his secrets, he knows mine. So I helped him. He might not have ever learned it was from me—and that would have been fine."

Ruth turned again to the bench, "your honor, please instruct the witness to answer."

"Ms. Whittaker, these are your questions. But will the court reporter please reread the question, and Judge Bleaker, you are instructed to answer the precise question asked."

The question came again and Nelson answered that yes, the payment occurred during the time his firm's case was before the judge.

"Mr. Bleaker, is it your testimony, I take it, that you were just helping a friend?" Ruth asked with sarcasm.

"Essentially, yes."

"But your friend had a $500 million class action pending before him that you and Mr. Spellman had brought. Don't you see any conflict there?"

"I don't. By your standard, in a case that could last ten years, I could never so much as buy the judge lunch or pick up his golf tab on occasion."

"That is exactly what I am saying, Mr. Bleaker. What else did you do for Judge Flood?"

"Objection to form, overbroad in time and scope, irrelevant, vague."

"Anything else, counselor?" the judge asked Walter in jest. "Objection sustained. More precision, Ms. Whittaker," Judge Donahue offered.

"At some point, did you discuss with Judge Flood his joining your law firm?"

"Yes."

"And when was that?"

"A few times in passing in the Fall of 1993, then at the end of that year."

"And these conversations were during the pendency of your case against the railroad?"

"Mr. Spellman's case, you mean?"

"Your firm's case, Mr. Bleaker."

"I don't recall exactly, but I talked to him many times, often in passing, about how nice the firm was, how good the private practice of law could be. And perhaps, yes, during the pendency of my firm's case. But I will add—"

"You answered my question, thank you," Ruth said. She continued: "And when did Judge Flood decide to come to your firm?"

"I recall it was right about the time he retired. After the class action case you referenced had settled."

"But at some point, did your firm pay to Judge Flood some form of advance on his employment?"

"Well, not an advance. But yes, a signing bonus, I guess you would call it."

"And what was that?"

"I paid off his mortgage."

"And how much was that?"

"Oh, around $300,000."

"And you paid that out at Mr. Spellman's direction, correct?"

"No, no. Again, that came out of my account."

"And did the firm reimburse you."

"No."

"So, over the course of a few months, you decided to just give Judge Bleaker close to a half million dollars?"

"Well, yes. I mean, well, the practice of law has been very good to me and—"

"Don't you mean Judge Flood had been very good to you?" Ruth countered.

"Funny thing, that. I actually looked back at my files and I never won a case in his courtroom. In about five tries. Always defense verdicts, or I settled. If anything, he was hard on me for having known him."

"Then why give him the money?"

"As I said, he was a good friend—going way back. And this firm was good to me in my transition from the bench to private practice, and I wanted to give him that."

"And so you delivered a payoff of his mortgage?"

"Yes."

"And you did that through an intermediary?"

"No, actually our accounting just moved the funds from my account to his bank. But it went through too fast and he was still working for the government when it cleared. That was my mistake. But it was a harmless mistake. He was coming to work for us just a few days later."

"And is Judge Flood still working for you now?"

"No."

"Did you fire him?"

"No. He quit."

"Did he give you your money back?"

"No, but you are right, it was my money—not the firm's. And no, I haven't asked for it. He needs it more than I do. He can have it."

"Was Mr. Spellman aware of your paying off Judge Flood's mortgage?"

"No. We discussed with regard to every attorney acquisition how we could make a splash. A guy like Bill—Judge Flood—is in high demand when he walks off the bench. Especially to the big firms in St. Louis. We knew we had to act fast to get him, and to make a unique and interesting offer he couldn't refuse. So Jack knew I would make a play for the judge once he retired. But I assure you that Jack didn't know what it was, and certainly didn't know it was going to clear in advance of the judge's retirement. As I told him, and I told the judge, I screwed that up." Nelson again turned towards the jury, offering with his face and shoulders a mea culpa for what he had done. "But none of that was on Jack."

11

THE THIRD-SHIFT BAILIFF HEARD A SHOT. Night was turning into day in East St. Louis, but even in the dawn the faint sound of rat-a-tat gunfire was not rare at the courthouse. But this was a single, booming sound, like a car backfiring, and it was close to the court. The guard turned the volume down on the radio on his security desk, but heard nothing more.

He walked to the front of the courthouse, peering through locked doors onto Missouri Avenue. He looked for cars, or for passersby, but the street was vacant. He walked back towards the rear entrance of the building. At the back of the parking lot, he saw his own car. Up against the building, he saw one other car in the parking lot, an old maroon Buick.

The car was parked in front of the sign marked Reserved: Chief Judge, with its wheels stealing some space from the U.S. Attorney's empty spot next to it.

The presence of the car in the lot at this hour struck the bailiff as odd. But the glare from the parking lot lights made it impossible to see inside the car from his vantage. He opened the courthouse door and headed down the steps to the parking lot. He pulled his weapon and looked out at the empty streets. He walked up to the old car and realized this was the car he had seen in this spot for years. It was the car of the former chief judge who was set to return to the courthouse later in the day to testify.

The guard approached the car, but stopped. He could see through the passenger window a shotgun barrel resting against the window of the driver's door. He squatted to see more. He gasped. The large, working hands—a hunter's hands—were the only attributes of the chief recognizable to him. He radioed the open police line that the chief was dead and sat down on the curb, his hands shaking as he holstered his gun.

The response came fast and loud as city police squad cars raced into the parking lot with their lights on, sirens blaring. The unmarked FBI cruisers and U.S. Marshalls arrived next, followed by a crime scene van. The parking lot was cordoned off and the early-arriving courthouse custodians and cooks were sent around to enter from Missouri Avenue.

As the officers worked their way into the car, they found on the front passenger seat the morning's newspaper. The front page headline was divided into two parts. One side of the page summarized the trial testimony the day before from Nelson Bleaker, with a promise from the prosecutor comprising the headline: "Chief Judge to Rebut Defense Half-Truths…." Next to that headline, and above a picture of a teenage William Flood, however, was another headline: "…But Had Ties to White Dukes."

Despite a week's worth of revelations about the judge in his professional life—including claims of improper conduct towards his subordinates, illegal campaign contribution tactics, and more—the paper had saved the purely personal revelations—the scandalous allegations, for the day of his testimony. Or perhaps, one of the detectives speculated, the paper had not so coincidentally just been provided the story.

Whatever the cause for the timing, the story was damning. The chief judge, well before he had gone to college and law school, had been a member of a local white segregationist club, the White Dukes, which had tried to slow the rising tide of blacks moving into East St. Louis.

Several former members of the organization were quite forthcoming to the paper in describing the pursuits they had participated in with young Bill Flood back in those days. Although none of the men testified to anything as horrible as a lynching or a murder—for which they could have still been tried—each recalled in vivid detail their days of running families out of town, through violence and intimidation. They recounted the stories only to the extent they included Judge Flood, and each made sure to note Flood had been a ringleader and avid participant in their club before he got some schooling and turned his back on them.

The paper, meanwhile, bootstrapped the article with an in-depth review of the judge's decisions in major criminal cases. It surmised that minority criminal defendants received from the chief longer sentences for the same crimes as their white peers—at least until the mandatory sentencing guidelines had taken most of that discretion away from him. The paper found too that the judge had been dismissive of the majority of civil actions that were brought for racial, gender and similar forms of discrimination.

In some effort at neutrality, the paper had found a few men willing to defend Judge Flood as a "man of his time," which was a euphemism for the subtle racism that endured in the East Side. Others noted the judge's Democratic political affiliation, which they argued was at least a proxy for the judge's more modern beliefs on issues of equality, affirmative action and the like.

But even those claims were eclipsed by detailed interviews with released convicts who felt some sense of vindication in learning what they thought they already knew—that they had been sent away by a racist judge.

The crime scene technician took the folded paper, which had found its way to the judge's doorstep even though he no longer subscribed, and slipped it into a plastic bag. A final set of photos were snapped and County Coroner Fred Donovan arrived to secure, remove, and transport the body.

As daylight broke, officers reopened the parking lot to a line of cars, including that driven by Ruth Whittaker, who noted the emergency vehicles near her parking spot. She parked some distance away and located an FBI agent she recognized.

"What is this?" she asked.

"Suicide," the agent replied. "And you aren't going to believe who?"

"No?"

"Judge Flood."

"No," she whispered, turning her head up to the sky. Shaking her head, she mouthed the words, "oh my God," and walked into the courthouse.

"Did you see the News-Democrat this morning?" the agent called after her. Ruth waived him off, figuring she could not care less about the coverage of her case in the paper.

12

"THIS IS YOUR PROSECUTION, Ms. WHITTAKER. But I have a jury room full of men and women waiting on us. How do you plan to proceed?" Judge Donahue was red-eyed, sad for the loss of an old friend, and saddened too by the coverage he had read about his friend in the paper earlier in the morning.

Ruth sat in an armchair in Judge Donahue's chambers, her hand covering her mouth. Nelson Bleaker, Walter McDonnell and Jack Spellman were seated on a sofa along the wall.

Ruth didn't know where to begin. She was certain that the stories in the paper were the workings of the defense team. And she knew these reports, which steadily eroded the great pride of the former chief judge, had killed him. She wanted, more than ever, to take down Spellman, but she was out of the tools with which to do so.

"Judge, if I may," Walter tried to fill the silence.

"No," came the response from the judge, "I want to hear from the United States Attorney."

"We are ready to move forward," Ruth finally concluded. She had no stomach for a delay, which she knew would allow the defense more time to pummel her case from the outside.

"We would object, your honor," Walter said. "The government has premised their entire case on the testimony of Judge Flood—and Ms. Whittaker has harped on that testimony from the very start. His sad loss demands at least a mistrial, and perhaps a directed verdict for my client."

"A mistrial, your honor, would be a travesty," Ruth countered. "The government has shown the elements of the crimes. We just lack some of our ability to show that clear motive. But if your honor would allow the grand jury testimony in, why then—"

"We would strenuously object to that, judge, and you know that would be grounds for the overturning of any conviction. We have the right to cross-examine the accusers in this case, and that was not afforded at the time of the grand jury." As he spoke, Walter walked over and sat in the seat next to Ruth. "Let the government come at Mr. Spellman after a mistrial—see what they have left of their case—but make them do it without any reference to the judge."

"So, they get to lure the judge into their firm, then push him off the cliff, and now just walk away?" Ruth asked incredulously.

"What are you implying, Ms. Whittaker?" Walter asked.

"You know damn well what I am saying. The m.o. of the defense has been to attack this case from the outside. You've played to the media for weeks, and you've torn down Judge Flood with story after story. And then this dirt you dug up today. You know anything about that, Mr. Bleaker, Mr. Spellman?" Ruth pointed to the men on the sofa.

Walter spoke for his clients: "Ms. Whittaker, you are out of line. And you are wrong on so many levels. You picked this fight with the judge, and with Jack and his firm. You did that. And you have no goddamned case, excuse me, no case here and you know it. You made a deal with Flood, and that deal fell apart. That isn't on us. You want to drag this through to the end, and lose? Fine; I'll take the win. But I suggest to you that you take a mistrial, and save your precious reputation."

"Alright, enough. Both of you. Save it," Judge Donahue said. "I've had enough of all of this. Mr. McDonnell, I read the papers. I have seen the campaign waged against Judge Flood, and I found it deeply troubling. This is not how cases are won or lost in this district. I am inclined to let this case move forward and see what happens to your client. I don't think you are entitled to a mistrial."

"Judge, if I may?" Walter interrupted the judge, who nodded towards him to continue. "I read the papers too. The judge was no saint. None of us are. But there is no allegation, one, that this defense team had anything to do with the revelations that came out, and two, that even if we did, there was anything wrong with making such disclosures. I am only saying that there is a long history in this district of the papers digging into power players, and those on trial. Hell, Mr. Spellman and his own family were raked over the coals in a case against his son a year ago. The papers are in the business of selling papers. And I don't hear anyone saying those allegations were untrue—and they would have been used in the cross-examination of the judge, I can assure you of that."

"Oh please," Ruth offered.

"Please yourself, Ruth. You flipped the judge, and you shouldn't have. The pile of his crap was a mile high, and it just took the press for you to see it," Walter countered.

"Enough. I don't want any more of this back and forth," Judge Donahue snapped. "Ms. Whittaker, if I move this along, what do you suggest I tell the jury about your key witness?"

"Simply that he died. End of story," Ruth offered.

"We believe a mistrial is demanded here. But if the court is not inclined to grant that," Walter said, "then we would ask, judge, that the jury be reminded that any comments about what Judge Flood would have testified to be stricken. Also, we would ask that Ms. Whittaker be prohibited from referencing him in her closing remarks."

"Ms. Whittaker, what is left of your case?"

"We've established the elements, your honor, of the crimes alleged against Mr. Spellman. We have a very good case even without the motive Judge Flood would have provided."

"No, I am not asking that. What else do you have to put on in my courtroom?"

"Nothing judge. Flood was my last witness. We are prepared to rest our case."

"And you, Mr. McDonnell. What is your defense in chief? You've already had a crack at every witness in this case."

"Jack Spellman would like to testify, judge."

"Really, Mr. Spellman? Do you think that is wise?" Judge Donahue questioned the defendant.

"Yes, judge. I have been advised against it, but I want to tell my story, and tell the jury that I have done nothing wrong," Jack said.

"It has the distinct benefit of also being true," Nelson offered.

"Fine. We will take a day off today, and get back here tomorrow for Mr. Spellman, then closing arguments. But might I suggest in light of all the atmospherics in this case, as I call them, that you perhaps consider striking a deal—and perhaps putting all of us out of our misery?"

"No chance judge," said Walter, who was shaking his head along with Nelson and Jack.

"We've tried judge, they won't accept anything that risks the millions from their class action settlement," Ruth added.

"Yes, well, so be it. I'll send the jury home for the day. See you tomorrow at nine sharp." He raised his hand and waived the back of it at all of the lawyers, shooing them out of his chambers and into the hall.

13

THE PAPERS BILLED THE FINAL DAY OF U.S. V. SPELLMAN as a prize fight. The specter of the region's top prosecutor going toe-to-toe with an attorney one writer called a "silver-tongued orator" and "the nation's hottest trial lawyer," filled the courtroom with observers.

Walter McDonnell had spent the prior day building Jack Spellman up to be the savior of the East Side. In the guise of answering the allegations against him in the case, Jack walked through his firm's accomplishments, its charitable undertakings, and his previously unsoiled reputation as a proud member of the plaintiff's bar.

He spoke glowingly of the work he and lawyers like him did for the common man, which the jury appeared to savor. Walter also got Jack to discuss the charitable boards upon which he sat, the sports booster clubs he had started for his kids' schools, and everything else he could squeeze through the U.S. Attorney's objections to relevance. Amongst this character building exercise, Jack also testified that he had done nothing with regard to the payments made on behalf of Judge Flood to his bookie and his mortgagor, and knew nothing at the time these events took place.

On the morning of his cross-examination, the television news was reporting that the U.S. Attorney's case against Jack was all but lost. Universal praise was heaped on Walter for having navigated a sticky case and positioning his client for acquittal.

The experts claimed the prosecution had faltered from the very beginning by the abrupt departure of Xavier Holden and the decision to move forward without a trial lawyer as capable as Walter. The experts pointed, for example, to various rookie mistakes during the trial that they thought weakened the U.S. Attorney's case. They all acknowledged, though, that Jack was taking a risk by having agreed to take the stand and subject himself to the prosecution's questions.

Ruth had not read or listened to the coverage, but she was acutely aware that her case would rise or fall on what she could get out of the defendant, who had brazenly taken the stand to knock down her case once and for all.

So, if it was a prize fight, the government seemed now to stand in the challenger's corner. For the first time in the trial, the courtroom was at capacity. The gallery behind Ruth was filled with prominent members of the local trial bar, including those dozens who had helped build the defense and media campaign that had brought the case to the tipping point in Jack's favor.

Ruth rose to the podium and turned to take in the courtroom. She recognized the various members of the media that filled the front rows. She saw her former boss at AgriFarm, David Meirs, in the back row.

Ruth was ready. She had waged for over a year a war on corruption in government, the judiciary and the trial bar. She had landed a number of notable convictions, but nothing on the scale of Jack Spellman. She wanted this conviction. She wanted her name in the Journal, and she wanted the adulation of David Meirs and his brethren.

She stared at Jack Spellman. She looked to the jury, which was waiting for her first words.

Jack shifted in his seat. He was nervous. He had implored Walt to let him testify, and over the strenuous objection of both his lawyer and his own wife, Jack had prevailed. Now, as he sat waiting for the U.S. Attorney to begin her cross examination, he considered whether he had made the right decision.

"Mr. Spellman," Ruth began, "you spoke yesterday as to your influence, isn't that correct."

"Yes, I suppose so. I—"

"Thank you. And is it fair to say that you consider your firm to be one of the more influential class action law firms in this country?"

"In certain areas, yes. We have had some—"

"Thank you." Unlike the testimony of Nelson Bleaker, Ruth intended to keep the defendant on a short leash.

"And certainly, in our neck of the woods, you are considered one of the most influential lawyers around, isn't that true?" Ruth asked.

"Yes, I suppose that stands to reason."

"Has that always been the case?"

"What?"

"Has your firm always been one of the most influential law firms in the country?"

"Well, no. We—"

"Thank you. And—"

"Judge," Walter interceded, "can the witness complete a response?"

"He can if it is called for. These questions appear to require succinctness. If that was an objection, it is denied."

Ruth continued: "And as for you, Mr. Spellman, you have not always been the most influential lawyer in town, wouldn't you agree."

"Certainly. Yes."

"Your firm is how old?"

"About 15 years old, give or take."

"And you started it alone, correct?"

"Essentially yes. Me and some associates. It was a small operation."

"But not so small anymore?"

"No, not as small. But still small. I have only two partners."

"Let's talk about those partners of yours. Nelson Bleaker, is he one of your partners?"

"Yes."

"And where did Mr. Bleaker work before he worked for you?"

"He doesn't work for me."

"Alright. Worked with you."

"He was the chief judge of the St. Clair County courts."

"And until his employment in your law firm, was he in that role?"

"Yes."

"And how many cases did you try before Judge Bleaker over the years?"

"I have no earthly idea."

"Can you give me your best estimate?" Ruth asked.

"A dozen."

"In fact, Mr. Spellman, let me show you what is marked as Government 136. It is a docket sheet from that court. Do you recognize this document?" She walked over to the witness stand and handed him the document.

"No."

"Do you recognize the cases on the document?"

"Some of them. Some of them appear to be cases brought by my former firm against various railroad companies."

"How many do you recognize?"

"Probably about, let me see, about twenty."

"And do you have reason to believe those other thirty cases were not your cases?"

"No."

"Objection, judge. Relevance?" Walter asked.

"Ms. Whittaker?" the judge asked the U.S. Attorney for her response.

"The defendant testified yesterday as to his influence in the community," Ruth argued. "I am working my way into his influence in the courthouses, which is central to this case."

"Objection overruled."

Jack answered: "I have no reason to disagree that these were my cases, but I have no idea how far along they got with Judge Bleaker, if they settled or—"

"Well, let me help you along, then. Here are exhibits marked Government 137-140, which are compilations of jury verdicts reported in those cases."

"Objection, judge, we've never seen these documents," Walter said.

"Denied; these are public documents, counsel."

"OK?" Jack offered.

"What are those totals, Mr. Spellman?"

Jack read from the sheets, which carried totals at the end of the document. Each was in the millions of dollars.

"What was your take of those cases?" Ruth asked.

"My firm took one third, and costs. I was not paid as such."

"But you were a partner, correct?" Ruth prodded.

"Well, a non-equity one. I got paid a salary and bonus. So those verdicts and settlements, they mostly benefitted the individual litigants, not me."

"How did you induce Judge Bleaker to come to your firm?"

"Objection, facts not in evidence," Walter yelled.

"Sustained."

Ruth tried again: "What was the offer you made to Judge Bleaker to join your firm?"

"I offered him a job that paid better than what he made on the bench."

"And didn't you make his DUI arrest go away?"

"Objection, foundation!" Walter yelled.

Ruth rephrased in advance of a ruling: "Were you aware at the time of your hiring him that the judge, Judge Bleaker, was under arrest for driving under the influence?"

"Yes."

"And did you work to make those charges go away?"

"No."

"And when you were about to hire Judge Bleaker, were you aware his wages were being garnished to pay child support?"

"I don't recall that. I knew he had been in a divorce, and had his girls heading off to college. He needed a better job, which I gave him."

"What else did you give him?"

"I think I leased him a car through the firm."

"A Cadillac."

"Yes."

"And where is Mr. Bleaker living at present?"

"In an townhouse."

"That you own?"

"Yes."

"And does he pay you rent?"

"No."

"So, let me summarize your testimony: You induced Mr. Bleaker off the bench with a higher paying job, a Cadillac, and a very nice townhouse on a golf course. Is that all?"

"That sounds about right."

"And you made that DUI go away, correct?" Ruth repeated, hoping to catch Jack off guard.

Over Walter's objection, Jack again denied that contention.

"Why Judge Bleaker?" Ruth asked.

"Why Judge Bleaker, what?" Jack countered.

"Why did you hire him?"

"He had class action experience on the bench. He had no other loyalties. He was a smart guy. I liked him. That enough?" Jack was losing his patience. Walter gave Jack a series of signs that he should to take it easy, slow down and listen to the questions.

"I don't know, was it? Did it help that he had sent millions of dollars to you and your cases over the years?"

"You could say that about a lot of judges. I have won a lot of cases over the years."

"But you didn't hire all of them did you? Strike that. And you didn't answer my question. Isn't it true there was a quid-pro-quo in place, that Judge Bleaker rewarded you over the years when he was on the bench, and you rewarded him when he stepped down?"

Walter offered an objection, which was overruled. "There was no such pact," Jack stated coolly.

"Oh, but there is a pattern, isn't there?" Ruth asked rhetorically, as she walked back to her counsel's table. She picked up a document, and without looking at her witness, asked: "You ever give Mr. Nelson the title to that townhouse?"

"No."

"Ever pay off a bookie for him?"

"No."

"Craig Rock," she said to Jack.

"Yes."

"Your other named partner?"

"Yes."

"And another former judge?"

"Yes."

"What kind of car did he get?"

"I think we first leased him a Cadillac, too."

"Popular car," Ruth stated with a grin.

"It's no Mercedes," Jack responded, knowing the car parked in the U.S. ATTY spot in the parking lot.

"Where did you find Mr. Rock?"

"He was a judge up in Madison County, north of here."

"And why did he want off the bench?"

"You'd have to ask him."

"Why did you want him?"

"Again, class action experience. He had nearly every asbestos, Agent Orange, and other class over there on his docket. He knows class actions, and he knows how to manage them."

"What kind of package did he get to join your firm?"

"Better wages than he made on the bench. A better lifestyle."

"Did you give him a condo?"

"No."

"Pay off any debts?"

"No."

"How many cases did you have before Judge Rock over the years?" Ruth asked.

"Not many. Maybe two or three?" Jack guessed.

"Let me show you a Madison County docket record," Ruth said as she offered the next document to her witness.

Jack reviewed it: "Looks like about 10. This was a long time ago."

"Sure, but I can see why you recall only two or three—do you see the verdicts on the page?"

"Yes. They total about $15 million."

"And two of them are major verdicts—they account for almost all of that total, isn't that right?"

"Yes."

"And did you have a prior understanding with Judge Rock that if he treated you well, you would treat him well somewhere down the road?"

"Objection!" Walter yelled.

"Sustained. Where is the basis for that, Ms. Whittaker?" Judge Donahue asked.

"I'll answer that," Jack offered, ignoring the ruling from the bench. "Juries gave these verdicts, Ms. Whittaker. Those are jury verdicts, not bench trials. Judge Rock had nothing to do with those awards. The same was true for Judge Bleaker."

"We'd all like to believe that, wouldn't we?" Ruth stated as she looked at the jury with a grin. "Now, tell me about the profitability of your firm when you were the only partner."

"We were not profitable."

"And now?"

"Now we are."

"Indeed IRS statements previously entered into this case estimate revenues amongst you and your partners at close to $45 million over the last three years, isn't that right?"

"That sounds right. But what you are not—"

"Thank you."

"—what you are missing is the expenditures we have to pay out in cases, not all of which—"

"You answered my question. Thank you. Now, these class action cases your firm brings, where do you bring them?" Ruth asked.

"In courts."

"Ah yes, thank you, very helpful," Ruth responded, "but primarily which courts?"

"This court, for one. St. Clair County, Madison County, and about thirty others at present."

"And what percentage are in this court?"

"Probably a third."

"And what about St. Clair?"

"A fifth."

"And Madison?"

"Same."

"So, let me do the numbers here. About seventy-five percent in these three courts?"

"I've never done the math, but that seems about right," Jack said succinctly. "I don't like to travel," he added.

"Why would you when the majority of your cases are in courts where you hired top judges into your partnership?" Ruth argued.

"There is nothing that prohibits that."

"And so, at some point, you decided to add to your ranks a judge from this courthouse, is that right?"

"Yes."

"And when was that?"

"Late last year."

"And who was that?"

"Bill Flood."

"That is Chief Judge William Flood?" Ruth clarified.

"Yes."

"And did you hire Judge Flood?"

"Yes."

"And he worked for your firm?"

"Yes."

"As a partner?"

"No, there was a probationary period we followed, per the ethics rules, and our own policies. So, up until he left our employ, he was of counsel to the firm."

"And that meant what?"

"He was paid a salary. He took on no risk of partnership, and shared in no benefits."

"And what was that salary?"

"$25,000 per month."

"That is quite a salary. Who approved that?"

"The partnership."

"Including you?" Ruth asked.

"Yes, including me."

"What kind of car did he get?"

"He didn't get a car."

"Did you pay off any loans for him?"

Jack sat up in his chair, noting finally that the prosecutor had reached the substance of the allegations against him.

"I, well, I did not."

"But your firm did," Ruth protested.

"Well, no. As Judge Bleaker previously testified, he was in charge of attempting to hire Judge Rock, er, Flood."

"It is hard keeping all these judicial hires straight, isn't it, Mr. Spellman?" Ruth chided him over Walter's objection. "It isn't 'Judge' Spellman, is it?" she asked only slightly in jest.

"It is decidedly not," Jack said.

"Alright, I just wanted to keep all these judges straight. So, you just testified that Mr. Bleaker handled the negotiations with Judge Flood, is that right?"

"Yes."

"And when did that begin?"

"As far as I was aware at the very end of 1993, after he—Judge Flood—had announced his plans to retire from the bench."

"And you are familiar, are you not, of the inducements Mr. Bleaker claims to have provided to Judge Flood?"

"Objection, overly broad, not limited in time or scope, vague and without foundation," Walter said as he stood, throwing out every warning he had to Jack to tread carefully.

"Overruled. What is your contemporaneous understanding Mr. Spellman?" Judge Donahue offered, helping the case along.

"I am now aware that Nelson directed his own money to pay off a gambling debt."

"And from where did those funds emanate?" Ruth asked.

"From his account," Jack said.

"And then they went where?"

"They went to a contractor of the firm. One that was doing work on Hayes House—our offices—that Nelson was supervising."

"And were you aware of how much that contractor charged?"

"At the time, no."

"When did you learn of that?"

"Only once you had indicted me," Jack offered.

"And at the time this payment occurred, did you have a case in front of Judge Flood?"

"Yes."

"And did that case go to a verdict?"

"No, it settled," Jack said.

"Why?"

"Because the parties agreed to settle."

"What kind of case was this?" Ruth asked.

"A class action against the SL&SP railroad. It had to do with their improper use of property," Jack started to explain the premise of his case to the jury, but was cut off by the U.S. Attorney.

"What was the settlement?"

"That is confidential."

"Not anymore it isn't. The class was paid $100 million, isn't that right?"

"Yes."

"And your firm took home how much?"

"$25 million."

"When did the settlement occur?"

"After the Seventh Circuit Court of Appeals affirmed the lower court's order certifying the class."

"And by the lower court, you mean Judge Flood?"

"Yes."

"So, at the time you were litigating this case, your partner was paying off a $160,000 debt owed by the judge?"

"Unbeknownst to me, yes."

"And then, after the settlement, you decided to hire Judge Flood into your firm, correct?" Ruth asked.

"Well, yes, that is the timing, but—"

"Thank you."

"When during this time did you speak with Judge Spellman regarding his employment with your firm?"

"Never."

"Never?"

"I did not speak to him regarding his employment until after he had announced his retirement."

"So you left that to Mr. Bleaker, is that right?" Ruth asked.

"As far as I know, he also did not convey an actual offer of employment until that time."

"But you heard the tapes, sir, where Mr. Bleaker offered or suggested to the judge employment with your firm months in advance of that, did you not? Indeed, those calls took place while your case was pending, didn't they?" Ruth had found her line of attack and moved closer to the witness stand.

"I heard two old friends talking about what fun it would be to work together, and that was about it. But again, I had no knowledge and there was no real, concrete offer," Jack protested.

"But your firm arranged the payoff of a bookie at that time, isn't that correct?"

"Mr. Bleaker testified that he did, from funds in his own account."

"And then, right around that time, the class certification order came out, didn't it?" Ruth asked.

"Yes, that is correct."

"And it favored you and your client?"

"Yes, but that was upheld—"

"Thank you. Now, did you ever discuss with Judge Flood his certification?"

"When? At the time of the order? No. In fact, I don't think we ever discussed it—then or anytime thereafter."

"Did you know that his law clerk had penned a very different draft of the class certification order, which denied certification?"

"No," Jack said.

Ruth showed the government's next exhibit to Jack. He was asked to read aloud the conclusions of the clerk's draft order, which stated that the nationwide class against the railroad would be a "nightmare" to manage and would not be certified. It was a startling piece of evidence, Jack thought, and he had never seen it.

"How do you account for that different draft order?"

"I can't," Jack said slowly while he contemplated his words and the exhibit. "But from what I can tell," he filibustered for time to come up with a credible response, "and for all I know, Judge Flood had his clerks draft items up each way, or he wrote one side, and had a clerk write the other. I have no earthly idea. Regardless, the order that was issued was upheld by the appellate court."

"You intended for that $160,000 payment to turn the tide on certification, didn't you?" Ruth asked.

"I don't know how I could have, since I didn't even know it had occurred," Jack reasoned, leaning forward on his chair into the microphone.

"And then you thanked the judge for certifying your class action by offering him employment and paying off his mortgage, isn't that right?"

"No. We offered him employment, but there was no quid pro quo. There simply wasn't," Jack said.

Ruth moved in for her final push: "But all evidence is to the contrary, isn't it?"

"No," Jack protested.

"And you paid the judge to send millions to you, and then you hired him—just like you did with Judge Bleaker, isn't that right?"

"It is not. We—"

"And just like you did with Judge Rock. Isn't that true?"

"No, it isn't," Jack yelled.

"You built a multi-million dollar firm—that's what you said."

"Yes."

"And you did that by hiring the judiciary."

"Well, in part, but—"

"And it was those judges, Bleaker, Rock, then Flood, that funneled millions to you, isn't that true?"

"As I said, those were jury awards—"

"Objection!" Walter shouted, rising to his feet.

"Sustained!" Judge Donahue ruled, reaching for his gavel to quell the yelling.

Ruth let the din in the room settle. She concluded gently and methodically: "Mr. Spellman, you testified that your firm is one of the most influential in the country. You testified that you are one of the most influential lawyers in the area. Are you to have this jury believe that you were unable—despite payments by you and your firm of $460,000 and the prospect of employment for an annual salary of another $300,000—to influence an old, broke federal judge into seeing your way in a class action case? Is that your testimony?"

"You would have to ask Judge Flood what influence I had on him," Jack said, staring down the United States Attorney.

"You know full-well why I can't do that now, don't you Mr. Spellman?" Ruth countered, over a speedy and sustained objection.

14

AS THE KIDS CHANGED OUT OF THEIR WORK CLOTHES, dirty from a morning in the Belleville Central Kitchen, and as Kathy started on the day's meal, Jack sunk into his leather recliner in front of the televised Thanksgiving Day parade. He started into the back of the newspaper with the sports section, reading that West would make State in football for the first time in many years.

The local business report was next. The top headline noted that the region's largest employer, AgriFarm, was adjusting considerably downward its forecasted year-end earnings and profit expectations. Principal causes, the paper reported, were "rising litigation expenses," as well as increases in related insurance costs, and a drop in demand for the company's top corn seed, Selector.

It would take years more, Jack figured, until AgriFarm caved to those mounting legal costs and would agree to settle with his potential class of farmers who had bought Selector. Still, he couldn't help but smile at the news of their revised forecast, no less the contemporaneous five percent dip their stock took before the trading day was halted early on Wednesday for the holiday.

Jack wondered how long it would take until AgriFarm brought back their former general counsel to halt the company's rising legal costs and exposure and return the company to its halcyon years. As U.S. Attorney, Ruth Whittaker had been roundly defeated in her most notable government corruption trial, Jack knew firsthand. And after a rash of gang and drug-related murders, there was talk about the need for a return to a more brass-knuckled violent crime fighter in the position. Jack relished the idea of seeing Ruth out of her current job and back in a civil courtroom facing him someday.

Tim sat down on the sofa adjacent to his father, while Wendy headed into the kitchen to grab the two of them orange sodas.

"Here comes Santa!" Jack bellowed.

"Yeah dad, we know what he looks like," Tim said, already bored.

"Dad, you want a Whistle?" Wendy asked, holding up the orange and white soda can.

"At 9 in the morning? No thanks."

"Suit yourself," she said.

"There's fresh coffee, Jack," Kathy offered from the kitchen.

"Now you are talking." Jack stood up and left his kids in the family room. He took the coffee from his wife and, from the doorway to the family room, watched his children drink their sodas and obligingly watch the parade that they knew he loved.

Kathy came up from behind Jack and slid her arms under his and around his waist. She tilted her head up towards his face and whispered, "it is so nice to be a family again. All of us here. Nothing else," she said, and Jack knew what she meant. Jack gripped her arms as she continued, "and no one else."

"Not 'till noon, anyway, when your crazy family gets here," he joked.

"You know you love them," she said, poking him in the side.

"You know I do."

the end